And Darkness Fell

By Christian S Tait

Published by Shetland Library
Lerwick, Shetland 2018
ISBN 978-0-905924-64-9

Cover photo:
'Group on Beach' by L. G. Scott, Grandfather of the author.

L. G. Scott's full photo collection can be viewed online,
in the photo archive on the Shetland Museum
and Archives website.
www.shetlandmuseumandarchives.org.uk

The book title is from
'Alfriston, Sunday, 3rd October, 1915',
a poem by Bernard Pitt 1881–1916
(Arras Memorial to the Missing)

Also by Christian S. Tait:
Spindrift
(Poetry; 1989; ISBN: 9780951548301)
Stones in the Millpond
(Poetry and war correspondence; 2001; ISBN:
9780904562507)

For my Grandfather,
Laurence Gray Scott 1879 – 1960.
He was, and is, my lodestone.

CONTENTS

For love is the creator
and cruelty is that which destroys.

Neil M. Gunn, Green Isle of the Great Deep.

The Jacobson Family Tree 1917

Both families came from the fictitious crofting district of Grindavoe

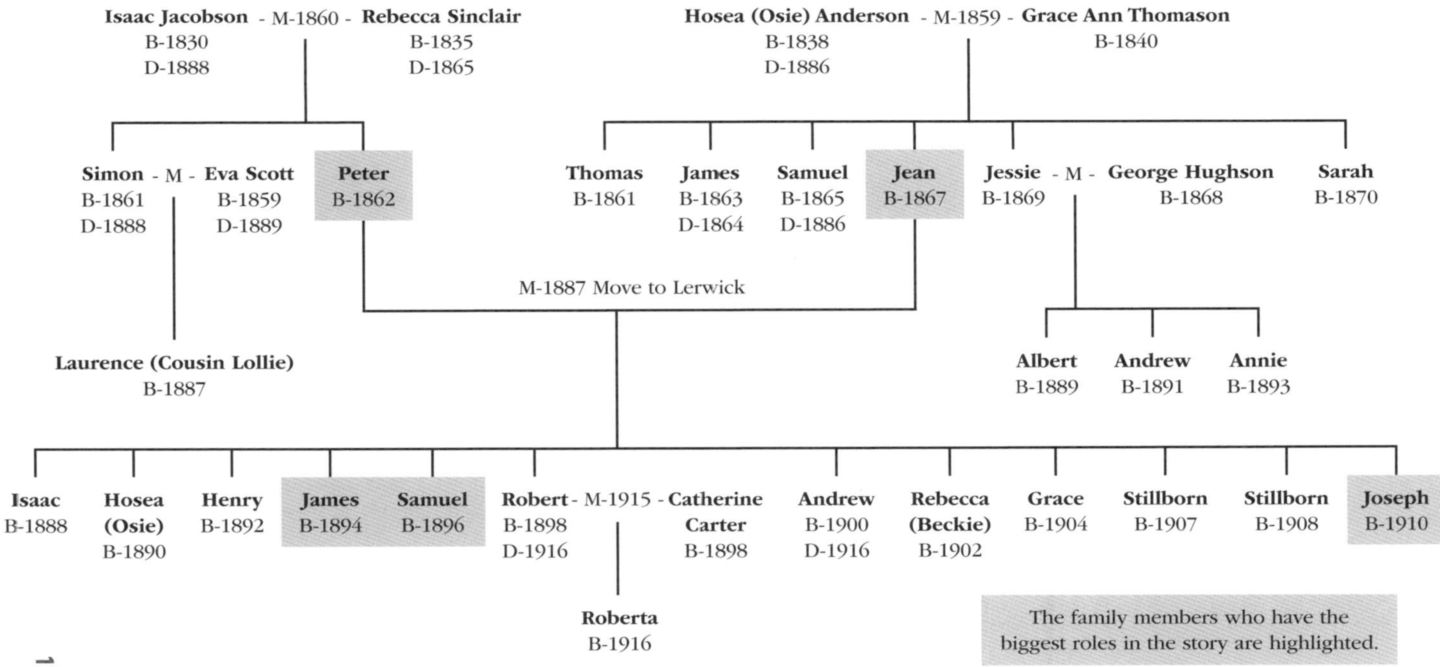

Prologue

Jamie Jacobson Remembers Summer 1899

Grindavoe! He and his little brother, Sam, had been sent to their grandmother's croft while their mother recovered from a difficult birth. Grindavoe. For him the whole experience had been dominated by the day of the whales. He savoured the words.

The day of the whales. The phrase had a biblical ring to it, as if it should be recorded in a gilt-edged book. It was certainly engraved upon his heart.

They were all in the park that morning, he recalled, turning the hay – Granny, Auntie Jessie, Auntie Sarah, himself and Sam - the two of them trying their best with the little rakes Uncle Geordie had made for the cousins when they were small. Suddenly the wife from Setter, the croft nearest the mouth of the voe, appeared over the brow of the hill. Chest heaving, legs flying and skirts flapping, she was like some enormous bird about to take flight. He and Sam had laughed delightedly and shouted,

'Look, Granny! Look!' The woman cupped her hands round her mouth, shouting, 'Whales! Whales! Whales comin inta da voe!'

A great wave of excitement passed over them like wind among corn. Jamie, too, had felt a quickening of his blood – though he didn't know what it was about. The rakes were cast aside and the haymaking forgotten. Auntie Jessie swept

Sam up in her arms and swung him onto her back in one deft movement, then ran, carrying him pick-a-back. Auntie Sarah had grabbed his hand, Jamie recalled, and had run faster than he'd thought possible, dragging him with her, and Granny had followed – desperation lending her speed. Once home, the Aunts had pulled on sea-boots and rushed into the barn looking for knives, old scythe-blades and anything that would cut through a whale's tough skin.

In every direction school bairns were running home as fast as they could, leaping over burns and clumps of heather, and shrieking with delight at getting an unscheduled break from slates and copybooks. The schoolmaster had dismissed them the minute he heard the news for he knew, as they all did, that everyone was needed – especially the bigger boys for, with their fathers and older brothers away at the fishing (or the war), it was up to the women and the bairns to 'caa' the whales ashore. And they could do it, for all but the youngest could handle a boat almost as well as the men. Everyone knew that this was an opportunity not to be missed, for the money they earned from the sale of the blubber could lift them above subsistence level for a few weeks – and the little they kept for themselves would be melted down to keep their lamps burning in the dark days of winter. They had to succeed.

By the time the cousins reached Grindavoe, Jessie and Sarah were already at the beach gathering stones which they placed in the boat. Albert and Alec threw off their school clothes, pulled on their working breeks, thrust their arms into the thick oiled sweaters that Granny held up for them and stamped their feet into the boots that little Annie had set out at the door. They were off.

'Come on, Jamie,' shouted Albert, the oldest cousin. 'No, Bertie! He's far ower young. It's no a thing for peerie bairns ta see,' their grandmother protested. 'He'll bide here wi Annie an Sam.' But Jamie was already on his way.

Albert lifted him aboard. Then the aunts and cousins pulled the boat over the halibut bones that served as "linns", smoothing its path over the stony beach to the water. The boys held it steady for the women. Then they jumped nimbly in. Albert, standing up, levered the boat away from the shore with an oar, making as little disturbance as possible. Gently, so gently, he eased it out into deeper water making hardly a ripple on the gleaming surface, for he didn't want to alert the pod and cause it to change direction. Then he sat down, resting on the oars, and they waited holding their breath. The only sound was the lapping of wavelets against the hull, and the occasional soughing as a whale breathed out through its blow-hole. 'Here dey come,' whispered Auntie Jessie, and sure enough the black fins moved steadily into the voe. 'Wait,' she said. 'Wait till der aa in…'

Their hearts pounded as the magnificent, gleaming beasts glided into the enclosed waters of the voe. Fifty or more, perhaps a hundred. Then the Grindavoe boat, along with several others, rowed out to form a line behind them, barring their escape to the open sea. Hunters and hunted moved steadily forward. At first the animals sensed no danger, but - as the water became shallower and the lead beasts felt the stony bottom graze their bellies – panic spread among them. They plunged and reared, tried to break through the blockade. They were quickly redirected with roars like war cries, and a pelting of the stones brought for the purpose. The line of boats moved inexorably forward, driving them on. Jamie had joined in the stone throwing and had shouted till he was hoarse. He remembered the rush of excitement. He'd never experienced anything like it before. The terrified animals were forced to beach themselves, or lie stranded in the shallow water. The voe was filled with shining black bodies, heaving, thrashing, struggling for breath. Then the killing began.

The crowd waiting at the head of the voe surged forward, and began to strike with their knives at the beached creatures. The boats maintained their blockade and their crews joined in the massacre. Standing up in the wildly rocking boats, they lunged with makeshift harpoons, or leapt into the churning water (as Albert and Andrew did). The most skilful aimed for the blow-holes, which would sever main arteries and give a quicker death, but the others hacked indiscriminately and the water became a cauldron of blood.

The high-pitched shouts of the women and children mingled with the excited screech of seagulls, which circled and swooped – waiting for an easy meal. 'Come an gie wiz a hand, boy,' Albert shouted, holding up his arms. Jamie hadn't needed a second bidding. Albert lifted him out of the boat, carried him close to the shore, and gave him a small knife. Jamie hadn't the strength to break through the animals' skin, but he struck again and again into the wounds opened by the others. A rush of power surged through his veins. He felt strong, free…alive. Everything was brighter, clearer. He had delighted in the flow of warm blood, letting it run over his hands in glistening rivers. The smell excited him. Was it fear? Or suffering? Or death? He stood up to his thighs in crimson water, thinking nothing – but nothing – could be better than this.

Mighty hooks were sunk into the creatures' flesh, and ropes looped round their tails. They were hauled ashore and lined up in rows. Then began the laborious task of stripping off the thick white layer of precious blubber. As it was near midsummer there was no true darkness. So they worked into the night, sleeves rolled up, arms, faces and clothing spattered with blood and grease. They stopped only to eat the food the older women had brought in straw kishies which they carried on their backs. Then they picked up their knives to slash again at the creamy-white treasure that could change their lives – at least for a while.

The menfolk returned from the fishing in the morning and took over the flensing from their exhausted wives and children who, after a short sleep, began preparing food for the celebration which would take place when the work was over. Every house was filled with the smell of bannocks baking on the hearth, and soup boiling in the pot that hung from the crook in every chimney. That night when the fiddles were playing and the dancing was fast and furious, Jamie moved among the crowd listening to snippets of adult conversation.

'Der no mony boys dy age could bear ta watch da killin,' they said, ruffling his hair, 'an dere du wis right in da heart o it wi dee ain peerie knife.' He'd felt brave, important… *special,* for the first time in his life.

Over the next few years he often thought of the day of the whales, and gradually it dawned on him that the others had not been celebrating the joyous act of slaughter. Their high spirits were due to the prospect of a temporary relief from crippling poverty. Unlike them, Jamie had enjoyed every moment. More than that. The anguish in the dying creatures' eyes had held for him a kind of beauty. By the time he was a youth he had admitted to himself that he had needs which had no place in a Christian home, for he realised that inflicting pain gave him a strange and sensuous pleasure. He knew he was different. This was his secret.

PART ONE

Chapter One
Home-coming

Monday 10th September 1917

The whistle blew, and the train drew to a screeching halt. Sam Jacobson glanced at the station clock, and confirmed the time with his pocket watch. Four thirty. Only fifteen minutes late, but it seemed like hours. A feeling of dread had settled in his stomach - heavy and cold as stone. This wasn't how it should be. Meeting his brother should be a joyful occasion, but all he could think about was the day that Jamie ran off to Australia, the day he realised he'd no longer have to bear the brunt of his brother's violent outbursts, or the cutting edge of his sarcastic tongue. Was it going to start all over again? He tried to reason with himself. *Dat was seeven year ago. I was only fourteen. Surely things'll be different noo at wir baith grown men.*

Shafts of sunlight slanted through the dirty panes of the glass roof spotlighting the soot smuts that drifted slowly down. *Like black snowflakes*, he thought. *Unnatural and ominous.* He shook his head - he was even beginning to think in English because he was away from home! *Fluckra. Black fluckra. Dat sounded better.* But the meaning was just as disturbing. His mood was bleak. He glanced around. Not a single "kent face" - and the babble of Doric that echoed around him sounded strident and discordant compared to the long soft vowels of his home-tongue. He shivered, and realised he was holding his breath. He let it out slowly, fighting for control. *Get a grip, man,* he urged himself. *Du's no a bairn noo.*

The crowd surged forward, carrying him along, unresisting till they were close to the barrier. He held back then, and let them stream past. Standing on tiptoe, he looked over their heads - eyes darting here and there searching for his brother. A river of humanity flowed along the platform forming little eddies here and there – jostling and waving, meeting and greeting, laughing and weeping. There were service men of every rank, their sombre blue and khaki relieved by proud, bright touches of tartan. There were businessmen in bowler hats; working men in cloth caps; well-to-do women in furs and feathers, and others making do with their threadbare best. Impatient children jumped up and down shouting, 'Can ye see ma Daddie?' and tugged at coat sleeves. All the world was there, but no Jamie. Had he missed the train? Or been unable to travel? That was possible, he supposed. "Neurasthenia" the letter had said, but gave no information as to what that was or how it affected him – only that he was "temporarily unfit for service" and had been granted four weeks leave for rest and recuperation. His status would be reviewed when he returned from furlough. What did that mean - and where was he?

The platform was empty now. There was little point in waiting. Jamie hadn't come. *Am I sailed aa da wye fae Lerwick ta Aberdeen for nothin*? His irritation, he had to admit, was tinged with relief. The tension in his neck muscles began to ease. He knew he'd have to face their reunion soon. But not today. As he turned to leave he took one final look along the empty platform. But it wasn't entirely empty, for a thin drooping figure appeared at a carriage door and climbed unsteadily down. Sam stared. Could that be Jamie? His heart lurched, and he felt a rising flood of horror as he recognised the stranger who was shuffling towards him swamped by a greatcoat that looked several sizes too big, and much too heavy for his fragile frame to bear. Grey-faced and sunken-cheeked, Jamie stared out from under the Australian slouch hat, whose jaunty style served only to emphasise his haunted look. Could this really be the older brother who'd made his childhood a misery? Sam drew in his breath sharply. Poor Jamie, what had this war done to him? This wasn't the bully he'd expected to meet. This was a vulnerable, broken man. Pity and remorse swept over Sam, brushing away the years of distrust and fear. He wanted to make a fresh start, to hug Jamie, to tell him it was all right – but how could he, when clearly it was not? Side-stepping to avoid the porter - who had abandoned his "portering", and was now raising a cloud of dust with a large broom - Sam approached with purposeful strides.

'Hello, Jamie,' he said, his voice husky with emotion. He cleared his throat and tried again.

'Hello, Jamie,' he said, more clearly this time - and reached out to take his brother's kitbag from him. Immediately Jamie stepped back and clutched it close with both arms, eyes dark with fear and suspicion. Somewhere a guard's whistle blew and a train pulled out of the station with a slowly accelerating chuff, chuff, chuff.

'It's aa right, Jamie. It's me, Sam,' he said gently, as if to a child. 'I was only goin ta carry dy bag for dee.'

But Jamie, would not, could not let it go.

'Come, boy. We'll get a cup o tay. Du'll need it efter sittin in da train aa day. Come, it's no far ta da tay-room, an we hae plenty o time for we dunna sail till six.'

Once they were seated at their table, Jamie suddenly spoke.

'Why did you come to meet me, Sam?'

His voice had a distinctive Aussie twang. No hint of a Shetland accent. No use of the familiar 'du' instead of you. No warmth or pleasure in his tone.

'Mammie was worried aboot dee traivellin sae far wi nobody ta help dee. So I cam ta keep dee company on da last leg o da journey.'

'I thought you were in Edinburgh learning to be a doctor.'

Sam ignored the sarcasm in his voice. Maybe he'd imagined it. And why was his brother using English instead of Shetland? Did he think that made him sound superior?

He waited while the waitress clattered a teapot, milk and sugar on the table, and a plate with some decidedly fruitless fruit cake. Then he explained.

'T.B. Jamie. Tuberculosis. Dey sent me hame ta end my days among my ain fock, but A'm still here. You canna keep a good man doon.' Sam smiled, making light of his life-threatening illness.

'So you're not serving in the war, then?' This time the sneer was unmistakable. Sam poured their tea, determined not to rise to Jamie's taunts.

'No,' he replied calmly. 'Dey widna tak me for a soldier. "Permanently unfit" dey said. I work for Mr Leask in da chemist shop noo – da nearest thing ta doctorin at I could get.'

He had nothing to be ashamed of. So why did he feel defensive? Maybe Jamie hadn't intended to goad him.

'Oh,' said Jamie, losing interest. He picked up his cup with trembling hands and slurped noisily, while the ladies at the next table looked disapprovingly and tut-tutted. 'Colonials,' one whispered to the other. 'They're a rough lot. Nae manners.'

'Aye,' replied her friend, 'Fit can ye expect when they're descended fae convicts.' Sam locked eyes first with one then the other, till their faces reddened and they looked away. Couldn't they see that his brother was ill? His reaction took him by surprise. He'd instinctively wanted to protect Jamie. *Me, protect Jamie?* He shook his head in disbelief. Nothing was as he'd expected it to be.

On board the steamer, Sam helped his brother down the steep narrow stair to their cabin, settled him in the lower bunk, then went on deck. He needed space to think. He inhaled deeply. The good salt air was a powerful antidote to the city smells which lingered in his nostrils – the choking thickness of coal-smoke that issued from the rows of chimneys crowning the grimy granite buildings; the horses, so many of them, and their mix of odours - their breath, their sweat and their muck which they left behind them in steaming heaps on the cobbles; the sharp fumes from the motor cars and the lorries that rushed up Union Street honking their horns and frightening horses and pedestrians alike, and the all-pervading stink of fish, overpowering near the harbour. None of these smells was new to him. It was the scale of things that was somehow wrong. The same could be said of the noise, and the crowd of grim-faced hurrying people. Never a smile. Never a greeting. *Give me Lerwick every time,* he thought.

No lights showed from the little fishing villages along the coast. He would have been in total darkness were it not for the almost-full moon silvering everything, and making the ship an easy target for any enemy vessels that might be lurking beneath cliffs or sheltering in the bays. Sam gave a rueful smile. The war and its bureaucrats could control many things, but no-one could control the moonlight. The war. The war. The bloody war. It was impossible to forget about it, not even for a minute. The fear had been with him since he left Lerwick the day before, for that morning a steamer had sunk off the Bressay Lighthouse. Blown up by a mine. Sam tried to calm himself by identifying the familiar and reassuring constellations. The stars fascinated him and always put his worries in perspective.

He made his way to the saloon, nodded at the men who were occupying themselves reading newspapers or playing cards, and found a quiet corner. Old men. He was fed up with being surrounded by women and old men. He craved the company of fellows his own age. There was always Jake, the young Police Constable – but once they'd exhausted war news and forensics they had little in common - only their youth, and the fact that they weren't on active service. He lit his pipe, adding to the haze of tobacco smoke. He was living inside his own head too much. He knew that. He blew a perfect smoke-ring, and fumbled in his pocket for the letter he'd received from a medical chum in Edinburgh in response to his request for more information on neurasthenia.

It's a new kind of illness, his friend wrote. *'Shell-shock' they call it, and it presents itself in many ways – mutism, trembling, loss of balance, terror, nightmares and so on. Research into its treatment is experimental. Some doctors treat it with electric shocks. That seems a bit brutal, don't you think? But we have our orders too. The army needs us to get them on their feet and back to the front as soon as possible. Another man is another gun. Sorry if I sound cynical, old chap, but that's how it is. The psychology brigade tries to get their patients to talk about their experiences and face up to them. This is slow and often doesn't work as the poor buggers' minds have shut down. The experiences they've had are just too disturbing to revisit. However, some patients do make a sudden and unexpected recovery. I hope your brother will be one of the lucky ones. Sorry I can't be more helpful, Sam, but I'll keep you posted about any new developments.*

Sam folded the letter and put it back in his pocket. It would be his mother's job to care for Jamie during his sick leave. His expression softened as he thought about her. She was a strong woman, of that there was no doubt. But how much strain could a person bear? He knew that she worried constantly about his father and his three elder brothers who were at sea facing all kinds of dangers, and she had already lost two sons to this terrible war. Sam admired the way she carried her grief with such quiet dignity. Life's blows were tests of faith and would be overcome with the Lord's help, she said. He wished his belief were as unshakeable as hers, for he was struggling to hold onto his faith in a God who allowed this to happen. Losing Andrew had left a permanent ache in his heart, but losing Robert was like losing half his own self for they'd been like twins, sharing everything, thinking the same thoughts. Even now he could hear Robert's voice whispering, 'Dunna believe everything du hears. Nothin is da wye it seems.'

What did he mean by that? Sam knocked out his pipe, went down to the cabin and climbed up to the top bunk.

His mind would not rest. Jamie's presence enveloped him, making him tense. Fearful. Guilty. He prayed each night for his older brothers - Isaac, Osie and Henry – who were at sea, and he'd prayed in vain for Robert and Andrew…but he'd scarcely spared a thought for Jamie. Poor Jamie - he was the frail one now. White moonlight shone through the porthole, accentuating the hollows under his cheekbones and giving his pale skin a waxy sheen. His eyes were wide open, like empty holes. Skull-like and disconcerting. *Get a grip, man,* he told himself, not for the first time that day.

'Try ta get some shut-eye, Jamie. It's been a lang day, and it'll be a lang night.' Jamie made no response, but turned on his side to face the cabin wall.

It was after eight o'clock when they approached Lerwick harbour – a bright but chilly morning. Sam turned his back to the wind and placed his feet firmly apart to steady himself against the rolling of the boat. Then, cupping his hand to shield the match, he began the comforting ritual of lighting his pipe. When it was drawing well he stepped forward to join his brother. Side by side they stood in silence – two men with very different thoughts.

The ship was in still water now, gliding past the familiar landmarks that never failed to lift Sam's heart for he saw this town as an old friend, full of stories, secrets and shared experiences. He loved its people, who wouldn't dream of passing anyone in the street without a cheery greeting, 'Aye, aye. Fine day'. He loved its quaint beauty. "Venice of the North" some people called it, with its sturdy grey houses built out into the sea. He loved the romance of it – the tales of pirates and smugglers who stored their contraband in tunnels beneath the street. He loved the noise and bustle of the harbour when it was filled with fishing boats, and the street when it was filled with Hollanders who clattered across the cobbles in their clogs, puffing clay pipes and leaving a smell of foreign tobacco in the air.

There were no Dutch "böms" anymore. Today the St. Sunniva was threading her way through a different kind of shipping - cruisers, destroyers, merchant ships and mine-sweepers, for close by - too close - German U-boats lurked under the water, sneaking in to lay their mines and fire their torpedoes, creating havoc at the very mouth of the harbour. The thought of them, and the fear, had never been far from his mind during the journey south and back, for the North Sea was a dangerous place. As Captain of the St. Rognvald, the Sunniva's sister ship, his father had to cross this stretch of water several times every week. How did he manage to remain so calm? *Dear Lord,* he prayed, *keep Daddie safe.*

Sam pulled up his collar against the wind. Soon there would be more change. He'd read in the paper that they were going to build homes to re-house the people in the shacks and hovels near the fishing stations, and provide decent homes for returning soldiers. But too many families would have empty spaces, and – he glanced at Jamie – too many families would barely recognise the strangers who returned to them.

Jamie clasped the deck-rail with thin, scarred fingers and stared at the shore with dull, dead eyes. He hated this place as intensely as Sam loved it. Hated the way that everybody knew everyone else's business. Hated the way the sombre grey buildings conspired with the sombre grey people to stifle his spirit and hold him down. Nothing had changed. He felt trapped. Couldn't breathe. He tried to loosen his collar, but his fingers were weak and trembling. What had he been thinking about, coming home for his leave? He should have known better. He dreaded being surrounded by kinsfolk and the lilting cadences of his home-tongue. All that *canna*, *dunna* and *winna* instead of *can't*, *don't* and *won't* and that antiquated *du*, *dee* and *dine* for *you* and *your*. It reminded him of the "thou, thee and thine" of the bible, and he wanted none of that either. When he left home he'd made a determined effort to lose his native dialect, not just to make his speech more intelligible to strangers but to rid himself of everything that would mark him out as a Shetlander. He was determined to be his own man, to carry no baggage with him. It was to be a new beginning, where no-one knew him…or his history. But now that he was back there would be questions, opinions, judgements. All the things he'd left behind when he set sail for Australia.

They were passing the New Cemetery now, with its carefully tended graves. He pictured the polished coffins where the dead lay in crisp white shrouds. Memories of France flooded his senses. He could feel on his hands the work-smoothed haft of a spade - the spade he'd used to shovel pieces of men into bloodstained sacks… and to dig the shallow scrapes that served as graves. His palms began to tingle. Now he could smell the stench, and see the sickening mess that modern warfare could make of human flesh and bone. Not the clean, heroic wounds of axe or spear-thrust... He shook his head violently, hoping in vain that the images would fly from him as drops of water fly from a wet dog. Ghost-buildings were gliding by. Nothing had any substance. The only reality was the war. Its sights and sounds filled his head, leaving no room for the here and now. Sam's voice broke into his thoughts.

'Bain's Beach, Jamie.' He pointed with his pipe stem. 'Mind when we were bairns?'

Of course he remembered – every little childish escapade – but that was from another life and held no significance for him now. His head gave an involuntary twitch as the heat of anger and frustration erupted inside him. Growing, burning; growing and burning. How could he relate to people from that other time, especially those who'd spent their war sleeping between soft clean sheets? The only real people were those who'd been with him at Messines and Bullecourt. People who knew what it was to live like beasts, surrounded by filth and putrefaction and the mind-numbing, never-ending noise of gunfire. People who lived with death at their shoulder. All the rest were shadow-people. His head twitched several times and his knuckles whitened as he grasped the rail more tightly and waited till the spasms passed. He shouldn't have come home. Already he knew it was a mistake.

Sam watched his brother struggle to master his feelings. A great wave of pity rose like vomit from his stomach to his throat, leaving a bitter taste. Pity was no good. He needed to understand in order to help, but there was a great void between them. Always had been. He laid his hand on Jamie's shoulder and felt his brother flinch at his touch.

'Look, Jamie. Dere's Mammie.'

He pointed to their mother, but it was hard to know if Jamie recognised her for his expression didn't change.

Black-clad like so many others, Jean Jacobson was standing in the lea of the steamer's store with the cluster of folk who were trying to pick out their relatives and friends among the travellers jostling for position on deck. *So much sadness*, she reflected. *You can feel it in da air.* She put up a quick prayer of thanks for her sons' safe arrival. *A'm keeping da Good Lord busy wi my prayers*, she thought. She edged her way through the crowd, and stood beside Ellie Johnson. They smiled at one another in greeting, but said nothing. This wasn't a time for words. Each knew what was in the other's heart, for though they had been mistress and servant for eighteen years, they were lifelong friends. Now they were both waiting to welcome a damaged son home from the war.

The boat completed her manoeuvre and eased herself beside the Victoria Pier. The air was filled with the shouts and curses of the dockers as they handled the ropes, securing the vessel and raising the gangway. Sam watched his mother raise her hand to pull her shawl tight around her shoulders as she waited for them to disembark. She didn't fidget or stamp her feet in spite of the bitter cold. Maybe it was her stillness that made her stand out from the crowd. He could make out her features now. She was a handsome woman, maybe even beautiful. He felt a rush of tenderness. Was she getting thinner? Her cheekbones seemed more prominent and there was a web of lines about her eyes. Those dark, angular eyebrows drew attention to her eyes. Blue. Dark blue, so dark they were almost purple – the colour of the sea before a storm, yet she was the calmest person he'd ever known.

Her boys were making their way down the gangway, Sam in front – ready to break Jamie's fall if he should stumble. Jean held her breath for a moment. How frail Jamie looked. There was none of his swagger now. Of all her brood he was the one who'd caused her most concern, for the harmless pranks of childhood became more serious as he grew older. He'd resented Peter's attempts to keep him on the "straight and narrow", and had been sullen and rebellious. Maybe if she'd had more time for him when he was a bairn? She knew he resented the time she'd had to spend with Sam who was always ill, and the little ones who always needed attention. She should have tried harder…but he'd been so difficult. He shook off all her attempts to comfort him when he wakened with nightmares. Glaring and sullen, and ashamed of his own weakness. She sighed. Things had gotten worse as he grew older - scenes and shouting - and her caught in the middle, protecting her son from his father's wrath, and Peter from shame and disappointment at their son's behaviour. Trying to show both of them her love and understanding. She remembered how thankful she had been if Peter was at sea when the police brought Jamie home, bruised and bloodied from yet another drunken brawl. They were tempestuous times, and the advertisements in the paper were very tempting, offering new lives and opportunities in the colonies. Jamie begged her for the fare to Australia. Was this the solution to their problems?

'I need ta get awa fae here. Aa I need is a fresh start,' he'd said. 'You'll see, Mammie. A'll mak my fortune, an you'll be prood o me.'

'Oh Jamie, Jamie,' she'd said, shaking her head. 'Money's no da answer.' Nevertheless, she'd emptied her "rainy day tin" and given him his fare. She'd also written to her brother in Victoria asking him to look out for the boy, and keep her posted on his progress. That was the only secret she'd ever kept from Peter…

'You're lucky ta get him hame in wan piece, Jean,' Ellie said, glancing at her own son who had lost both legs and was waiting to be carried down once the others had disembarked.

'I am dat,' Jean agreed, but when she clasped Jamie briefly to her and felt his unresponsive body in her arms, she knew his wounds went deeper than severed limbs. *Lord gie me strength ta bear his pain*, was her silent prayer – for she had looked into his empty eyes and seen into his empty heart.

The sombre little group made its way to the pier-head, and climbed into the carriage Sam had ordered. No one spoke. Each was wondering what the next few weeks would bring, and each felt instinctively that they wouldn't be easy. They barely noticed the cacophony around them…the carters urging their horses on, shouting greetings to one another as they came to collect the stores the boat had brought to fill the empty shelves; the dare-devil delivery boys whizzing round on bicycles, ringing their bells incessantly and laughing if people were forced to jump out of their way; the rumble of the wheels, and the sharp clip-clop of their own horse's hooves. It was quieter once they left the cobbled Esplanade and made their way over the compacted mortar of the Nort Kirk Closs, and past Annsbrae to the South Hillhead where they got down. Still silent, they walked the short distance over the flagstones to the gate in the high wall near the top of the close.

The click of the latch alerted their sister, Grace, who ran to the door to greet them, pulling the youngest Jacobson - a reluctant Joe - behind her.

'Weel Jamie, what does du think o wir Grace? She's quite da young lady noo, is she no?'

Grace blushed at Sam's words and gave him a quick smile, but at fourteen there was still too much of the child in her to conceal the shock she felt when she saw Jamie.

'Here, tak dis for me,' Sam said, handing her his overnight bag to help her through her awkwardness.

Joe eyed the stranger openly, his face bland and expressionless. Poor peerie Joe, with his golden hair and the face of an angel. *What is he thinkin?* Sam wondered, but there was no way of knowing.

'Joe doesna go ta school, Jamie, for he canna speak - but he understands every word we say.'

He smiled reassuringly at the boy, then turned back to Jamie.

'Du should see da picters he draas! Dey're better as mony a trained artist can do.'

Sam knelt down and took the little boy's hands in his, attempting to focus his attention.

'It's Jamie, Joe. He's wir big bridder, an he's come hame fae da war for a while. He's goin to sleep in my bed, in da doonstairs room wi dee.' Rising to his height again, he said, 'Tak Jamie's kitbag through for him.' The boy showed no emotion, but obediently reached out for the bag. Jamie made no attempt to stop him. Perhaps that was a good sign.

With an aching heart Jean watched her two sons, man and boy, make their way slowly through the passageway to the front room. It had ceased to be the parlour and had served as a bedroom since the day Sam had come home from Edinburgh, too weak to climb the stairs. Joe had elected to sleep there too. Perhaps he didn't like the isolation of the attic, for all his brothers – barring Sam – were at the war, and there was a row of empty beds...

Breakfast was a subdued affair for Jamie didn't come through to join them, and each was trying to work out why it was that his homecoming was making them all edgy. Once Grace had gone to school, Sam to his work and Joe to the harbour - armed, as usual, with his drawing book - Jean busied herself in the scullery preparing the dinner. When the stew was simmering, she sat down beside the kitchen range with a cup of tea - and her thoughts. As ever they turned to Peter. They were drifting away from each other, and it was breaking her heart for she loved him with a passion that had grown stronger with the years. Their love was the foundation of her life – the well from which she drew her strength. She had to reach him before it was too late. She sipped her tea, grimacing at its bitterness for she hadn't got used to doing without sugar. The war touched their lives at so many different levels. It was over a year since Robert and Andrew had died at the Somme, but the pain didn't get any less. She glanced at their photographs on the mantelpiece. Such boannie boys. So young. Her throat constricted. If only she and Peter could comfort one another, but he was unwilling to share his sorrow, thinking it would only add to her burden. *Can he no see it hurts me mair ta shut me oot? A'll hae ta mak him see dat next time he's hame.* A single tear trickled down her cheek.

'Are you all right, Mammie?'

She hadn't heard Jamie come into the kitchen.

'Dat am I, boy. It's just da onions. Mutton stew for denner da-day. Dat's what du needs. Good home cookin an plenty o rest.'

'I expect you're right,' said Jamie, but in the silence that followed they both knew it would take more than that to exorcise his ghosts.

Chapter Two
Settling In

Jamie sat by the kitchen stove. It was almost noon. He'd only been home a few hours and already it was getting to him. He didn't belong here. Never had. The clock on the wall ticked loudly, keeping time with the aching pulse in his temple, making his head hurt more. The pendulum swung back and fore, back and fore holding his gaze, hypnotising him. Nothing was real. He watched his mother go about her chores, dusting and sweeping – singing snatches of the songs she used to sing before he went away. He remembered them, but the memories meant nothing. He was an outsider, looking in. He'd always been an outsider. His brain was numb. His heart was numb. He had hoped...he shook his head. Hoped for what? Whatever it was, it was too late, and the hope faded as soon as it had formed.

The clock's mechanism whirred and it began to strike the hour. Jamie put his head in his hands and held tight, as each stroke exploded and reverberated in his brain. 'Aa right, Jamie?' his mother asked as she came over to check the stew. He nodded and tried to return her smile. She lifted the lid of the bubbling pot. A cloud of steam escaped, and with it a rich meat-laden smell. This was real. Too real. A cold sweat broke over him. Retching, he stumbled through the scullery into the tiny yard at the back of the house where he vomited until his muscles ached. He leaned against the wall in the shelter of the peat-stack, lit a Woodbine and inhaled deeply while he waited for his gut to settle. The ground rose and fell beneath his feet - mimicking the motion of the boat – and, from time to time, he felt the jolting and shuddering of the train which had brought him north from London. He was being thrown up and down, from side to side… and the noise…the clickety-clack of the wheels grew louder, louder till it became a barrage of deafening gunfire. He was caught in a vortex that was whirling him round faster and faster, disorienting him.

Suddenly a girl backed out of the shed that served as a washhouse. She was carrying a basket of clothes. He tried to focus on her for she was here. Now. She was real. Breathing heavily, she dumped the basket beside a large tin bath on a trestle table. Then she went back into the building. Gradually the world stopped spinning and his panic subsided. After a minute or two, the girl reappeared - this time with two steaming buckets of water, which she poured into the bath. Straightening up, she wiped her brow with the back of her hand. It was then she noticed him.

'Mercy me, boy!' she gasped. 'Du gied me a turn – standin yonder like a ghost.'

He watched as she dried her hands on her apron and crossed the green briskly.

'Du must be Jamie. Dey telt me du wis comin da-day. Du looks…different.'

She smiled and held her hand out in greeting, but he didn't respond. So she let it fall by her side.

'It's fine to see you,' she said, rather formally.

He could see she was embarrassed, but did nothing to put her at her ease.

'Du doesna ken me, does du? But dat's nae wonder. It must be six, no seeven year since du ran aff ta Australia.'

She laughed, 'I was only eight so I suppose A'm changed a lot too!'

No response.

'A'm Kirsty, Ellie Johnson's lass. Does du mind me noo? I used ta come here wi her when she came to do da washin. Noo A'm dy Mammie's live-in maid. I started last week.'

He knew she was waiting for him to acknowledge her, but still he said nothing.

'On Mondays I do da washin an on Tuesdays I do da ironin. Dat's unless Monday's a day o rain – same as it was yesterday – dan everything's a day late. Da rest o da week I run errands an help wi da cleanin'.

Her cheeks were flushed now. Bright red. He could see she was disconcerted by his lack of response to her chatter.

'Du is Jamie, is'n du?' A note of uncertainty had crept into her voice. His eyes flickered and he gave an almost imperceptible nod.

'My bridder Davie's been sent hame an aa. He was on da boat last night. Maybe du saa him? He's lost his legs.'

She waited a second…then rushed on.

'Dat's why my Mammie had to stop workin for dy Mammie. She has ta bide hame wi Davie noo, an dat's why A'm here.'

What possible interest did she think that was to him? Still she prattled on. She was speaking more quickly now. He was making her nervous. He was beginning to enjoy this.

'For such a mornin A'm had! I raise at six an lit da fire under da boiler, dan I ran doon ta da boat ta help Mammie wi Davie's wheeled chair - I kent she'd never manage ta push it up da closs on her ain - but ean o da neebours wis gotten dere afore me. Folk are sae good-hearted... I made dem a cup o tay, dan I ran aa da wye back here ta get on wi my wark.'

Silence.

'A'll better do dat, dan. Get on wi my wark, I mean.'

He lit another fag, took a long drag and blew out a column of smoke. She bent over the bath and began to rub the garments vigorously on the washboard. He studied her coldly, objectively, as if she were an insect pinned out for inspection. After a few minutes she paused, breathing heavily, and eyed him – openly curious.

'So what's up wi dee, dan? I dunna see ony wounds.'

'My chest,' he said curtly. 'It was the gas.'

That was as good a story as any and would put an end to her questions. He was tiring of this game.

'Oh,' she said. 'It's a peety it's no somethin we can see. Folk respect a wound dey can see. Tak wir Davie, noo. Everybody can see at he's a hero.'

He could hear the pride in her voice. The knot in his stomach tightened. What did she know about it? There was nothing heroic about getting your legs blown off, screaming in agony and calling for your mother. He'd seen it often enough, could see it clearly now. He shook his head to dislodge the pictures in his mind. He felt the tremor start again. What was wrong with him? He couldn't eat, couldn't breathe properly and found his balance all out of kilter. He started at the slightest sound and he couldn't sleep – dare not sleep - for they came to him at night, crowding in on him…those wounded boys whose cries he'd ignored, the dead he'd trampled over and the Fritzes he'd killed.

He concentrated on the movements of her arms and the regular little grunts she made with the effort of it; saw the beads of sweat that formed on her brow; watched her dash them away with the back of her wrist. Down, up; down, up. Christ, she was mesmerising him like that bloody clock had done. His head gave an involuntary jerk. Perhaps it was the washing, or the tumble of dark hair, but she reminded him of the French girl at that farm beside the woods. She'd laughed at his clumsy attempts to flirt with her in the estaminet. Humiliated him in front of his friends…next day they'd found her alone, washing clothes in the river.

'Come on, Jamie boy,' his pals said. 'What are you waiting for? It's time to get even.' They'd run down the embankment, taunting her with insults. He could still hear her muffled screams as they dragged her into the trees. Hear his own coarse laughter. See her torn clothing. Well, she'd been asking for it, standing in the water with her skirts all tucked up. Chanting obscenities and stamping their feet, they'd urged him on… and all the while her eyes were fixed on his with a look of hurt and puzzlement, pleading with him to stop. She was still looking at him. Why didn't she scream? Why didn't she hate him? Puzzlement was worse than hate. You knew where you were with hate.

'Come on, Jamie. Gie me a hand.' Kirsty's words brought him back to the present. All the clothes were back in the basket – a neat pile of twisted cylinders.

'I need clean water for da rinsin.' She pointed at the bath. 'You tak wan end an A'll tak da idder.'

In spite of himself, he gripped the handle.

'Lift on "three",' she said, and counted. It was no good. She raised her end, but he hadn't the strength. The water sloshed over, soaking his feet. He reeled back, cursing. His face grew hot with fury. This girl had humiliated him too. Nobody got off with that. Nobody. He'd find a way to pay her back.

'Do it yourself, bitch,' he said in a hard, tight voice. 'It's what you're paid for.'

'Denner-time, Jamie.' Sam had come home for his mid-day meal, and had witnessed the little drama. Jamie glared at them and shuffled indoors, but he had noticed the hurt in her eyes, and the reproach in Sam's. A servant and a "Mammie's boy", too weak to serve his country. Who were they to judge him?

'A'll gie dee a hand,' Sam said softly.

'A'm sorry, Sam. A'm sorry.' Kirsty's eyes filled with tears. 'I didna ken he was sae frail.'

'Dunna blame deesel, lass,' he said gently, as they poured the soapy water down the drain in the wash-house floor. He stood up panting for, though he was much stronger than before, any exertion made him breathless. She took the empty bath outside while he filled the buckets with cold water and carried them out to her, one at a time.

'Tell me, Kirsty – why does du wash da claes ootside? If du did it in da wash-house du wid save deesel a lot o liftin.'

'Du'll think A'm daft, Sam," she replied, glancing at him sideways as she began to rinse the clothes, 'but on fine fresh days like dis I canna bear ta be inside. I like ta feel da wind tuggin at my hair an da cloods are dat boannie, shaestin ean anidder ower da sky, an I dream…' Her expression grew serious and her earnest grey eyes sought his, as if checking for any hint of ridicule, 'Promise du'll no laugh…'

'I widna mak fun o a body's dreams, Kirsty. Du kens dat.' Reassured, she went on, 'I look at da cloods an try ta see things in der shapes. It fairly maks da time pass, an it helps me ta forget hoo hard da wark is. Wan day I saw a muckle white clood at minded me o a sailin ship – a three-master, wi wind in her sails. I dreamed I was on her, sailin tae a foreign land.' Her eyes sparkled as she relived her fantasy.

'Sometimes I see faces in da cloods - fock oot o story books – an I speak ta dem an dey speak ta me. Dey look me right in da eye as if I was somebody worth speakin tae…'

'You are somebody worth speakin tae, Kirsty Johnson,' Sam interrupted rather gruffly, 'an don't you forget it.' Then he smiled at her and gave her a quick hug. 'Come noo. We'll hae ta get wir denner or A'll be late back to wark.'

'Sorry,' he said, as he saw the family seated round the table – their food starting to grow cold. 'We didna mean ta keep you waitin.' Over the last few years, with his older brothers away at the war, Sam had sat at the head of the table whenever his father was at sea. Now, according to family protocol, it was Jamie's rightful place.

'Du should be sittin here, Jamie.' He pulled out the chair for him. 'Du's da head o da hoose noo.'

'I'm fine where I am,' mumbled Jamie. Sam caught his mother's eye. She gave a little nod. 'Sit doon, Sam, an ax da blessin.'

'But Jamie should…'

'Get on with it for God's sake,' Jamie interrupted sharply.

Grace gasped in horror. She'd never heard anyone in this house take the Lord's name in vain. She half-expected a thunderbolt to strike him down. Yet neither her mother nor Sam corrected him. *He's lucky Daddie's no hame. He widna let him aff wi it.* Was this what they'd meant when they said everyone would have to "make allowances" for Jamie, considering what he'd been through and all?

'Sam,' his mother prompted.

With quiet dignity he gave thanks for the food and for Jamie's safe return and asked God's blessing on the household.

Jamie stared at the heads bowed in reverence. How could they swallow all this religious nonsense? They were so gullible. His feeling of alienation swamped him again. He didn't belong here. Didn't want to. His breathing got faster and, as they began to eat, the tremor in his hands got worse, making the spoon clatter against his plate. The weight of their pity bore down on him, as did their studied efforts to ignore the percussive rattle, and to keep the conversation "normal". Only Joe watched openly as half of each spoonful dribbled down over his chest. Jamie couldn't bear the candid eyes of the child who said nothing, but seemed to see into his very soul. The urge to strike out at him was almost uncontrollable. Jean laid her hand on his arm.

'Maybe you should go an lie doon, Jamie. You could do wi a rest. A'll bring dee somethin ta eat in a peerie while.'

Grateful for the excuse to leave the table, he went through to his room and sat on the bed cradling his head in his hands. God, how he hated that boy. It was obvious he wasn't "the full shilling". Didn't even go to school. Yet everybody seemed to accept him and love him unreservedly, and what had he done to deserve it? He'd always be a burden to them. Couldn't they see that? Come to think of it, everyone seemed to love and respect Sam, and he'd been a passenger all his life too. Where was the justice in that? He took off his wet shoes, and lay down on the bed. Maybe Sam did bring in some money now that he was working in the chemist's, he admitted grudgingly, but he'd never done his fair share of the chores when they were children – not like the rest of them had had to do. He'd always been their mother's favourite. She'd molly-coddled him through his coughing and wheezing, saved the top of the milk for him, knitted warm clothes for him, and sat up with him through his fevers, and they'd all had to do with less so he could stay on at school and go to university. Much good that had done him, for he'd had to abandon his course and come home, ill again. And now he was excused war service! Perhaps you had to be a half-wit or an invalid to have it easy in this life. He hated them both – "Mammie's boys" who had no idea what it was like in a real man's world.

Christ, he could do with a drink - but there was no alcohol in this house. He remembered only too well how his father felt about the "demon drink". No, he needn't expect any of the family to help him out. They all knew the rules. He'd have to bribe the servant-girl to get him some. Better still, he'd scare her into it. Kirsty, that was her name. He remembered her vaguely, but she was just a skinny schoolgirl when he went away. She'd filled out now. He'd noticed the curve of her breasts when she was bending over the wash-board, and the neat waist emphasised by the big white bow of her apron. Yes, he'd scare her into it. He smiled to himself, imagining her terror - but there was no humour in his smile, only cruelty in the curl of his lip.

'I'm not a child,' he protested when his mother came through with a cup filled with the meaty liquor from the stew, and held it up to his lips.

'No, son. But du's still in need o nursin, so du'll just hae ta swallow dee pride an let me look eftir dee for a while.'

'I can manage,' he said and took the cup from her and, holding it in both hands, gulped down the hot liquid. Soon he began to feel drowsy. This was the dangerous time. If he gave in to sleep they'd come – come to stare at him with that look in their eyes…as if they pitied him. Pitied him? Why on earth should they pity him? He was alive and they were dead, so why didn't they damn well stay dead? He must not sleep. He tried to fight it. His eyelids kept closing, and every time they closed he started violently and they flew open again.

'Bad dreams, Jamie?'

Reluctant to admit to them in case it made him seem less of a man, he said nothing. Jean nodded.

'Du aye was troubled wi dreams when du was a bairn, so it's little wonder der troublin dee noo, wi aa du's been through.' She stroked his hair gently.

The knot of rage began to burn beneath his breastbone. He wanted to dash her hand away and scream, *What would you know about it? You have no idea what it was like!* But something in the softness of her touch and the tenderness of her voice got through to him and his bitterness subsided.

'Du haes ta sleep, Jamie. Everybody haes ta sleep.' She closed the curtains to keep the sun's glare out of his eyes.

'I canna sleep, I darena sleep,' he whispered, slipping into the dialect now his guard was down. He was exhausted, vulnerable and near to tears. 'Dey aye come when I try ta sleep.'

'So, so. Dunna upset deesel,' she murmured. 'Dey'll no come when A'm here. A'll bide wi dee, like I did when du wis a bairn, but A'll hae ta fetch my spinnin wheel for I canna sit hand-idle.' She patted his hand. 'A'll be back in a minute.'

Tying on her spinning apron, Jean went to the back door and called to Kirsty, who was hanging out the washing.

'A'm goin ta sit wi Jamie for a while. Wid du mak some bannocks when du's finished wi da claes? Der some buttermilk in da pantry.'

'Yiss,' replied Kirsty, clearly delighted to be given the responsibility, 'an I could mak some oatcakes. Dat wid be a treat for him, an Sam likes dem too.'

Jean smiled. 'Du's a treasure, Kirsty Johnson. I dunna ken what I'd dae wi'oot dee.'

Kirsty watched Jean go back indoors. *She's dat good ta me*, Kirsty thought, *an so is Sam.* He was special. He was so brave. He'd shown no fear when he'd come home so near to death. That made him as much a hero as any man at the battlefront. She'd watched him regain his strength, watched his colour return to normal, noted how his handkerchief was no longer spotted with blood when he coughed. The doctors had said there was nothing they could do. It was up to him, they said, to prolong his life by adopting a very Spartan regime – bland food, fresh air and exercise. No excesses, no 'intemperate' emotions. "Moderation in all things" had become his motto. She'd heard the gossips say it was unnatural for a young man to deny himself like this, but Kirsty admired him for it. He had made himself well enough to work again. She reckoned God must have saved him for a special purpose.

The world was a better place because he was in it, she thought, for he was a good man. Not stuffy or solemn – but kind and caring. *Aabody likes him. Especially me. He was dat good ta me when Jamie swore at me.* She smiled, remembering. *I think my hert tirled clean ower when he hugged me.* She could still feel the pressure of his arm around her shoulder and the roughness of his jacket against her cheek. He was her hero. Always had been, even when she was a peerie bairn, and now that she was all grown up she loved him with all her heart. That was her secret, and would have to remain so, for a clever man like Sam would go up in the world and would need a lady by his side.

Coming out of her daydream, Kirsty shook her head. *He's no for da likes o me*, she told herself ruefully. His wife would need to be educated and know about the world so she could talk to him and his clever friends, and she'd need to have smooth white hands and do fine needlework. She glanced at her own hands, which were already becoming reddened and rough. She'd be so embarrassed if anyone were to guess what was in her heart for they'd think she was a stupid ignorant girl, who didn't know her place. No, her feelings for Sam would have to remain locked in her heart for ever, for she couldn't bear it if they were to ridicule her and put an end to her beautiful dreams.

She pegged up Grace's striped pinafore and watched it dance in the wind. It was hard to be so much in love, knowing it could never be.

Back in the room with Jamie, Jean sat at her wheel in the half-light. Soon the footboard was moving up and down with a steady clack, and the wheel softly whirring round. Her practised fingers teased out the thread from the fluffy rowers, and as she worked, she sang – simple honest songs that had been passed from generation to generation. The rhythm of the songs and the rhythm of the wheel placed her at the centre of a comforting continuum where she could look forward and back, bonded with her daughters (and with those who had gone before) by this humble everyday task. Her presence filled Jamie's sleeping mind, and he slept as he had not slept for month upon tormented month.

Chapter Three

Da Day o da Whales

Late afternoon sun was filtering through the curtains when Jamie woke. His mother was still beside him.

'Der nae need for dee ta rise, Jamie. Rest while du can. A'll get Kirsty ta tak dee tay through.'

'Thanks,' he said, reaching for his cigarettes as she gathered up her things and went through to the kitchen. He was relieved not to have to face the ordeal of eating with the others. He lay, one hand behind his head, watching the smoke form patterns in the air above him. He was strangely calm. After a while Kirsty arrived with his tea-tray which she set on the wash-stand. He studied her coolly as she eased herself past the bed and reached up to open the curtains.

'We hae ta mak da best o da sun while we can, Jamie. Da days are getting shorter noo, an der a nip in da air.'

She linked her arm through his and helped him sit up. He noted her strength, and the warm feminine scent of her as she adjusted his pillows. Ripe for the picking, she was – but he could wait, and he'd savour the waiting.

'Here du is,' she said cheerfully as she handed him the tray. 'A fine fresh egg, three an a half minutes. Just da wye du likes it. Beckie sent dem in fae Grindavoe, an some fresh butter at she kirned hersel.' She smiled and added proudly, 'I made da bannocks.'

With that she turned on her heel and had gone before he had time to ask why his sister, Beckie, was staying at their grandmother's. No matter. He'd find out soon enough.

When he went through the meal was over, but everyone was still seated at the table.

'Sit doon, Jamie.' Jean patted his empty chair. 'Du's just in time for da readin.'

His heart sank. He'd forgotten about their evening ritual. He wouldn't be so quick to come through tomorrow night... all this religion was something he'd happily do without. He watched Sam take the Family Bible from the shelf and begin to leaf through the gilt-edged pages. This book was the keystone of their lives. All their names, their dates of birth – and death - had been entered in the front page in their father's painstaking copperplate. Faith and family were bound together between its leather covers.

'What'll it be tonight? Ony suggestions? Jamie?'

He shook his head.

'Mammie?'

'Du kens my favourite, son.'

He smiled. 'Da Beatitudes it is dan.'

In spite of himself, Jamie found he could not shut out Sam's voice, which had a resonance he hadn't registered before. The reading was expressive and, combined with the hypnotic repetition of "Blessed are they..." was very persuasive. He could see, in a way, why they all fell for it. They were easily swayed by pretty words.

'Dat was lovely, Sam,' Jean sighed. 'Blessed are they that mourn for they shall be comforted'.

Then, as was their custom, she led their evening prayers, asking the Lord to watch over Peter and their older sons – Isaac, Osie and Henry.

'Give them calm waters and safe harbour. Be with our Beckie too, Lord, and the Grindavoe folk, and help our daughter Catherine to accept thy will.' She prayed for the souls of Robert and Andrew, and finished by giving thanks for the love and fellowship at their own fireside.

I can't take much more of this, thought Jamie. *They're like children – eager to hear the same fairy story over and over again.* He wished he could escape, but he knew he had to stay. His recovery depended on their care and attention - so enduring the prayers was the price he'd have to pay for it. In the meantime he'd eat the food his mother prepared for him, the treats the neighbours brought and the fresh eggs his aunts sent from Grindavoe. It was his turn to have the top of the milk now! He knew he'd soon feel the benefit of the nourishment and, if he could manage to sleep a little, he'd feel stronger in no time. He'd play along with them, hiding his true feelings – after all, that was what he'd done most of his life. In fact, he reflected, it was only when he was away from home that he'd been able to drop his mask. Sometimes in the bunkhouse with the other drovers, but more especially at the battlefront. *Christ, I wish I was there now.*

After prayers Grace and Joe remained at the table so they could carry out their usual routines. She settled to her homework, and he played with his dominoes. With infinite patience he lined them up on their ends, then gave the first one the gentle push that started the sequence of falling. One by one they fell till none was left standing. The inevitability of it seemed to satisfy him. Every night was the same. Three times he'd line them up. Three times he'd make them fall. Then he'd pack them away and work on his drawings till bedtime.

The others drew their chairs round the stove. Jean opened the door so the glow of the smouldering peats shone through the bars. Then she and Kirsty settled with their knitting while the men smoked – the rich honeyed scent of Sam's pipe tobacco mixing with the sharp pungency of Jamie's Woodbine.

'Why is Beckie at Grindavoe?'

Jean felt a wave of relief to hear Jamie initiate conversation, for he'd hardly said a word all day. He was coming back to them. The sleep must have done him good.

'A'm sorry, son. I forgot at du doesna ken aa da faimily news. Poor Auntie Jessie's brokken her leg, so dey axed if Beckie could go an help wi da hay, an next month dey'll hae ta lift da tatties.'

'Couldn't Auntie Sarah help?'

'No. She has enough ta dae lookin eftir Granny - she's a poor body noo, an her mind is wanderin.'

'Well, what about young Annie?'

'She's in service at da big hoose, an dey need da money at she sends hame. It's no easy for dem wi Uncle Geordie away at da war.'

She gave a mischievous smile. 'Beckie says Auntie Jessie's hobblin aboot on a staff tellin everybody what ta do.'

They all laughed, for they knew Auntie Jessie liked to be at the helm.

'We aa miss Beckie, but it meant we had room for Kirsty ta bide here, an she's a real godsend.'

'She is dat,' agreed Sam, glancing at her affectionately and making her blush.

'What about the boys? What happened to Robert and Andrew?'

There was a shocked silence. Had he not received his mother's letters? Had he not even bothered to read them? Everyone knew she'd written to him faithfully every week since the day he'd left home. Jean's fingers fell still and her eyes grew distant as she explained that they'd both lost their lives at the Somme.

'And the others? I take it they're doing their bit…' He looked pointedly at Sam.

'Yiss,' he answered smoothly, ignoring the jibe, 'Isaac an Osie are on troopships. Dey're based at da sooth coast, an geng back an fore across da Channel takin soldiers ta da war, an bringin dem back on leave, or ta da hospital. As for Henry, his trawler was converted tae a minesweeper. He works here, keepin a passage clear inta da harbour, but we dunna see much o him when he's ashore for he's coortin wi a Scallawa lass.'

Jamie turned to his mother.

'And who is Catherine? The one you prayed for? Why did you call her your daughter?'

The mood changed, and for a moment the only sound was the soft hiss of the kettle simmering on the stove. When she spoke, Jean's voice was heavy with sadness.

'Catherine is Robert's wife, Jamie. His widow. Catherine Carter she was. Does du no mind her? She's a boannie, lively lass, an smart as paint. Her faither has da carriage business. Does du no mind? Robert worked for him in da stables. Catherine liked da horses, but she was aye mair interested in da motor cars. Her daddy lairned her ta drive. A lot o fock towt hit wisna very ladylike, but she didna care.'

Jean concentrated a moment while she broke off the grey thread and joined in the white. When she took up her tale again there was a touch of laughter in her voice.

'I mind her snoring up King Harald Street toot tootin at da boys on der bikes an gaffin fit ta burst. She must a been doin twinty mile an hour. Sometimes she took Robert wi her if he wisna ower busy – an him just a stable boy. But she didna care. Her fock brocht her up ta hae a mind o her ain.'

She paused for a moment, lost in her memories, then went on, 'Dey're weel-aff folk, da Carters, but no prood. Robert an Catherine got married when he was hame on his draft leave no last Christmas but da wan afore.' She sighed, and her busy fingers fell still. 'Poor bairns, dey only had twartree days tagidder, dan he had ta geng back ta da war. She never saa him again…'

The clock ticked several times, loud in the silence. Then Jean went on to explain that Catherine had gone to London, where she joined the Red Cross and trained to be an ambulance driver.

'You see,' she said, 'her idea was at if she could only get ta France, she wid be able ta fin Robert when no idder body could. Naebody kens whaar she is.'

She picked up her knitting again, and spoke more cheerfully, 'Du haes a peerie niece, Jamie. Roberta. She's a year aald noo, born da day da word cam aboot Robert, "missing, believed dead". She bides wi Catherine's folk. She's a lively peerie ting, an a bit spoiled – but wha could blame dem? We keep her on Saturdays, so du'll see her dan.'

Sam picked up the story.

'It's like dis, Jamie. Catherine doesna believe at Robert's dead. She canna accept it.' He struck a match and held it to his pipe, tamping with his matchbox and sucking hard to get it going again. 'Truth ta tell, it's da sam wi me. I keep hearin him tellin me things at simply canna be…'

'So, so,' said Jean. 'Dis is Jamie's first night hame. It should be a happy time. We shouldna be dwellin on sad things.'

'Does du mind wir first trip ta Grindavoe, Jamie?' asked Sam, trying to lift the mood of the evening. '1899 it was, just efter Robert was born.' He turned to his mother, 'You were poorly, Mammie. Aafil poorly.'

'I was dat. I had a real bad fever.' She looked at Kirsty. 'Dy midder helped at da birthin, an cam every day ta look efter me an run da hoose till I was on my feet again. Isaac an Osie an Henry wid a been, let me see… eleeven, nine an seeven – aald enough ta gie her a hand when dey cam hame fae school. But as for da pair o you! Du was aye a handfoo, Jamie. Never could dae what du was telt. An Sam, du was aye coughin an wheezin. So da twa o you were packed aff ta Granny's, for Ellie had enough on her plate wi'oot you!' There were murmurs of agreement. 'Du wid a been tree year aald, Sam. Can du mind dat far back?'

'Weel, I can mind Auntie Jessie comin for wiz wi da horse an kert. It was a lang journey – or so it seemed ta me, daddin up an doon on da rough tracks an gettin farther an farther awa fae hame an fae you.' He smiled at his mother. 'I mind feelin seek, an greetin when I gied ta bed.'

Jamie sneered, 'You always were a timid fellow. You stayed with Granny all the time and never went far from the house.'

'Dat's true.' Sam didn't rise to his taunts. 'She was good ta me. I was happy enough when I settled in. Hoo much can du mind, Jamie?'

'I mind da day da whales cam…'

But his reminiscences were interrupted by Grace and Joe, who got down from the table and brought his drawings for everyone to admire. Everyone was totally focused on Joe. Jamie felt the heat of anger burning again. Nobody was interested in what **he** had to say. He spoke again.

'I mind da day da whales cam...' But still they ignored him.

'He has a special gift, Jamie,' Jean said simply, and smiled at Joe with pride and affection.

'See dis' said Sam, tipping the sketch book so Jamie could see the drawing of the busy harbour, so many ships. There were cruisers, trawlers, sailing ships, all waiting to be inspected. Every one was perfect right down to the last detail. 'Man, I wish I could draa like yon.'

Kirsty pointed to the cobbled esplanade. 'Da stanes look real. Shinin. You can see at it's been rainin.'

'Bedtime, Joe,' said Jean, glancing at the clock. Obediently he gathered up his pencils, sketchbook and dominoes and went through to the bedroom. Kirsty filled an enamel jug with hot water and followed him.

'Mind an wash ahint dee lugs,' she said as she poured the water into the basin. When Joe was settled, Grace read him his bedtime story. Meanwhile Jean made the "eight o'clock's" – the cup of tea they always took at that hour.

Jamie drank his tea, then shuffled through to his room. Joe

was already asleep, so Jamie got into bed, blew out the candle and lay in the darkness with his thoughts.

Grindavoe. Eighteen years had passed, yet he could remember every detail of the day of the whales. He relived its sights, sounds and smells and sensations until at last he fell into a troubled sleep. At first his dreams were of pilot whales – rows of them. Dead. Lined up on the beach. Then he saw the blood and carnage, heard the raucous screams of the gulls and the harsh croak of the 'corbies' which had flocked to pick the carcases clean. Soon the rows of whales became the rows of broken bodies that lined the roadside after each battle, waiting to be taken to some makeshift dressing station... and the carcases became the corpses disinterred by exploding shells. Birdcalls became the screams of the dying, the stabbing of his little knife became the thrust of his bayonet - and his ghosts were there again. They poured under the door, through the keyhole, through the fabric of the walls. Nothing could stop them. They rolled towards him like a cloud of poison gas, surrounding him, suffocating him. Gradually their faces took shape, became recognisable – chaps from his platoon who lay in the bloody fields of France clutching their wounds and pleading for help as their young lives ebbed away. Always the same faces. What did they want from him? Why wouldn't they leave him alone?

Panting and sweating, Jamie woke to the sound of his own moaning. Little Joe was standing beside the bed staring down at him with those wide, expressionless, innocent eyes. Rage welled up, violent and uncontrollable.

'What do you think you're looking at?' He took a swipe at

the boy. ‘Bugger off’, he snarled. ‘Just bugger off’.

Joe evaded the blow and fled to the kitchen shocked and frightened, but unable to tell anyone what had happened.

Chapter Four

Vikings!

Lack of sleep, and his abrupt awakening, had made Jamie edgy and irritable. He washed clumsily in the warm water that Kirsty had brought for him, slopping it over the wash-stand. Looking in the mirror, he scarcely recognised the gaunt face staring back at him. You weren't allowed mirrors in the hospital. Bad for morale, they said. He could understand that – some of his fellow-patients had hideous injuries - missing features and appalling burns. But even his own appearance was disturbing. He dipped the soft brush in his shaving mug and worked up a lather, preparing to shave. The tic which made his head jerk became more pronounced. He held his breath, trying to control it. Opening the razor, he set his feet apart to steady himself and put the blade to his cheek.

Just then there was an almighty bang that rolled round the sky like thunder, echoing off the hills and rattling the window panes. He started violently, cutting his chin as the razor flew out of his hand. Reaching for a face-flannel to stem the bleeding, he gave vent to a string of oaths as Kirsty burst into the room.

"Did du hear yon?" she asked, her eyes wide with horror.

Did she think he was deaf? He glared at her, but moderated his language to a muttered 'God-dammit, God-dammit, God-dammit' – he was not going to be drawn into conversation with a skivvy who didn't know her place.

'I hope it's no anidder mine. A'm heard at da boat at gied doon on Monday was a steamer – nothin ta do wi da war. Just an innocent cargo boat takin coal ta Sweden.' She gave a toss of her head. 'It's just no right.'

Jamie dabbed at the trickle of blood, then bent down to retrieve his cut-throat.

'Here, let me do it,' she said, taking it from him. 'Dunna worry. A'll no hurt dee, I shaved my faither often enough when his hand was shaky.'

She sat him down, put a towel round his neck and proceeded to give him as good a shave as he'd have got in any barber-shop. Her competence infuriated him. Little Miss Perfect, she was – this cuckoo-in-the-nest – but not for long. He'd see to that.

'Dat's better,' she said, patting his face with the towel. 'Come through for dee gruel noo. It'll help dee get up dee strength.'

Who did she think she was – speaking to him as if he was a bairn? He was glad she made herself scarce while he ate, hunched over his plate to reduce the distance the spoon had to travel. He didn't want her feeling sorry for him. In spite of his mood he ate with relish. Hot salty gruel and fresh sweet milk! At the front the water was carried in empty fuel cans, and everything smelt and tasted of petrol. He'd practically forgotten what uncontaminated food was like. Kirsty returned as he pushed his empty plate away.

'Good!' she said, taking it to the scullery. 'Go an sit at da fire noo,' she called over her shoulder, 'I need da table for da ironin.'

She put two irons on the stove to heat and, chattering all

the while, spread a thick blanket on the table, topped it with a sheet and began to sort the clothes.

'Dy Mammie's geen ta da fish market ta see if she can get a fry. Good food is hard ta come by wi dis war on.' She dipped her fingers in a jug of water and, with a deft flick of the wrist, sprinkled droplets on a too-dry nightdress. 'It's wonderful how she manages.'

Jamie fought to control his irritation. She was little more than a bairn but she was ordering him about, telling him where to go and what to do. His mother was too soft on her. They all were, but he'd have to play along for now - because he needed her. He watched as she bustled over to the stove, picked up an iron and spat on it, listening to the hiss to judge its temperature. She gave a little nod, and began to iron. He took out his cigarettes and matches and concentrated on the business of lighting up, so that he didn't have to look her in the eye. Then, trying to keep his tone friendly and casual, he asked, 'Tell me about your Davie, Kirsty. Does he like a drink?'

'Aye, he's just like my Daddie – fond o da hard stuff. Afore da war dey were aye drunk on payday, an da money spent afore dey got hame. Poor Mammie, what a struggle she had ta pit maet on da table! She still does, for things are no better wi Daddie awa an Davie no able ta work. If it wasna for dy Mammie helpin her oot, I dunna ken what would become o dem…' She paused, with a little worried frown, then a sudden smile lit her face. 'It's a good job A'm workin. She'll be real glad o my wages.' She placed the finished garment on the clotheshorse, and began to work on the next. 'Wan thing is certain, Jamie. A'll never marry a man at drinks.'

Jamie stole a sideways glance at her determined little face.

'But you wouldn't grudge a man a drop to ease his pain, would you?'

Kirsty considered a moment, then agreed somewhat reluctantly, 'No, I suppose no – if it was only a drap, an wid truly do him some good.'

She put the now-cool iron back on the stove, and took the other one.

'So you would get some for me then?' he asked. 'A tot of rum or a dram of whisky would fairly help me sleep. You could ask your Davie…'

'Heavens, no Jamie!' she exclaimed in tones of horror. 'I couldna bring drink inta dis hoose. Surely du kens dat? I'd never do dat. Never!'

She thumped the heavy iron down on the damp linen as if to emphasise the point, raising a cloud of steam.

We'll see about that, he thought. *She's had her chance to do it the easy way…*

Aloud, he said curtly, 'I'm going for a walk. Tell Mammie I won't be long.' With that he left the house, banging the door with a strength that surprised them both.

He shuffled along the pavement as far as the Town Hall and back, forcing his legs to move step by weary step. From time to time he paused to catch his breath. No one stopped to pass the time of day with him. Embarrassed by his awkward gait and the strange twitching of his head, they didn't know what to say. So men raised their hats to him with a 'Fine day, Jamie!' and women lowered their eyes and walked briskly on. No matter, he had nothing to say to them anyway.

He wished he were back in France. He'd felt more at ease in the army than anywhere else, ever. The chaps had looked up to him, respected his courage. Officers had held him up as an example to fellows who got in a funk about going over the top. He was somebody there. He had no fear of death - so how could they say he was shell-shocked? Surely that was for chaps who'd lost their nerve and abandoned their posts, or refused to carry out orders. He'd never done that. He was mortified by this diagnosis and protested to the medics that they'd got it wrong. They'd tried to reason with him…

'You were found unconscious in a shell-hole,' the Padre told him. 'The shockwaves of the explosion must have shaken your brain like a pea in a tin. It needs time to recover, so be a good chap and rest like they tell you.'

All that, combined with the persistent noise of gunfire and the lack of sleep, had taken its toll, they said. Hell, he'd got more sleep on the battlefield than he did now. There he could sleep standing up if he had to, and feel refreshed after a minute or two…now he couldn't sleep at all. The minute he closed his eyes the ghosts came to torment him. But he'd done nothing wrong. He'd only been following orders when he left them to die. Surely they knew that? And he'd been serving his country when he bayoneted that young Hun. All that blood and those staring eyes. But he'd done nothing wrong. Nothing.

His thoughts were interrupted by the tapping of a walking stick. He listened. He recognised the side-to-side rhythm of it. It must be…he glanced over his shoulder. Yes, it was… the blind scholar. The only person he'd truly respected when he was a boy, and the only person who'd respected him. He waited till he drew level.

'Good morning, Mr. Burgess. Fine day!'

'That it is, young man. Now don't tell me. I never forget a voice…it's Jacobson, isn't it? Jamie. I've got it now. So you're out of the war, eh lad?'

'Yes, but I'll be going back to France as soon as I'm fit. I've to report for another medical as soon as I get back from leave.'

'Don't be in too much of a hurry, son. You've done your bit.' His sightless eyes seemed to stare into the distance. 'We've lost too many of our fine young men.'

They walked a few steps in silence till they came to the top of the lane. Burgess stopped.

'This is your turn-off, is it not?' he asked, as his stick indicated the gap in the wall.

'Yes, sir.' Then he added rather hesitantly, 'It's good to see you again.'

Burgess smiled. 'Come and see me some day next week if you'd like to talk. I take it you're still interested in our Viking heritage?'

'Yes sir. I am…and I'd like that.'

'Would Wednesday suit you?'

'Wednesday will be fine. Thank you. I'll look forward to it.'

'Wednesday it is, then. Good-day.'

Jamie's heart felt lighter. Haldane Burgess had been his hero when he was a boy. *This was the man who gave talks, wrote papers - and even books – on the Vikings. Yet he made time in his busy schedule for me…when nobody else would. Lent me books. Treated me like an equal. It'll be good to talk to him again.*

'Dat was weel-timed, Jamie,' his mother greeted him. 'Dinner's ready. Will du tak it here, or will Kirsty bring it through?'

'Here will be fine,' he said, and sat at the table.

'Fresh fish wi mealie tatties an Grindavoe butter. Du'll no a tasted onything sae good for many a day!'

She went to the back door to pour the potatoes and shake them in the fresh air in the time-honoured way.

'Sam'll be here in a minute,' she said, returning with the steaming pot.

Sure enough, Sam arrived on cue.

'Da toon is fairly buzzin wi news aboot da explosion,' he said. 'A trawler. Struck a mine. Sam place as on Monday – no far fae da Bressay Light.'

'A terrible business,' said Jean. She didn't want to make too much of it in front of the children.

'Naebody seems ta ken for certain if onybody survived…'

'Pray for dem, Sam, when du says da grace.'

'I saw Haldane Burgess when I was out for my walk,' Jamie volunteered as they began to eat. 'He's asked me round next Wednesday.'

'Dat's splendid, son,' said Jean warmly, glad of the change of subject. 'He aye was good ta dee.' She turned to Joe. 'Mr Burgess telt Jamie aa aboot da Vikings when he was no muckle aalder as dee.'

There was no expression on the child's face.

'Jamie could tell dee some o his Viking stories when he feels up ta it. Du wid like dat.'

Joe nodded.

'They're not just stories,' Jamie muttered.

A look flashed between Jean and Sam as if to say, *He's touchy. We'll hae ta handle him carefully.* Swift though it was, Jamie picked up the silent signal and his hackles rose. His eyes narrowed. How dare they patronise him. He didn't want to be treated as if he were a bairn or a halfwit.

'Sorry, Jamie. I didna mean at dey wirna true...'

Her voice tailed off, and Sam came to the rescue, turning the conversation to the latest reports from the war.

Jamie took no part in it. They were talking about a fantasy fed to them by journalists who reported only what the ministers in war rooms wanted them to hear – men who had never been near a trench and knew nothing about the filth, the lice and the never-ending danger from bombs, shells and sniper-fire - all for a few yards of ground, which would more than likely be recaptured the next day. All that talk of heroism! There was nothing heroic about being killed by a sniper's bullet, or mown down by a sweep of machine-gun fire. As far as he was concerned the only opportunity for heroism was in hand-to-hand combat, when you got near enough to see the fear in their eyes. The chance didn't come often, and you had to make the most of it. That was what bravery was about, but they'd never understand that. So let them have their fairy-tales if it made them feel good.

'Go through for dee rest noo, Jamie. Du'll need it efter dee walk. A'll be through in a minute.'

Jean helped Kirsty to clear the table, then hurried through to protect her son from his demons. His eyes were closed and, though his breathing was a little fast, he wasn't as restless as the day before. Jean nodded. He'd eaten most of his dinner and his meeting with "da blind scholar" had given him something to look forward to. She was full of hope. His interest in the Vikings had saved him once before. Perhaps it would save him again, she thought as she looked on her sleeping son.

Behind closed eyes Jamie's mind was racing. Vikings! Meeting Burgess had brought back floods of memories. He was just a bairn, maybe six or seven, when he first heard of them. That was the first time he was allowed to go out with his older brothers on Up Helly Aa Night. Of course at that age he knew little about the origins of the festival, which marked the end of the Yule celebrations, and which was gradually incorporating more and more elements of Shetland's Viking past. All he knew was that he was infected by the excitement in the air. He'd been so proud to go with his brothers, pulling their home-made longship through the streets, vying with other groups of lads as to whose galley was the best. Finally they set it alight, and watched spellbound. He could feel it now – the smell of the smoke, the heat of the fire, the flames leaping up into the night sky. There had been something elemental about it and just enough danger to make them feel reckless and brave. They had danced round their dragonship cheering until they were hoarse – but as one they fell silent when the cardboard dragon's head took light. They'd watched mesmerised as the edges curled before it fell sideways as if in death. A strange mixture of sadness and pride brought them close to tears. Embarrassed, they raised a mighty cheer to break the mood and put an end to the emotion, which they didn't understand. Then they ran home and gulped down the cocoa their mother had made to warm them before they set off again to watch the adult procession. Their little “Up Helly Aa” was, after all, only a pale imitation of the real thing.

‘Look after peerie Jamie, noo,’ Jean told Isaac, ‘an nae climbin on da Fort waas. It’s a big drap doon…’

‘No, Mammie. We’ll be careful,’ they chorused as they ran out the gate.

He remembered struggling to keep up with his brothers as they rushed headlong over the Hillhead, past the Town Hall and into Fort Charlotte. They edged close to the wall between the big cannons, ignoring the disapproving ‘mind how you go!’ of the people whose feet they trod on, for it was dark as pitch away from the glimmer of the street lights. Isaac lifted him onto his shoulders so he had a bird’s-eye view of the torchlit procession as it followed the Viking longship that was being drawn northwards along the narrow street that ran between the rocky cliff-face and the sea. In the ship was the chief guizer, the Guizer Jarl, dressed as a Viking warrior. Following him were a crowd of masked men – each group, or “squad” as they were called, in a different disguise. Colourful, fanciful, humorous or topical, they brought an exotic carnival feel to the dark winter night. The boys watched, fascinated, till the last guizer passed and the night grew cold and dark again. As the line of torches made its way up Harbour Street the boys raced up to the Town Hall to catch another glimpse as the procession passed along the Hillhead. Then, fast as they could, they snaked down a steep close to the Market Cross and threaded their way to the front of the crowd that had gathered to wait for the burning. They stared up into the night sky, watching the fiery glow that indicated the progress of the procession, and listening to the cheers of the on-lookers growing louder by the minute.

'Here dey come! Here dey come!' he'd shouted jumping up and down with excitement.

The men formed a circle round the galley. The Guizer Jarl stood at the prow silhouetted against the ring of fire, then climbed out after a rousing 'Three cheers for Up Helly Aa!' This was the signal for the men to throw in their torches. Soon the flames were creeping hungrily up the mast, devouring the crow's nest and nibbling at the raven banner. Hissing and crackling, they consumed the painted boards, revealing the ships skeleton. Quickly they spread to the dragon's head. To Jamie's young eyes it looked as if it were truly breathing fire! The brothers stood at the front of the crowd, their cheeks burning with the heat of the blaze. Jamie was transported to a magical world of myth and adventure, filled with exotic characters all larger than life – but none as impressive as the Viking Chief.

So many emotions – excitement, sadness, pride and wonder! Every time it was the same heady mix, but over the next few years something else crept in – the conviction that there was something more to it, something secret that he was striving to understand. It wasn't until he was twelve that everything fell into place in his mind and in his heart. That year not only was the Guizer Jarl dressed as a Viking. So too were the rest of his squad. They took young Jamie's breath away for they looked so brave, so fierce in their winged helmets with their axes and their shields.

As they marched they sang the new song – 'From grand old Viking centuries Up Helly Aa has come/Then light the torch and form the march and sound the rolling drum/And wake the mighty memories of heroes that are dumb/ The waves are rolling on…' He particularly liked the bit about the 'mighty memories' for he was convinced that he could tap into them if he concentrated hard enough. He wished with all his heart that he could have been a Viking. If only he could turn back the clock.

That week, at school, the English Master had set them a task. 'Write a letter to someone you admire. Say why you admire him.' He had nudged them towards the great men of the past – explorers, philanthropists, missionaries, scientists, but Jamie was having none of it. He knew who he would address his letter to. He smiled, for he could still see his mother trying to hide her look of astonishment when he sat down to do his homework without being told, and spent the evening engrossed in it.

Dear Mr Burgess, he wrote, *I know that you made up the Up Helly Aa song for my mother gave me the printed words and your name is on it. I got it for my birthday. It's the best thing I am ever gotten. I think the words is first rate. I am copied it into a speshal note book and I am done some picters too. I know you are an expert on the Vikings and I want to know all about them. I want to put it in my note book too. I winder if you can help me I would be very greatful. Yrs sincerely, James Jacobson. P.S. Why is there a mast with a hand on it on the galley at Up Helly Aa? I am axed my brothers but they dont know. J.J.*

He'd overheard his mother tell his father about it when he came ashore at the weekend.

'It looks as if wir Jamie is turned ower a new leaf,' she concluded.

'Praise the Lord,' Peter had replied. 'He surely has answered wir prayers.'

When the schoolmaster had marked his work Jamie made no complaints about the liberal sprinkling of red lines, but spent another busy evening correcting his spelling errors and translating his "Shetland" grammar into the King's English.

The following day he went to school cheerfully, without his usual morning sulks and grumbles.

'This is good work, James,' his teacher had told him. 'Would you like me to pass it on to Mr Burgess? I expect he would be interested to see it.'

'Oh yes sir. Thank you sir.'

He gave Jamie a sheet of writing paper and an envelope.

'Copy it out in your fairest hand, and I'll see he gets it.'

That afternoon Jamie had run home whooping and throwing his cap in the air with a feeling of pure elation.

A few days later a typewritten letter arrived addressed to him. Master James Jacobson! No one had ever written to him before. He was strangely nervous. He hardly dared open it.

'Here, use this.' His mother handed him his father's paper knife and he slit the envelope open with trembling hands. Mr Burgess had thanked him for his kind remarks about Up Helly Aa song and offered to give him an hour's tuition every week. In lieu of payment Jamie was to read a chapter to him at each session.

Jamie passed the letter to his mother, and fidgeted impatiently while she digested its contents.

'Can I go, Mammie? Please let me go,' he'd pleaded.

'We'll hae ta wait an see what Daddie says,' she'd replied, but her smile told him she would present his case in the best light.

On Saturday his father came ashore for the weekend. That evening Jamie tip-toed downstairs in his bare feet when he was supposed to be asleep, for he knew his mother would be telling his father about Mr Burgess's offer as soon as they were alone. He listened shamelessly at the kitchen door.

'I dunna ken, Jean,' his father had protested once he heard the story. 'We dunna want ta accept charity, do we? An learnin aboot a bunch o heathens…it doesna seen right. Noo if he wanted ta learn aboot da Good Book, dat would be a different thing…'

'I ken hoo du feels, Peter, but surely ony study is good if it stops him runnin wi yon wild crowd aboot da nights. It's hard for me ta keep doon on him when du's no here. Du kens what a headstrong boy he is. Da book wark would keep him safe in da hoose.'

The click of her knitting needles filled the silence while he pondered her words.

'I hear what du's sayin, Jeannie, but it doesna feel right. A'm heard at Burgess was studying ta be a minister, an changed his mind. He turned away fae da Lord. Is dat da kind o man we want wir son ta spend his time wi?'

Jamie's feet were like blocks of ice now and he was shivering, but he kept his ear to the door, willing his mother to win his father over.

'He's a good man, Peter. He had nae quarrel wi da Lord's

teachins. It was da man-made rules he didna like – at least, dat's what A'm heard. Besides, he kens wir a Christian family. He'll respect dat. He'll no say onything ta alter Jamie's beliefs.'

There was another silence. Jamie remembered thinking, *Beliefs? What beliefs?* As he blew on his fingers and tucked them under his armpits to keep them warm. Then he heard his mother's voice again.

'Onywye, wha are we ta judge him? Judge not, that ye be not judged. Does it no say dat in da Good Book?'

'Aye lass, dat it does.'

Seeing that he was beginning to relent, she gave a little laugh. 'Think on it, Peter. Jamie will hae ta improve his readin if he's ta read oot lood ta Mester Burgess. Dat must surely be a good thing, an would da Lord no be pleased ta see him helping a blind man?'

Peering through the keyhole, Jamie saw his father's stern face relax into a smile.

'Oh Jean, Jean. My boannie Jean,' he said, shaking his head. 'Du aye fins a wye ta get roond me.'

Jamie's heart leapt for joy when he heard his father relent. He crept silently away, and lay in his bed shivering. His mind was exploding with excitement, for he knew a new chapter of his life was about to begin.

Chapter Five

Thoughts and Secrets

In the evening Jamie unearthed his old Viking workbook and sat at the fire with his mother and Kirsty, studying the notes he had made all those years ago. Sam joined Grace and Joe at the table, and began to prepare a talk he was to give at the Debating Society the following Saturday. He wanted to do it well for several reasons.

Firstly, it was an honour to be asked and he wanted to prove to himself that he was up to it. Secondly, he knew his father would be pleased that he was arguing in favour of prohibition – a subject close to their hearts as both were passionate supporters of the Temperance Movement. *Maybe it'll lift him oot o himsel for a peerie while.* This was Sam's fervent hope, because his father had been like a ship without a rudder since the death of his sons. He shared his grief with no one, not even Jean. All he would say was, 'We must accept the will of God,' but Sam suspected this devout man was finding it hard not to question His reasons.

I ken how he feels, Sam thought, for he too was struggling to find justification for whole-scale slaughter in the name of peace. How could a loving God allow such things to happen, especially when both the Germans and the Allies claimed the Lord was on their side? It simply didn't make sense. *A'll never understand it, even if I live ta be a hunder.* He stared into space and tried to focus on the job in hand, but he kept seeing his father's shuttered face. *A'll mak him prood o me,* he vowed. *My speech'll gie wiz somethin ta speak aboot. Dan wance he's opened up a bit, maybe I could tell him aboot my sorrows. Dan maybe he would be able ta speak aboot his...*

Sam's heart was filled with love for this plain, blunt man, whose private thoughts were shared only with his wife...*but no dis time,* Sam reflected. He knew his father was trying to spare her the added burden of his pain as well as her own. *How can he no see at his silence is addin ta her sufferin, deprivin dem o da comfort dey could gie wan anidder? Somehow,* he resolved, *A'll get dem ta open up ta each idder afore da weekend is oot.* It was difficult to construct his argument when these thoughts kept intruding.

Jamie's meeting with Burgess, and the rekindling of his interest in the Vikings, was disturbing. Sam's mind kept drifting back to his brother's last year at school, when he visited Mr Burgess every week and spent his evenings writing up the stories he was reading so avidly now. Sam knew better than anyone that Jamie's "interest" had been (and probably still was) more than it seemed. Young as he then was, Sam had sensed it was unnatural in its intensity. It was an obsession, a sickness even - and it had served to fuel Jamie's fascination with violence and cruelty.

Each night, after they went to bed, Jamie had recounted the latest Viking story. Right from the start Sam was aware that Jamie gloried in their gory deeds. And Sam had realised that Jamie, in his fevered imagination, dreamt of becoming just like them. Sam was appalled to learn that his brother had no sense of horror regarding the ruthlessness of Viking raids on the coastal villages round Britain and Ireland. They killed all men who stood in their path, and ravaged the women. Little children were subjected to the utmost brutality. All this seemed to excite him. Even the desecration of churches and the murdering of holy men didn't shock him, though it terrified Sam who couldn't understand why God didn't strike them down. How was it that Jamie never paused to wonder how men could do such things? How they felt no guilt at causing such suffering, and showed no fear of divine retribution? These were real men, Jamie said. Men after his own heart. He wasn't interested in those who were peaceful traders... or those who settled to farm the captured lands, sparing the lives of the original owners. Nor did he have any time for those who renounced the pantheon of Norse deities in favour of the White Christ and his teachings. All he cared about were the deeds of fearless warriors, particularly the "berserkers" – the men who worked themselves into a furious bloodlust and rushed into battle without armour, or any fear for their own safety. Their courage was legendary, almost mystical - and Jamie practically worshipped them.

His passion had scared Sam, who saw these Norsemen as lawless people. Their actions and attitudes were totally opposed to everything he believed in. Many a night Sam's sleep was disturbed with dreams of clashing swords, screams, war-cries and rivers of spilt blood, for Jamie's stories filled his mind with such vivid pictures. Once or twice Sam had pointed out that they were breaking God's commandments. Were they not afraid of going to Hell? Jamie had merely laughed. No, he said. They feared nothing. They didn't believe in God, or Hell. They had their own gods who knew how to enjoy themselves - and if a warrior died bravely in battle he would go to Valhalla, the Viking heaven, and feast and drink with them forever. 'An dat's what A'm goin ta do,' he'd added.

Now Sam glanced at his brother and wondered if so much had changed. Perhaps this war had given Jamie the opportunity he'd longed for – the chance to fight like a berserker; to commit acts that, in peacetime, would be considered the worst kind of barbarism. Shame stabbed at Sam's conscience, and he silently asked the Lord to forgive him for his uncharitable thoughts. He had no right to criticise anyone who put his life on the line for King and Country - but was that truly Jamie's motivation? The niggling doubts would not go away.

Robert had believed in the war. Sam knew that, because they had talked about it long and hard the night before they went to volunteer - or rather, Robert had talked and Sam had listened. It was the right thing to do, he said. Everybody knew that, even the minister. It was important to help "little Belgium" in her "David and Goliath" fight against the Hun, and the threat to our own freedom was real. Besides, Germany should not be allowed to get away with "frightfulness" that was at odds with human decency. 'What does du say, Sam? Will du come wi me an do dy bit?'

'A'll come. Let me come,' Andrew interrupted. He'd been eavesdropping to their conversation, and couldn't contain his excitement. 'I want ta geng wi you.'

'Du's no aald enough,' said Sam gently…

'But A'm big for me age,' Andrew protested. 'Please.'

'Let da boy come, Sam. Let him see a bit o da world. It'll do him good,' said Robert.

This was the first – and last - time that Sam had not been totally in tune with Robert, and he'd found it confusing and upsetting. In his secret heart Sam did not believe in the rightness of this – or indeed of any – war, but he didn't voice his objection for he couldn't bear the thought of having a disagreement with Robert. They'd always thought as one before…so he kept silent, and the following morning they'd gone to enlist.

It was ironic that Andrew, who lied about his age, was immediately accepted - but Sam, who was old enough, was turned down on account of his tuberculosis. He was still ashamed that his initial reaction had been one of relief. Being declared "unfit for service" saved him from having to act against his conscience. It also spared him from having to stand up and be counted with the "Conshies", who refused to fight on moral grounds. He was a hypocrite, he knew that, but he couldn't bear to speak out and hurt those he loved and who loved him. They'd have been appalled to find that he didn't want to fight for King and Country. *What kind o man am I if I canna stand up for my principles?*

Meanwhile Jean and Kirsty, busy with their knitting, talked easily to each other about anything and everything. Kirsty loved the evenings. She looked on them as her "learning time", for they gave her a chance to ask Jean or Sam about things she didn't understand.

'I wish I was a man,' she suddenly declared, taking them by surprise.

'What on earth for?' asked Jean, trying not to laugh because the girl was so serious.

'Weel, dey can vote, so dey can help ta change da bad things in da world.'

'What bad things did you hae in mind?'

'Weel. Sam says at everybody should hae da chance ta mak something o demsels – no just da rich folk. An I think at women should hae dat chance too. I mean, do you no wish you'd done somethin excitin an worthwhile wi your life, Mistress Jacobson?'

'Bringin up ten bairns is excitin an worthwhile enough for me, lass,' Jean laughed, besides, when would I a had time ta dae onything mair?'

Kirsty blushed and her hand flew to her mouth. 'A'm sorry Auntie Jean...I mean, Mistress Jacobson. I didna mean at you...'

'I ken dat, jewel.' She smiled at the girl affectionately. It amused her that Kirsty had chosen to address her formally once she became her housemaid. In fact the girl had insisted. She was proud of her position and saw this as part of it.

'I canna caa you "Auntie" noo,' she'd said. 'It wouldna be right.' But occasionally the more familiar courtesy title slipped out – when she was excited or, as now, embarrassed.

'I think we hae a buddin Suffragist here, eh Mammie?' said Sam, glancing up from his paper-work with a smile

'What's a Suffragist?' asked Kirsty.

Jean explained as best she could, then added, 'Catherine joined dem in London. Dey helped her get her VAD job wi da Red Cross.'

'What's VAD?' asked Kirsty.

'Oh, questions, questions! It's Voluntary Aid Detachments. Da Red Cross trains women ta be nurses or ambulance drivers an sends dem ower ta France. Of coorse, Catherine can drive, so she got a job as a driver.'

Kirsty's eyes grew dreamy, 'I wish I could dae something ta help – something idder as mak gloves, I mean…'

'Du will, lass, on Saturday,' Jean said, diverting her thoughts to the outing they were going to have on Saturday afternoon, when they were going with a group of ladies from the church to gather sphagnum moss. This would be used as a dressing for soldier's wounds. Apart from being useful work, it would be a social occasion. Picnic baskets would be prepared, and carriages hired to take them to the hill at the west of the town. Kirsty was looking forward to it immensely, and prayed that the weather would hold for it was a bit late in the year for picnics.

Jean was less enthusiastic because she knew that Mrs Wemyss, the minister's wife, disapproved of her "attitude" to her servant-woman, and would tell her so if the occasion arose. She'd done it before when she'd seen the comfortable friendship that existed between her and Ellie, Kirsty's mother. 'It's all very well being fair and courteous to these people, Jean,' she'd said, 'but if you allow your daughters to become, er…familiar with your cleaning woman and her child, they'll pick up nasty habits and common manners.' She'd patted Jean's hand. 'Now we wouldn't want that, would we?'

Jean sighed, wondering what Mrs Wemyss would say if she knew Kirsty was sharing a room with Grace, and that

Beckie considered Kirsty to be her very best friend! She gave a vigorous tug at her wool, which fell off her lap. *God forgive me,* she thought as she bent down to retrieve the ball of wool. *I canna fin it in my hert ta like yon woman. A minister's wife she may be, but dere's no muckle Christian spirit aboot her. Have dey never heard at wir aa equal in da eyes o da Lord?* She concentrated a moment on picking up a dropped stitch, tut-tutting to herself, for mistakes were rare, then she continued with her musings.

She looked at Sam, at his little frown of concentration, and a familiar glow of affection wrapped round her, for he held a special place in her heart. *He's like Peter. Dey face der hardships head on an come oot da stronger for it.* She thought about her husband. He wasn't coping this time. *Man an wife should be helpmates, but he's lockin me oot, an he's makin heavy wadder o it.* She knew that healing would only take place in the circle of each other's arms and the drying of each other's tears.

She put down her knitting and blew her nose.

'Time for da eight o'clock's,' she said briskly, pulling forward the kettle to boil. 'It's aa right, Kirsty. A'll get it,' she said as the girl sprang up to help. She needed to keep busy for she was anxious about Peter's home-coming in the morning. Her heart beat faster thinking about him, as if she were still a love-struck girl, but there was fear too. Fear that his grief was changing him into somebody else – somebody she hardly knew.

'Cup o tay, Sam?'

'No thanks, Mammie,' he said, gathering up his books and papers. 'A'm goin ta hae an early night.' He leaned over and kissed her cheek.

'Jamie?'

'Yes please. I'm dying for a drink.' He shot a sarcastic look at Kirsty.

His need for alcohol was driving him mad, but he'd have to get through this weekend somehow. On Monday he'd get Kirsty in the wash-house alone, and he'd have no difficulty in making her see things his way. He too was thinking about Peter's home-coming. He dreaded meeting his father again. Always disapproving. Always trying to clip his wings…*Maybe he'll be proud that I've fought for the 'old country', and he'll treat me with a bit of respect.* But the flicker of hope quickly died as his customary bitterness reasserted itself. *He'd be better pleased if Robert or Andrew had come home and I was lying dead in the battlefields of France.* He snorted aloud, then disguised it as a sneeze. *That's one thing we're agreed on, for I'd be in Valhalla now, feasting with my own kind.*

His mind was in turmoil. He was resentful that he'd survived for he was sure the next world was better than this, and he wanted to get there to be in the company of Odin, Thor and the other Norse gods – feasting, drinking, gaming, fighting and taking his pleasure with beautiful women. That was his destiny. He'd known that since he was a child. *I must have another chance at a warrior's death…if they won't have me back in the army, I'll become a mercenary. There will always be a war on somewhere in the world.* He didn't care about the cause, as long as he could fight. Some day Odin's raven would report that Jamie Jacobson was no coward, and had died a hero's death. Until then he'd make his life on earth as near to the Viking heaven as possible. *Things are clearer in my mind now*, he told himself. Next week will be better. *There's my time with Haldane Burgess to look forward to, and I'll have that Kirsty-bitch where I want her. So I'll get a drink when I want it, and I'll tell my "stories" to Joe.*

He smiled as he recalled telling them to Sam when they were bairns. He'd been soft and easy to scare! Sometimes he'd put his hands over his ears, or pulled the blanket over his head because he didn't dare listen...and he used to sob in his sleep. It would be the same with Joe. Things were looking up.

Chapter Six
Shockwaves

Saturday dawned with a thick fog, and the boat docked a little late. Jean was chilled with waiting, and not a little weary. The last few days had been difficult to say the least, but she was determined to keep things on an even keel. She didn't want a repeat of the scenes and unpleasantness that had taken place before Jamie left home. Subtlety wasn't Peter's strong suit, she thought ruefully, so she needed to alert him to Jamie's 'touchiness' in case his plain speaking should trigger one of Jamie's moods.

She watched him come down the gangway, old before his time. He'd lost his confident bearing, and the spring had gone from his step. Her love for this man was like a physical pain squeezing her heart. She ached with it, wishing she could help him. As he stepped towards her she smiled her welcome, and put her arm through his. When they'd moved away from the pier she broached the subject, trying to explain how edgy the boy was, and how careful they had to be not to upset him.

'It's shell shock, Peter, but he canna accept dat. He thinks it's as good as sayin he's a coward, an du kens he'll no hae dat!'

'No,' Peter agreed with a wry smile. 'He aye had ta be da tough man. So hoo does it affect him – dis shell-shock?'

'Weel, he's thin an weak, his hands are shakky an he's unsteady on his feet - an he's braaly jumpy. He canna sleep for faer o da nightmares. Der nothing dey can do for him. It'll just tak time.' She sighed. 'At least he's hame an safe for a while.' She glanced up at him, adding, 'But he's set his hert on goin back.'

'Is dat right? I must say A'm surprised ta hear it, for he aye liked ta get far better as ta gie. A'm blyde at he still wants ta serve his country, an doesna see dis as a wye oot. Dis war'll maybe be da makkin o him yet.'

Satisfied that Peter's attitude to Jamie was now more accepting, she changed the subject.

'Sam's speakin at da Debatin Society da night,' she said. 'Will du come? It would mean a lot ta him. He's arguing for Prohibition. Du'll be prood o him. I ken I am.'

Peter smiled down at her.

'Yea lass, A'll come, though A'll likely no understand what dey're sayin if dey use yon lang English words. My schoolin didna run ta dat – but A'll come for da boy's sake, an ta please dee. He aye was dy favourite.'

'No, Peter. Du kens fine weel at I hae nae favourite. I love aa wir bairns, though I will admit some are easier ta love as idders.'

'What wye dat?'

'Hit's like dis, Peter - tak peerie Joe. My hert goes oot ta him because he needs protection. An as for Jamie…he needs love as much as onybody, but he can neither gie it or accept it.' She laughed, shaking her head. 'Does du mind when he was a bairn hoo he would bristle like a bantam cock an fight me aff if I tried ta gie him a cuddle? Weel, he's muckle da same yet, but he's my bairn an A'll aye love him, no matter what.'

Peter looked down at her.

'Du has a generous hert, Jean. Du never did hadd his wild wyes against him.' His expression hardened. 'I canna forgive him for da pain at he pat dee through – da police never awa fae da door. Aye fightin. Aye drunk. Da shame o it…an me no here ta help dee. God forgive me for sayin it, but it was a relief when he geed ta Australia.'

'Hate da sin an no da sinner, Peter, an pray at he comes ta repent his sins. Dat's my wye o thinkin.'

They lapsed into silence. Jean wondered what Peter would think if he were to read her brother's letters, for they had charted Jamie's unsteady course, lurching from one job to another – always leaving under a cloud. Bunkhouse brawls, suspicion of theft or terrorising the aborigine servant-girls, who disappeared into the bush and were never heard of again. *He's a black sheep, Jean,* he wrote. *You'd do well to forget him, for you won't hear anything good.* But she could not cut him out of her heart. Constantly she reminded herself, *hate the sin but not the sinner,* and she remembered him daily in her prayers.

'Yiss, A'll always love him no matter what,' she repeated, as though to steel her resolve, and continued more cheerfully, 'Wi Sam an Grace it comes natural for dey're like me, wi der love o books an learnin.' Her voice grew soft, and her eyes focused somewhere in the distance. 'It was da sam wi Robert, though he said mair in his paintins as he did wi words…like Henry does wi his fiddle.' They walked a few steps in silence. 'Andrew was different. Aye up for a fun. Aye playin plunkies an makkin wiz gaff. You couldna help but love him for he made da hoose a lightsome place.' Her voice faltered. 'I miss dem,' she whispered, 'every minute o every day…'

'Da Lord kens best,' Peter said, his tone flat and expressionless.

Jean sighed, 'I suppose du's right.' This wouldn't do, she'd have to lighten the mood before they reached home.

The hill was much steeper now and she was out of breath, but she forced herself to sound more cheerful. 'Isaac an Osie, dey're deep-sea men like dee, so du understands dem better as me.' Her words came in short snatches. 'You're good at weighing things up, an makkin quick decisions. Beckie's like dat too, an Grace. You're practical folk – no dreamers. You see things clearly…black an white.' They stopped for a little while till her breathing settled. 'Folk like me,' she said, 'we see things in colours an patterns an get side-tracked by da beauty or da sadness, an aa da possibilities…'

Her voice tailed off, and she pressed Peter's arm more closely to her side in a gesture of affection. 'It's a good job we hae dee at da helm ta keep wiz right.'

'Aye, but things dunna seem ta be sae black an white for me noo, Jean. Da world is a grey an misty place an I canna see da wye ahead.' He gave a heavy sigh. This was the nearest he'd come to sharing his feelings with her in a very long time. Her eyes were bright with tears of relief.

'God will shaa dee da rodd, Peter, an der'll be clear skies at da end o it. Du'll see.'

He opened the gate for her and, as she led the way up the path, a break appeared in the clouds.

'Look, Peter. What did I say?' She pointed to a tiny patch of blue. 'Enough ta makk a Dutchman's breeks!'

They were both smiling as they went into the house.

Kirsty had made the breakfast and laid the table. She looked at Peter rather shyly as she served the gruel, for she was a bit in awe of this quiet man who was very much the head of the house. She put the pot back on the stove and hovered uncertainly until he said kindly, 'Sit doon, Kirsty. Du's wan o da family noo.'

'Thank you, Captain Jacobson,' she murmured, and took her place beside Grace. *Wan o da family! I wish at dat was true.* It was a wonder they didn't hear her heart pounding with Sam sitting right across from her.

Peter asked for God's blessing. Then, trying to put some warmth into his tone, he said, 'It's good ta hae dee back, Jamie. Shell-shock, I hear. Weel, I dunna ken muckle aboot it, but A'm sure it's nothing ta be ashamed o. Wi da Lord's help du'll soon be fightin fit again.'

Jamie could have wept with rage and frustration. His fury was swift as lightning, just as unpredictable, and just as dangerous in it's intensity.

'Shut up! Shut up!' he screamed, lapsing into the dialect as he lost control. 'You hae nae right ta say A'm shell-shocked. You're always getting at me. You drave me awa wi your preachin an prayin, an you're at it again. It's always "wi da Lord's help dis, an wi da Lord's help dat." Well, He's never been ony help ta me. So shut up, do you hear? Just shut up!'

With that he rose unsteadily from the table, spilling his gruel, and lurched away through to his room.

There was a stunned silence. Jean was torn in two. She wanted to run after Jamie and hold him, rock him, whisper the comfort-words all mothers use to take their children's hurt away. But, glancing round the room, she took in the horror on all their faces and knew the others needed her too.

Grace and Kirsty were holding hands, their faces white as sheets.

Joe's expression revealed nothing, but he was beating the table with his spoon in a regular, repetitive rhythm, and rocking back and fore.

Sam was paralysed by the effect Jamie's outburst had had on everyone. His eyes met Jean's in a look of agonising indecision. *Tell me what ta do, Mammie,* was his unspoken plea. *Tell me what ta do.*

And Peter. Oh, God. Poor Peter. His expression was one of complete bewilderment. She knew he didn't understand what had happened, or why. He'd been trying to show sympathy, to say the right things, strike the right note. But it was impossible for him to be other than plain speaking and honest. He shouldn't have mentioned shell-shock, but it was too late now. The damage was done and it was her fault. She should have made the situation clearer to him, explained how easy it was to trigger a violent outburst.

'Go ta Jamie, Sam. See if du can calm him doon,' she said with quiet authority. Automatically he did as she asked.

Sam found Jamie standing with his back to him, punching the wall with his clenched fists to emphasise his words.

'Shell-shocked', he said. He as good as called me a nithing. He canna get away wi dat. It's the worst thing he could say. Every Viking kens dat. He'll hae ta pay da price.'

Sam listened, aghast. "Nithing" was the Viking word for coward – the worst possible insult, and had to be avenged.

Dear God, did Jamie really believe he was a Viking? He must be losing his mind.

Suddenly Jamie became very quiet and still. The delusion, if that was what it was, had passed. He leant his fevered forehead against the wall.

'Christ,' he groaned through gritted teeth. 'I wish I could get my hands around his neck and force him ta apologise. He had nae bloody right ta say I was shell-shocked. Naebody does.'

He turned to face Sam. His expression was indescribable. He was a soul in torment.

'Everybody kens at shell-shock is just a fancy name for funk, Sam. The Brits tried ta use it for a defence in the military courts when blokes were accused o desertin der posts, or refusing ta obey orders. Said dey didna ken where dey were because da noise an da smoke had fuddled der minds, or dat dey didna hear da orders...Haig was havin none o it an had dem shot just da sam. So du sees, Sam, der nae such thing as shell-shock.'

Suddenly he slumped. Sam held him up or he would have fallen to the floor. Great rasping sobs tore through him. Sam waited till the worst was past. Then, keeping his voice calm and even, he said, 'Jamie, listen to me.'

He led him to the bed, sat him down and drew up a chair for himself, so their eyes were level.

'Look at me, Jamie. Look at me.'

He waited till Jamie made eye contact.

'Der is a condition – a kind o illness – at's brought on by noise. Lood noise at goes on an on wi nae let-up, or by da shock-waves at comes fae bombs when dey explode. Dey affect a body's hearin an his balance. A'm heard dey can even brakk bones – da shock-waves, I mean – an dey can caase terrible pressure on da brain, an it aa gets worse when fock are been livin on edge an getting nae rest.'

He paused to let Jamie digest this, then went on, 'It doesna matter what name dey gie it, Jamie. It's real, an it has nothing ta do wi whether you're brave or no. Man! We baith ken at du's nae coward, but dy body needs time ta recover…an sae does dee mind. Du's nae different fae onybody else.'

Jamie said nothing, but Sam knew he was listening.

'Things'll get better wi time.'

'Dat's what dey aa say.' Jamie's voice was barely above a whisper, and he made no protest when Sam took off his shoes for him and swung his legs in over the bed.

'Rest noo, Jamie.' He pulled the covers over him. 'A'm heard at da "talking cure" is helpin a lot o chaps. Think aboot it. A'm a good listener.'

Sam walked quietly out of the room leaving Jamie to make whatever he could of what he had said. He was overwhelmed with sympathy, maybe even love, for his brother. Yet he felt a burning sense of outrage that Jamie should have hurt their father with his cruel and blasphemous words.

Nothin is straightforward when it comes ta folk an der feelins, he thought ruefully.

When Sam had left the room to comfort Jamie, Jean drew a deep breath.

'It's time you aa kent mair aboot Jamie's condition,' she said, and waited till she had their attention. 'Daddie's right. It is shell-shock.' She smiled reassuringly at him, 'but it's a strange illness, an naebody seems ta ken hoo ta treat it.'

'So hoo do you ken aboot it, Mammie?' Grace asked.

'Sam wrat tae ean o his Edinburgh friends, axin aboot it, an he shaad me da letter at he got back. It said at some o da poor boys at hae it look as if der gone ta pieces wi fright – trembling, shakkin an staggerin aboot. Some o dem canna speak. Some canna bear noise. I canna say at I really understand it, but dis I do ken – dey are not cowards. Dey're wounded just as much as ony man at's lost an airm or a leg…but der wounds are in der minds. In der brains.'

'Oh, I see,' said Grace slowly, as she worked it out. 'I ken at it's wir brains at tells wir bodies what ta do, so if wir brain is hurt an canna work right, neither can onything else. Is'n dat right, Mammie?'

'Somethin like dat, jewel, but it's complicated. It affects der moods an feelins too…'

'Dat's what I want ta do,' said Grace with quiet conviction, interrupting her mother.

'What does du mean, lass?' asked her father. 'Du's no makin sense.'

'A'm goin ta be a mind doctor.'

'Du means a psychiatrist,' said Sam, coming back into the room.

'Weel, caa it what you like, dat's what A'm goin ta be – if it's aa right wi you, Daddie? Can I go ta university an study ta be a psych, psych…?'

'Psychiatrist,' said Sam, smiling.

'We'll had ta speak aboot it, Grace - but I'd be fair prood if du could do onything ta help poor boys like Jamie. I had no idea…'

'He's restin noo,' said Sam, and he laid his hand on his father's shoulder, then kissed his mother's cheek. 'A'm late. Mr Leask will be wonderin what's come o me. Will you be…'

'We'll be fine.' His father's voice was strong and confident, and when his eyes met Jean's his gaze was steady. 'We'll be fine,' he repeated.

Sam knew that it was true. Peter was sitting straight and tall. They would be fine. Sam could not voice his goodbye for the lump in his throat. Maybe God had put them through this crisis to shock his father out of his black despair. As he hurried down the lane he looked at the sky and mouthed a heartfelt, 'Thank you.'

'You too, lasses,' said Peter. 'Away you go an get some fresh air. Da day has fairly brightened up.'

Kirsty looked undecided for she still had chores to do. Jean nodded. 'Tak Joe wi you, an Roberta. She should be here ony minute noo.' She turned to her youngest, who was calmer now. 'Du would like dat, eh Joe?'

Joe nodded and ran to fetch his jacket. Jean had noticed a strange bond growing between him and her little granddaughter, who arrived on cue, brought by the Carters' maid. Jean leaned in over the gleaming perambulator and tickled the little girl, who giggled and squirmed.

'Du gets mair like dee Daddie every time I see dee, does'n she, Peter?'

Kirsty, Grace and Joe appeared dressed for outdoors.

'Go,' she said, shooing them to the door like chickens. 'A'll see ta da dinner an da picnic – onywye, da Captain an me…we hae a lot ta speak aboot.'

When they were alone Peter took her in his arms. There was no need for words. He had come back to her, and that was all that mattered.

Jamie lay on the bed trying to get to grips with what had happened. He was deeply disturbed by the morning's events. His mood alternated between one of total physical and mental exhaustion and one of savage violence. In the former he was wandering in a featureless wasteland where nothing survived – never had and never would – where he even doubted his own existence. In the latter he was very much alive. He was filled with tremendous energy and wanted to scream and rage and destroy. In the brief transition between these two extremes he tried to force himself to remember what Sam had said, for some of it made a kind of sense. All he could recall was, "Du's no a coward".

He knew he was no coward, but that wasn't good enough. He wanted everyone to acknowledge it too. How? He needed to have his courage publicly recognised. When it came, the solution was so obvious that he laughed out loud. He needed a medal to prove it to the world, so he'd get one when he went back to France. Most chaps got their decorations for "Putting their lives at risk in order to save others." Well, there was no problem there. He could crawl out into No-Man's-Land and bring back the wounded as easily as the next man, or go on daring raids and perform heroic feats. That was the better option. His father wouldn't call him a "nithing" when he had a medal pinned to his chest.

Chapter Seven

Signs and Portents

Kirsty and Grace returned from their walk in high spirits, and had clearly put the morning's episode behind them. They could hardly contain their excitement, which seemed to affect little Roberta, for she laughed with them. Jean was pleased to see Kirsty in frivolous mood, for life's hardships – and that drunken father of hers – had put an old head on her young shoulders. *She's a fine lass, and bright too,* she thought. *I hoop she gets a better man as her midder did…*

The girls rushed over to the dresser when they spotted the picnic basket, and Grace lifted up the clean white cloth to see what her mother had put in it. Their eyes widened with delight – bannocks with rhubarb jam, a slice of seed cake and, as a very special treat, three shiny red apples that Jean had acquired in exchange for a pair of her hand-knitted gloves.

'Ai-pils!' they exclaimed, pronouncing the word in the Shetland way. 'Ai-pils!'

They each grabbed one and bent down to show this treasure to Roberta.

'See, Berta. Ai-pil!' They said it slowly, one after the other. 'Say it, Berta. Say it'

'Ai-pil,' said Roberta, and laughed as everyone clapped their hands.

Peter picked up his little grand-daughter and threw her up in the air, and caught her again.

'So du's lairned a new word, is du, jewel?' he asked and his deep laughter mingled with her excited shrieks.

'What's aa da noise aboot?' asked Sam as he came in from work.

'Ai-pil!' said Roberta again.

'A new word!' said Sam. 'My, du is a clever lass.'

'Dis ean's for dee, Joe.'

Jean produced the polished fruit from her apron pocket. Joe took it from her and ran over to his little cousin

'See, Berta,' he said, joining in the game. 'Ai-pil!'

For an instant time stood still, the sound of his voice ringing in the air. It was a little miracle. All eyes were on him. Instinctively Jean knew she must draw attention away from him before he became conscious of their reaction. He couldn't bear people to look at him.

'Pit da aiples back in da basket, lasses, an come an tak up your dinner. Sam, geng an ax Jamie if he's comin through, or if he wants it in his room.'

Her heart was pounding as if it would break through her chest. He had spoken! Joe had spoken! It was only a couple of words, and he might not speak again – but it proved that he could. Praise be to God.

Jamie appeared, and the mood of hilarity dissipated as he took his place at the table. Conversation was stilted at first, for they were anxious to avoid upsetting him – and they were all trying not to stare at Joe. But Jean had a kind of energy about her that had been missing for too long, and her mood of confident optimism spread around the table, touching everyone. She noticed that Peter's eyes rested from time to time on the two silver-framed photographs, which stood on the mantelpiece – each with a black ribbon across one corner. Up till now he hadn't been able to look at them. Could this mean he was beginning to come to terms with his grief? He looked ten years younger than the man she'd met off the boat this morning. That was surely a good sign.

After dinner was cleared away, Jean and the girls set off to meet up with the other women at the manse. Two carriages were about to leave.

'Come along, Mrs Jacobson. There's just enough room for you and Grace,' called Mrs Wemyss, 'and the little one.'

Quickly Jean assessed the situation. Kirsty was not welcome – not good enough to ride with the ladies of the town.

'Thank you, Mrs Wemyss, but I'll wait for my friend.'

'As you wish.' Mrs Wemyss' eyes narrowed and she shook her head and gave the other ladies a pained look – as if to say, 'Well, I tried...' Then she tapped the driver on the shoulder. 'We're ready now, Thompson. You may drive on.'

'Oh dear,' murmured Jean as the carriages moved off. 'I've upset her again.'

At times like this she felt as though she were neither fish nor flesh nor good red herring. She no longer belonged among the ordinary working folk, nor was she fully accepted among the gentry. She was trapped in her own No-Man's-Land. She felt a pang of guilt. Peter had worked so hard to get on, progressing from cabin boy to Master Mariner in such a short space of time. She was proud of him and appreciated all the refinements his position afforded them. They had a nice house with good-sized rooms and big windows that could open. And on fine days she did open them and let the fresh air through the house – she could do that now they lived near the top of the hill, well away from the stink of the germ-laden garbage middens that accumulated near the foot. They didn't have a bath or an inside privy as the more well-to-do did, but they had plenty of running water, and she no longer had to queue at the well, as she'd had to do in the early days. *Yes,* she reminded herself, *I hae a lot ta be thankful for.* With careful management she could feed and clothe the family well. She could even put a little aside in the tin on the mantelpiece from time to time. They wanted for nothing.

She remembered how Peter had insisted – after her illness when Robert was born – that she should have help in the house for the workload was heavy with seven sons to care for. He didn't want her worn out with the daily toil as their mothers had been, he said. The idea of employing a servant didn't sit easy with her, but she had to admit that an extra pair of hands would be a great help. So she had agreed to it on condition that their employee was Ellie. *Dat wye A'll no be da mistress, an she'll no be a servant. We'll just be friends helping ean anidder.* Ellie would ease the pressure of the work in the house, and she would help Ellie by giving her employment that was better paid, and not so back-breaking or painful on the fingers as gutting fish and packing them in barrels. She winced as she thought of the salt stinging in the open cuts on Ellie's swollen fingers.

Peter had wanted her to have a "better" life. And so she did in many ways, but it brought its problems too. This business of knowing one's place and behaving accordingly. She'd have no truck with that. She was still the same person she'd always been, and refused to change her attitude to people she'd known all her life just because she was better off and had "advantages". *But dat doesna hinder dem fae changing der attitude ta me,* she reflected sadly, for her friends from the old days no longer stopped to pass the time of day with her when she met them in the street, and she'd noticed a subtle shift in their behaviour when she visited them. She was given the best cup, the best chair, and they didn't share their troubles with her as freely as before. It was hard work to win their confidence. However, just as she refused to set herself above ordinary working folk, so she refused to respect her so-called "betters" on account of their fancy houses, fashionable clothes and the number of servants they kept. The only people she looked up to were those who earned her respect through their integrity, their honesty and the way they conducted their lives...and nobody deserved it more than Ellie.

On cue, Ellie appeared at the top of Burns Lane, red-faced and puffing. She had been tasked with making the tea, so she was carrying two heavy black kettles. On account of their weight she was to travel in the cart which would later transport the full sacks of moss. The other women from the "poorer classes" had gone ahead on foot to collect some peats and get a fire going, ready to boil the tea-kettles for the picnic.

'Come, lasses!' Jean called, climbing nimbly into the cart. 'Dis'll be a fun!'

The girls lifted Roberta up to her. Then Grace got in. Kirsty ran to meet her mother and took the kettles from her. She handed them up to Grace, who stowed them safely then took Ellie's hands and pulled while Kirsty pushed from behind. Laughing they settled themselves comfortably on the bundles of Hessian sacks, which would soon be filled with moss. As soon as Roberta heard the horse's hooves she began to make clicking noises with her tongue. The girls kept the little company entertained with rhymes and songs. Everyone was in carefree mood.

'It's like when we were young, Ellie,' said Jean.

'Yea, we could mak on at we're at Grindavoe again, fetchin in da hay, or bringin hame da peats.'

The two women reminisced happily about their young days, when they'd been neighbours, friends - and equals. It was a day stolen from another time, a carefree time before they grew up, and their lives were changed for ever – changed by a fishing disaster that had claimed Jean's father and her brother, Samuel. That July gale had blown up without warning and a number of boats had been lost, leaving several houses with widows and fatherless children. It had devastated the little community. Jean's mother had never got over it – and neither had Ellie, for Samuel and Ellie had been planning to marry at the end of the fishing season. Already the young friends had begun to look on one another as sisters. But that was not to be. The Lord must have had his reasons...

When they got to the chosen site, Kirsty and Grace were dispatched to fill the kettles at the nearby stream. By the time they returned the ladies had already made a start. They worked in pairs, one to hold the sack open, and the other to fill it. Kirsty and Grace joined them. Soon all the sacks were bulging with the damp starry moss, and it was time for the picnic. Of course everyone was aware of the purpose of the afternoon's work – and there wasn't one among them whose life hadn't been touched by the war – but the sun shone and the birds sang and they were glad to put the harsh realities to the back of their minds for an hour or two. The mood was festive, frivolous even. There was light-hearted banter and gossip – even a sing-song, which everyone joined in. One of the drivers gave a splendid rendition of Harry Lauder's "I love a lassie".

All too soon it was time to clear away the picnic things, douse the fire and load up the sacks. The carriages led the way home along the aptly named Ladies' Drive, followed by the cart, with Kirsty and Grace perched on top of the sacks munching their apples. Their faces were flushed with the fresh air and the excitement, and a sleepy Roberta lay between them sucking her thumb. Next came the servant-maids and shop girls, arms linked, and stepping briskly. Sometimes they marched, singing as they went, sometimes they dawdled, exchanging confidences about their soldier-lads and their hopes and dreams. Bringing up the rear, Jean and Ellie strolled down the hill in companionable silence.

Jean glanced at her friend and her heart swelled with love and respect for her. The year after Samuel drowned Ellie had married Geordie Johnson, and Jean had married Peter. Geordie had been a likeable enough rascal before the drink got the better of him, Jean admitted. He'd made Ellie laugh – and Lord knows there was little enough laughter round Grindavoe in those days – so who could blame her for settling for him, though her heart was at the bottom of the sea with Samuel? The two young couples had moved to Lerwick with such high hopes.

Jean stole a sideways glance at Ellie. Her face was lined beyond her years and her red, swollen hands were becoming twisted and rheumaticky with a lifetime of doing other people's dirty work. All she wanted now was that Kirsty's life would be easier and more fulfilling than her own had been. *I ken she canna hae da education at wir Grace'll hae,* Jean told herself, *but A'll do my best ta see she uses yon quick mind o hers. She can lairn aboot da world fae books da sam as me.* Silently she resolved to do everything in her power to help the girl.

As if she'd read Jean's mind, Ellie suddenly broke the silence.

'Does du ken, Jean, every day I thank da good Lord at my Kirsty is aside dee, in a good Christian hame – awa fae da drink an aa at goes wi it? She looks on dee as a second midder...'

'An I look on her as a third dowter. A'll see at nae harm comes at her. Du can depend on dat.'

Behind them the afternoon sun was a fiery red, reflected in the water of the harbour in front of them, and spreading its glow over the hills of Bressay beyond. It truly had been a day to remember. In the troubled days that lay ahead they would often think back to that golden afternoon.

When Jean and the girls returned, Peter listened to their excited chatter, then reported that Joe had been out all afternoon and had produced some excellent drawings, Jamie – as far as he knew - had stayed in his room. He had been out on his "Saturday rounds".

'Dey wir blyde ta see me,' he told them, and Jean was obviously pleased, Kirsty thought, for her expression was one of surprised delight. Kirsty was curious as to what his "Saturday rounds" were, and resolved to ask her mother if she could explain the following day.

Conversation was relaxed at tea-time.

'I see in *The Shetland Times* that there's to be a sale on the 27th,' Peter said. 'It's surely goin ta be a grand affair for it's ta be in da Drill Hall an da Public Park...aa kinds o edibles an knitwear. Dey're hoopin ta raise a lot a money for da Red Cross an da Hospital Funds. It's ta be a Public Holiday, so aabody can geng.'

'Anidder day oot, lasses,' Jean said, and the girls nodded and beamed. Their social life was certainly looking up.

Jamie contributed nothing, but since he seemed calm enough, Jean had no qualms about leaving Kirsty to get his "eight o'clocks", and to see that Joe went to bed at a reasonable hour. So she, Peter and an excited Grace went to the Debating Society with Sam to hear him speak.

He argued his case well, making his points clearly and with conviction, swaying the "don't knows" to his side, and even bringing some of the "cons" to his way of thinking. His parents looked on with quiet pride when folk crowded round to congratulate him. Even Mr Wemyss shook his hand and said, 'Well done, lad!'.

When the others had left for the Debate, Joe settled as usual with his drawings and dominoes, Jamie became engrossed in his old notebooks and Kirsty sat down with her knitting. No one spoke. At eight o'clock she made the tea. Then, just as she was about to take Joe through to bed, Jamie said, 'I'll tell him his story tonight.'

Kirsty felt uneasy, but she could think of no good reason why he shouldn't. Besides, she hadn't the right to stop him. So she said nothing. Jamie turned to the boy.

'Mammie said you'd like to hear some of my Viking stories, eh boy? Come with me.'

Joe made no response, but obediently stood up to follow Jamie through to their room. Kirsty picked up her knitting, but try as she might she couldn't concentrate, nor could she quell her nagging suspicions. Something was wrong. She was sure of it. When she could contain herself no longer, she tiptoed through to satisfy herself that all was well. The door was ajar. Jamie, at the climax of his story, was standing by the bed acting it out.

'They don't call my axe 'Skull-splitter' for nothing,' he snarled, bringing the imaginary weapon whistling through the air to land on the boy's pillow, right beside his head. Joe lay as if turned to stone, unable to move. His eyes were huge and dark with fear. He was making little whimpering noises.

Without a second thought, Kirsty stormed in.

'Is du no caased enough trouble for wan day?' Her voice was cold with anger. 'Get awa fae da boy.'

She held out her hand to Joe. 'Come,' she said gently. 'A'll get dee a fine hot cup a cocoa, an A'll mak up a bed for dee up da stair aside Sam. A'm no letting dee bide wan minute mair wi dis…dis heathen.' She glared at Jamie. 'Du should be ashamed a deesel – a grown man, gluffin an innocent bairn.'

With that she swept toward the door with the boy in tow.

'Take care, bitch. You should mind your place. You're only a servant in this house, you know, and you can't speak to me like that.'

His tone was threatening, but anger made her bold. She stopped in her tracks and retorted,

'A'll speak ta dee however I like. A servant I may be, but A'm every bit as good as dee. At least I dunna go around hurtin folk at canna stand up for demsels.'

Her heart was beating fast as she and Joe left the room.

She left Joe sipping his cocoa while she went to the linen cupboard to collect clean sheets and blankets, but before she could take him upstairs, he took hold of her skirt and pulled her towards the bedroom.

'Du doesna want ta sleep yonder, does du?' she asked, amazed.

He shook his head. Mystified, she let him lead her. Quickly he ran across the room and, lifting the corner of the mattress, pulled out his sketchbooks. Then, hugging them to his chest, he ran from the room. Together they climbed the steep stairs to the attic.

When the little party returned from the Debate, they found the kitchen deserted. Kirsty must have gone to bed, Jean thought. It had been a tiring roller-coaster of a day. She filled an earthenware hot water bottle for Sam and went upstairs with it. There she found Joe tucked up in bed. Kirsty was sitting in the candle-light, singing to him softly.

'Joe was faird for Jamie efter dis moarnin's carry-on,' she whispered. 'I thought he'd sleep better up here wi Sam. I hoop you dunna mind...?'

'Mind? Of course no. Du did da right thing.'

Jean stroked her son's cheek. It was only when he was asleep that she could allow herself to caress him, for when he was awake he shrank away from physical contact – even with her. *Poor peerie boy,* she thought, and kissed his warm cheek.

She took Kirsty's hand. 'Mercy, lass, but du's ston cowld! Come an warm deesel at da fire afore du goes ta bed.'

She blew out the candle and led the way downstairs.

'How did Sam's talk go?' Kirsty asked.

'A'll leave him ta tell dee aboot it,' Jean replied, smothering a yawn. 'Come, Peter. It's been a heavy day. We'll leave da young eans ta see da fire is restit.'

So Kirsty sat by the stove, and listened to Sam tell her about the success of his maiden speech.

'Mr Henry – dat's ean o da leadin socialists – said, 'Have you not thought about getting into politics, lad? We could do with a young fellow like you. You have a very persuasive tongue.' He mimicked Mr Henry's rather pompous "English" speech, making Kirsty laugh.

'Weel, why no, Sam?' she said, with a twinkle in her eye. 'Onything's possible. Is'n dat what du's aye telling me? Think aboot it – Samuel Jacobson, MP. It has a kind o a ring tae it.'

'Noo, noo Kirsty. Wan swallow doesna mak a summer, an wan speech doesna mak a politician,' he laughed. 'We shouldna get ideas above wir station.'

'Dat's true,' she said, suddenly deflated. 'Weel, A'll better see ta da fire an get some peats in for da morning.'

'If du banks up da fire, A'll get da peats.' He laid the remaining two peats beside the stove and, as he went outside to fill the empty basket from the stack, his thoughts were of Kirsty. *She's a fine bairn, an easy ta speak tae.*

It was a beautiful night. The sky was a great black bowl pierced with tiny stars that seemed to pulsate with life. He lit his pipe and stood for a moment letting the peace wash over him. Suddenly the aurora began to play across the northern quarter. At first the display was extraordinarily bright, then it became a deep crimson. Blood-red. *Da aald fock wid say it's a bad omen...but hoo can it be when it's sae boannie?*

'Kirsty,' he called in a stage whisper. 'Come an see da Merry Dancers.'

When she didn't appear, he called a little louder - still no response. So he knocked out his pipe and carried the peat-basket into the kitchen.

'Kirsty...' he began, but there was no one there. He felt a pang of disappointment. The room seemed strangely bleak without her.

Chapter Eight
Sunlight and Shadow

On Sunday the fine weather continued. The Jacobsons – except for Jamie – went to church in the morning. Peter was filled with a quiet joy for he and Jean were one again. He was acutely aware of her arm, her hip, her thigh pressed against his as they sat straight-backed in the family pew. As they intoned the Lord's Prayer, he opened his eyes and watched her lips shape the words *Hallowed be Thy Name, Thy kingdom come, Thy will be done…* Suddenly, inexplicably, he felt God's presence with him and found that, at last, he could pray again. He wanted to shout 'Hallelujah' but, fighting to control his elation, he breathed a silent prayer of thanks to his Lord and Saviour for reaching out to touch his heart once more. Nothing could harm them now.

Kirsty had gone home as soon as she'd cleared the breakfast things, for it was her day off. 'Du needna hurry back,' Jean had said, 'for Jamie will be here ta keep an eye on Joe while wir at da Kirk.' Northwards she went along the Hillhead, then turned right into the close. The farther she went downhill the smellier it became. She picked her way carefully, and held up her skirts to avoid the worst. She took off her shoes before entering the house so she wouldn't truck dirt over the floor, but she took them in with her and put them on the sack behind the door. If she left them on the doorstep they might not be there when she was ready to leave. *Livin fae hand ta mooth maks folk desperate, but I could never tak onything at didna belang ta me nae matter hoo bad things were,* she thought.

Ellie's face lit up when she saw her daughter. Kirsty kissed her and held her hand for a minute. Glancing round she could see that the house could do with a good clean for Ellie was overburdened with other people's washing and Davie's constant demands. Praying that the Lord would forgive her for working on His day, she put on an apron and kilted up her sleeves, 'Sit doon, Mammie, an rest while you can.' Ellie, protesting that she "wisna dat tired", lowered herself stiffly into her chair and promptly fell asleep.

Kirsty scrubbed and swept and polished. As she worked she sang gospel songs partly because they were cheerful and she loved the predictable rhythms and simple sentiments, and partly because she thought the singing of hymns might make the Lord overlook the fact she was breaking the rules of the Sabbath.

By the time everything was done to her satisfaction, the pot on the stove had come to the boil. She wakened her mother, wheeled Davie through to the table and served up the watery stew.

'I hae a question ta ax you, Mammie…' Kirsty began.

'Du aye has questions, joy. What is it dis time?' Ellie looked at her affectionately.

'Da Captain said yesterday at he was been oot on his "Saturday rounds". What did he mean, Mammie? Hit maks him soond like a doctor!'

'Du's no far wrang, lass. He is a "doctor" in a wye.'

'What do you mean?'

'Du said he was been on his rounds?'

Kirsty nodded.

'Jean will be blyde aboot dat. He's no been for ower a year. Eftir da boys died he hadna da hert ta geng…hadna da hert for onything.' She paused, lost in her memories. Then said, as if to herself, 'So he's been oot on his "rounds" again. Weel, weel, dat surely is a good sign.'

'Da "rounds",' Kirsty prompted gently.

'Oh yea. He aye used ta geng alang da aald folk an dem at wir poorly at da weekends when he was hame - dem at couldna afford ta pay da doctor, or ta buy der pills fae da chemist – an he wid gie dem his ain hame-made pooders an potions for nothin.'

She went on to explain that his remedies could cure sore stomachs, aching muscles, restore their appetites and help them sleep.

'So du sees, jewel, he was like a doctor.'

'But wha lairned him ta mak his medicines?' asked Kirsty, fascinated by her mother's tale.

'His grand-midder. She was a spey-wife…'

'A witch?!' exclaimed Kirsty. 'Was she a witch?'

'Na, na,' laughed Ellie. 'She never cast spells, or did onything ta harm onybody, but she kent everything aboot flooers an plants. She used ta tak Peter wi her when he was a peerie boy, whenever she geed oot collectin leaves, an flooers, an seeds, an roots. She telt him what eans could help da different ailments.'

Kirsty listened in amazement while her mother described how the old lady had taught her grandson how to cure roots above the peat fire, then grind them down to make draughts or ointments, or to make infusions from leaves.

'Peter has a real talent for it, an da folk swear by his cures. He's helped a lot o folk ower da years. He's a good man, Peter Jacobson, an A'm blyde at he's comin back ta himsel.'

I wonder if dat's why Sam wanted ta be a doctor, an Grace too?, Kirsty pondered as she cleared away the plates.

In the afternoon they wheeled Davie along the Esplanade.

'The sun will do dee good,' they told him, 'an da fresh air.'

'What's da point?' he grumbled. 'My life is finished.'

'Du's no ta speak like yon,' said Ellie. 'It's early days yet, an A'm heard dey're doin wonderful things…'

'Maybe for da rich folk,' Davie interrupted rudely, his voice harsh and bitter, 'but no for da likes o me. No. A'll be sittin in dis chair till da day I die. A'm good for nothin. A'm finished.' His voice faded to a whisper. 'Finished.'

His chin sank onto his chest and he stared morosely at his pinned-up trouser legs and refused to look at the boats, the birds, the sun on the water – and pointedly ignored the well-meaning people who tried to chat to him. Their cheerfulness infuriated him. How did they know things would get better? Who would employ him? What lass would have him now? Did they have any idea of the pain he suffered, not just in the red raw stumps that would not heal, but in his toes – the toes he'd left in his boots in France? They could keep their "look on the bright side".

After tea Ellie said to Kirsty, 'I could maybe geng ta da kirk da night.'

'Dat you can, Mammie. A'll bide wi Davie till you get back.'

She smiled and waved as Ellie set off up the lane, but she was uneasy about Joe being alone in the house with Jamie. So when Gilbert Petrie came to the door she greeted him warmly.

'On leave is du, Gibbie? Come awa in. Davie 'll be blyde ta see dee.'

Gibbie had been one of Davie's drinking cronies before the war. They'd signed up together, and served in the same platoon.

'An what aboot dee? Is du no blyde ta see me?'

'Yea, Gibbie. A'm blyde at du's safe.'

'Hoo aboot a kiss, dan – ta mak me feel welcome? Just wan peerie smoorikin?'

Nimbly she evaded his advances. 'I widna let dee kiss me last time du wis hame, an A'm no goin ta let dee noo,' she laughed.

'Oh weel. Du canna blame me for tryin.' Smiling broadly he turned to Davie and gave him a good-natured punch on the shoulder. 'Hello, Davie boy,' he said. 'Du certainly got deesel a "Blighty wan". Bad luck, old chap.' His face clouded over. 'Seriously, du's better aff oot o it.'

'Tell me aboot da boys, Gibbie. Did Jock Fraser make it? An what aboot Old MacDonald?'

'I can see at you hae a lot ta speak aboot, so A'll leave you tae it …' She was glad of the excuse to get back to Joe. 'Dat's if du'll bide wi Davie till Mammie gets back fae da kirk, Gibbie? We dunna like ta leave him on his ain…'

'Nae bother, lass. It'll be like aald times.'

When Kirsty got to the Jacobsons' she found Jamie studying his notebook and Joe putting finishing touches to the picture he'd sketched on Saturday afternoon. All was well. Her instincts were wrong. She must try to think more kindly of Jamie. After all, he'd suffered so much.

Monday morning was a flurry of activity. The Captain had gone to supervise the loading of the ship, and Jean had shopping to do. Meanwhile Kirsty was busy with the laundry. Jamie felt his pulse quicken. The coast was clear. He tip-toed across the yard to the wash-house, and let himself quietly in. Kirsty was bending over the copper, lifting out the steaming linen, feeding it into the mangle item by item. The latch gave a sharp click as he shut the door behind him. Startled, she looked over her shoulder. Jamie! She didn't trust him, but there was no escape for he was leaning against the door - leaning against the door and looking at her. His eyes were wide, coal-black, and she sensed a strange energy about him. Her heart began to pound and, trembling, she dropped a pillow-case on the floor.

'Noo see what du made me do,' she said, playing for time as she picked it up with the wooden tongs and put it back in the boiler. She kept her back to him, for she didn't want him to see how scared she was. Danger hung in the air, making her scalp prickle, turning her blood to ice.

'Well, bitch,' he began. His voice was deceptively casual, 'Are you going to ask that brother of yours for some whisky for me?'

She glanced again. His arms were folded and he was leaning back, one foot crossed over the other. Completely at ease.

'No I am not,' she said firmly, sounding a great deal more

confident than she felt. She busied herself with the washing. 'Du kens fine weel I canna do dat, Jamie. A'm telt dee dat afore.'

Suddenly he was behind her – so close she could feel his breath hot on the back of her neck. The speed of his movement and the suddenness of it took her by surprise. Unnerved her. How had he managed to move so quickly? It hardly seemed possible.

'This is your last chance, bitch. Are you going to do it?' His tone was ugly now. Threatening.

Kirsty said nothing.

'Well?' His lips were almost touching her ear and she could feel the rough stubble of his chin scratch against the side of her jaw, 'I canna do it, Jamie,' she repeated. 'Dy folk are been right good ta me an A'll no do onything ta upset dem.' She drew herself up and stared straight ahead, thankful that she couldn't see his face, for the wildness in his eyes had terrified her. 'Du canna mak me.'

There was a spark of defiance in her that both excited and enraged him.

'Can I no? Can I no?' he snarled, reverting to the dialect as he always did when he was out of control. 'We'll see aboot dat.' With one arm he circled her waist, pinning her arms to her sides, and with the other he pushed her head down into the steam, so her head was just above the bubbling water. Her cap fell off and floated like a white, frilly mushroom on top of the froth. She closed her eyes tight. The smell of the suds was choking her.

Her hair had escaped from its pins, and hung down in an unruly tangle. Jamie grabbed it and twisted it round his hand like a rope. He pulled her head back with a savage jerk and held it there while she gasped for breath.

'Changed your mind, bitch?' He was leaning over her, in control again. She couldn't move. Her eyes were wide with terror as she stared into his upside-down face. She had to do something. She fought to get free, kicking back, striking his shins again and again with her heels, but he didn't seem to feel any pain. Just laughed and tightened his grip. Jamie, who could barely walk, was filled with unnatural strength.

She tried to scream, but the position of her head restricted her voice and the effort hurt her throat.

'Yell all you like, bitch. There's nobody here to hear you,' he said, and laughed a crazy laugh that struck terror in her heart.

What was he going to do to her? There was nothing she could do to save herself. She knew he had sensed her despair for he suddenly let go of her hair. She felt faint, felt her knees buckle and she bowed her head.

'What do you say now? Had enough? Or am I going to have to stick your head right into the water, then no man will want you?'

'I canna do it, Jamie,' she repeated, her voice dull and leaden. 'Dy folk are good folk...an A'll never do onything ta hurt dem, nae matter what du says...or does.'

He was silent for a moment. Then, changing his tactics, he said slily, 'I've been watching you. I've seen how you look at Sam...'

Horrified, she raised her head. Her feelings for Sam were her special secret. How had he guessed? Her dreams were her lifeline, her escape from the prospect of a lifetime of poverty and hard work. Her dreams were what helped her to keep cheerful. Her beautiful dreams. And this monster had invaded her secret world.

He grabbed her hair again and gave it a vicious tug.

'Seekin eftir him like a bitch on heat,' he sneered. His tone as well as his words were coarse. She was near to tears. He'd made her feel dirty, ruined everything. He slackened his grip of her hair a little, but his hold round her waist was as firm as ever – his fingers biting into her arm.

'You think you're well in here, but what will my mother think if she finds out that you're after her precious Sam, eh? She won't want a servant-girl sniffing round her favourite son. It would be the sack for you, my girl...and what would *he* think? He's an educated man.' His voice was heavy with sarcasm. 'Do you really think he'd have anything to do with the likes of you?'

He yanked her head back again and leant forward to look into her face, 'So how about it, are you going to get me some of the hard stuff, or will I tell them your...peerie secret?' He let go of her hair, and laughed that cruel laughter.

She took a deep breath and tried to master her rising panic. Sam must not know, nor must his mother. What would they think of her? She couldn't bear them to think she was stupid or cheap, or to laugh at her. She felt embarrassed and ashamed even imagining it. She valued their good opinion more than anything...except, of course, being near to Sam. What if she were to lose her job? She'd have no money to give to her mother who depended on her - and she'd hardly ever see Sam. It was the end of everything, utterly hopeless.

'It was only a dream, Jamie,' she murmured. 'Only a dream.'

'So what do you say now?' He was getting tired. He released his grip on her.

'Will you do it, or will I tell them?'

'Aaright,' she whispered, rubbing her arm where his fingers had dug in. 'Aaright.'

'What did you say, bitch? Speak up. I can't hear you.' He was playing with her now, and enjoying it.

She spun round, eyes blazing. 'Aaright,' she screamed. 'Aaright, A'll do it.'

Through her tears she could see his look of triumph, and sense his sick pleasure.

'That's better,' he said, moving in close, so close his nose was almost touching hers. 'Before tea-time then, or you know what'll happen.'

She could feel his spittle wet on her face.

'I hae nae time aff in da eftirnoon,' she protested.

'You'll find a way,' he said, and moved away.

'I hae nae money. Du'll hae ta gie me money. Davie'll no gie me it for nothin,' she said, trying to assert herself, to show he hadn't broken her.

'There's money in the tin on the mantlepiece, isn't there? Help yourself.'

She gasped. 'I couldna do dat. I could never do dat. Never. Hoo can du even think such a thing?'

He smiled, relishing her horror. 'I seem to remember you said "never" before…you would *never* bring drink into the house – and where did that get you?' he stared at her, narrowing his eyes. 'You have till tea-time, bitch.'

With that he turned his back on her, and shuffled into the house. Now that he had got his way his manic strength had left him.

Chapter Nine
Deception and Despair

Kirsty's mind was in a whirl. As she scrubbed and rinsed, and rinsed and scrubbed she tried to figure out what to do. She wasn't entitled to time off on Monday since she'd had most of Sunday free. She'd have to think of a reason. Reluctantly she approached Jean.

'It's been a really good dryin day.'

'It is dat,' agreed Jean. 'Da wind's geen roond ta da nort – a fine stiff breeze.'

'Maist o da washin is in an ready for ironin. Yon's da last lot at's on da line, so I was wonderin…' She hesitated.

'What was du wonderin? Oot wi it, lass.'

'I was wonderin if I could run hame an gie my Mammie a hand dis eftirnoon? She canna get on wi her wark for Davie's aye shoutin on her, wantin dis an wantin dat, an da folk are sayin dey'll pit der washin ta some idder body if she canna do it faster.'

The words came tumbling out, and Jean noticed that Kirsty was avoiding her eyes. *She must be feelin awkward aboot askin for time aff, poor bairn.*

'Away du goes, lass. But come back in time ta mak da bannocks for da tay. I might be a bit late. A'm goin ta see Aggie Simpson. She's gotten word at her boy is dead.'

She seemed to be lost in thought for a minute, then came to herself with a little start. 'Tak some a yon fine fresh milk at Jessie sent in da day. A'm sure we can spare a peerie coarn.

She'll be blyde o it for der no muckle ta be had in da toon. A'm heard at dey're goin ta bring in mair fae da country soon – by motor-car – so it'll likely cost a pretty penny.'

'Thank you, Mrs Jacobson,' said Kirsty, running to get her coat.

'Du kens yon blue quilt at's needin mendin? Tak it wi dee. Dee Mammie'll soon fix it, an it'll be fine ta pit ower Davie's lap when he's oot in his wheel-chair. He'll fairly feel da cowld when he canna move aboot.'

Struggling a bit with the unwieldy bedcover clasped in her arms, and the little milk-can swinging from her fingers, Kirsty made her way home. Her conscience was troubling her. She hadn't exactly told a lie about her reasons for going home, but she hadn't told the truth either. She'd have to persuade Davie to give her drink today, but he wouldn't give her it for free a second time. She knew that. Where was she going to get the money? She'd never put her hand in the "rainy day" tin, no matter what Jamie said, so she'd have to find some other source of cash. Maybe she could sell the quilt - but what if Auntie Jean found out? 'God help me,' she muttered, close to tears. 'I hate dee Jamie Jacobson. Du's a wicked fellow – and du's makkin me a wicked body too.'

With some difficulty she turned the doorknob and pushed the door open with her elbow.

'Hello, Mammie,' she called, trying to sound cheerful. 'Auntie Jean sent me doon wi some sweet milk for you. It cam in fae Grindavoe dis mornin.'

'Grindavoe milk!' exclaimed Ellie. 'Noo dat is somethin worth getting. Mind an thank Jean for me.' She emptied the creamy liquid into a jug, and as she rinsed out the pail, she commented, 'I dunna ken what it is aboot dis Lerwick milk, but it's no half sae good.'

Kirsty smiled to herself. Auntie Jean and her mother were two of a kind, always claiming that anything from Grindavoe was sure to be the best!

Crossing her fingers to cancel out the lie, she said, 'Auntie Jean telt me ta mend dis quilt, an she said I might as weel do it here aside you, as up da hill aside her. She kent you'd be blyde o da company.'

'An she was right. Pit da kettle on, an we'll hae a cup a tay an a blether when A'm hung oot da claes.'

Kirsty took the washing basket from her.

'A'll do it, Mammie, dan your hands'll no get cowld again.' Besides, it was a good five minutes' walk to the drying green.

When they'd had their tea, Kirsty began to repair the quilt while her mother got on with her ironing.

'Hoo is Davie da day?'

'Sleepin it aff, I expect. Yon no-good Gibbie Petrie filled him wi whisky da streen. By da time I got hame Davie was lyin on da floor, blind-drunk – an Petrie was nae-whaar ta be seen. Just as weel, for I'd a gien him a piece o my mind.'

'Oh, Mammie, it was my blame. He seemed sober an he promised ta bide wi Davie till you got back. He said it wid be like aald times.' She snorted. 'It was like aald times aaright. I should a kent better as ta leave da twa o dem tagidder.'

'Dunna blame deesel, lass. Gibbie Petrie is a grown man, an he should a hed mair sense – leavin Davie on da floor like yon. I had some job getting him inta his bed.'

Kirsty watched her mother fold the laundry from the clothes horse, then wrap it in a clean but well-worn sheet.

'Wha's yon for?' she asked. 'I could maybe deliver it for you on my wye back. It's far ower heavy for you ta carry.'

'Du neednа worry aboot me, jewel. I can manage fine. Mrs Herculeson fae King Harald Street gied me her aald baby carriage. 'You can wheel your laundry in it, if you're not too proud,' she said. It fairly saves my back, but I do get a bit a tormentin. Wan bright spark looked in at da bundle o claes - "My, but he's da face o his faither" said she!'

The two of them laughed, picturing the "baby". It was good to share a joke together, to push their troubles away for a little.

After a while Kirsty folded up the quilt and put it on the chest, which stood behind her chair.

'A'll leave dis here, Mammie, an finish it da next time I come.' She picked up the milk pail. 'A'll just go an see Davie for a minute afore I go.'

She opened the door and stood on the threshold, covering her mouth and nose with her hand for the stink of sweat, vomit and whisky caught in her throat. Bracing herself, she went in and shook her brother gently.

'Waaken up, Davie,' she said, and shook him again – more vigorously. 'Waaken up. I need ta speak ta dee.'

He muttered, and flailed his arms, but she couldn't rouse him. There was an empty bottle on the floor, and another, half-full, clutched in his hand. She eased his fingers open, took the bottle and poured its contents into the milk pail, then laid the second empty bottle on the floor beside the first.

There were tears in her eyes as she came out of the room.

'I couldna waaken him. He's foo a drink.'

'Dunna greet, lass. He was a drouth afore da war an he'll likely need it mair noo ta deaden his pain.'

'A'm sorry, Mammie,' she said, drying her eyes - but her tears were not for Davie, they were for herself. What was happening to her? She had deceived everyone, and now she'd stolen the whisky. She was letting down everyone who loved and trusted her. Choking back her tears, she made her way up the lane. *What else could I do, Lord? What else could I do?*

Back at the Jacobsons', she put the pail in the wash-house and went straight to the pantry. She rummaged round till she found an empty ginger beer flask. Feeling like a criminal, she crept furtively back to the wash-house and transferred the whisky from the pail to the flask, which she then hid behind a jar of caustic soda. Then she washed the pail several times to get rid of the smell before taking it into the house.

Trying to appear as though nothing was amiss, she put on her apron and collected the ingredients for her bannocks. As she was measuring out the flour by the handful, Jamie appeared.

'Well?' he asked.

She told him where to find the flask.

'Leave it yonder till dey're in der beds,' she pleaded. 'Please Jamie, dunna let dem smell da drink on dee, or it will be bad for dee as weel as for me.'

'Fair enough.' He could afford to be amenable now he had a hold over her. Besides there was a kind of sweet agony in the waiting, knowing the liquor was there and he could get it when he chose. He smiled as he saw her dash away her tears of shame with the back of her hand, leaving a dusting of flour on her reddened, burning cheeks.

When Jean returned she noted Kirsty's distress. Things must be bad at home, she reckoned, and she's such a feelin-herted bairn.

'Da bannocks smell lovely, Kirsty,' she said cheerfully. 'Mak anidder batch, if du likes, an dan du can tak dem hame ta dee midder da moarn. It'll save her a bit o time.'

Jean's kindness only compounded Kirsty's feelings of guilt. She couldn't sleep that night for her troubled mind couldn't rest. In the space of a few days Jamie had turned her life upside-down. She didn't know who she was any more. Her sense of sin was overwhelming and she felt sick to her stomach. Her scalding had given her some colour – she'd noticed that when she was brushing her hair – and she was glad, for she was sure that underneath it she was as pale as a ghost, and no-one must suspect there was anything amiss. *Three mair weeks till he gengs back, an every day mair whisky. Whaar am I goin ta get it an, mair ta da point, hoo am I goin ta pay for it?* There seemed to be nothing but darkness ahead. Close to despair, she prayed *Please God, help me,* and the words echoed in her head like a mantra. *Help me, help me, help me, help me…*

Kirsty woke with a pounding headache. Silently she carried out her morning chores and started to do the ironing. She tried to appear calm, but her brain was working feverishly, tackling the problem from every angle. The flask in the wash-house might last him today, if he hadn't drunk it all last night. She'd have to sell the quilt this afternoon if she didn't find some other way. What could she do? Beg, borrow, or steal? Well, she wasn't going to beg, and she wasn't going to steal. That left borrowing. At least with borrowing you had a chance to put things right. But who would lend her money? Her thoughts were chasing one another round in her head, making her feel dizzy. Every time she moved, the tin on the mantelpiece caught her eye – taunting her, reminding her. Jamie's presence filled the room. She couldn't think straight with him sitting there behind the *Shetland Times*. He was 'catching up on the war news', he said, but she knew he was only pretending to read. His eyes were on her. Watching and gloating.

In the scullery, Jean was preparing the dinner. She missed Peter more sharply than she'd done of late, for now that he'd come back to her she couldn't bear to be parted from him. Not for a minute. Their time together was specially precious, for so much had been wasted…and all of a sudden she was painfully aware of their own mortality. They were getting older, more vulnerable. What if his concentration lapsed, or his memory failed him at a critical moment? She had always been aware that the sea was a dangerous calling, the unpredictable whims of the weather could turn a mirror-calm sea into a maelstrom in a matter of minutes. Like generations of Shetland women, she'd always taken that in her stride – trusting in her husband's skill and experience and the Good Lord's watchful eye to bring him safely home. But these were different times and there were new hazards, man-made ones, that he had to face on every voyage.

Of course she'd known from the start of the war that the North Sea was heavily mined – but now, after three years of calm acceptance, she was in a panic. Last week's explosions off

Bressay had unnerved her. Her hands trembled and she could hardly breathe. It was different when you heard the explosions with your own ears, saw the crippled ships. That brought it home to you. You couldn't pretend it wasn't happening. Submarines! She hated them. Sinister things, lurking under the sea, attacking from below. That wasn't honest warfare. But then, the Germans didn't pay much heed to the rules of war. Everybody knew that. You just had to think about the 'Lusitania' and all those innocent folk. Women and bairns too. No, nobody was safe. Peter was putting a brave face on it. There was no doubt about that.

She chop, chop, chopped the carrots efficiently and noisily as if the sound would drown out her fears. She had to get a grip on herself. She added the vegetables to the barley she'd soaked overnight, poured in the stock and bustled through to put the pot on the stove. Immediately she felt the tension in the air. A sixth sense was telling her there was danger here too. *A different kind o minefield,* she thought. She glanced at Jamie. He seemed to be at ease. In fact he looked more relaxed than he'd been since he came home. *A'm just a fanciful aald wife,* she scolded herself. And yet, Kirsty wasn't her usual cheerful self. There was none of her usual chatter. No singing. She seemed subdued, and her face was flushed. *Come ta think o it, her face was braaly red yesterday. Maybe she's sickenin for somethin.*

'Is du feelin aaright, Kirsty?' she asked with a little worried frown.

'A'm fine, thanks. Just a bit hot wi da ironin.' She forced herself to sound cheerful.

'Du's no ta drive deesel ower hard, lass. What does it matter if it's no finished da day?' She laid her cool hand on Kirsty's hot brow.

'Geng an stand oot in da yard for a peerie start. Dat'll maybe cool dee doon.' She gave the girl a gentle push towards the door.

Leaning against the door-jamb, Kirsty closed her eyes and held her burning cheeks up to the wind. As her skin cooled and the stinging grew less painful, her fighting spirit returned. *He'll no get da better o me,* she vowed. Returning to her ironing with renewed confidence, she began to sing – a wordless foot-tapping reel – as if she hadn't a care in the world. She was pleased to note that Jamie's wolf-like leer had changed to a disgruntled scowl. It was a very minor victory, but it reminded them both that the battle was not yet over.

Chapter Ten

Brothers and Sisters, Daughters and Sons

When Kirsty went home that afternoon Davie was waiting for her, alone.

'Whaar's Mammie?' she asked.

'She's geen ta deliver her laundry. She kent du wid be comin soon. Tak me ta da shop, Kirsty.' He was unshaven, and his eyes were fever-bright. There was a kind of wild desperation about him.

'Is it drink du's eftir?'

'Yea. It's da pain. Du has nae idea what it's like. Please, Kirsty,' he pleaded. 'It's da only thing at numbs it. Tak me ta R an C's.'

'Right,' she said, assessing the situation. Perhaps she could turn this to her own advantage. 'Der nae need for dee ta come. A'll be quicker if I geng mesel,' she said decisively. 'Gie me da money.'

He fumbled in his pocket and gave her the coins.

'A'll be as quick as I can.'

'Thanks,' he muttered, his voice breaking, as tears were not far away.

As she ran along Commercial Street she was working out her plan. She'd water it down. That's what she'd do. That way there would be more. Davie would still have a full bottle - albeit diluted – and she'd take the extra to top up Jamie's flask.

That would get her through another day, and maybe if she was lucky she'd be able to use the same trick again! She wouldn't have to sell the quilt. Not yet.

When she got back Davie was shaking, hardly able to wait for the relief the liquor would afford him.

'Hurry, lass.' He held out a trembling hand.

'A'll gie dee it when du's safely in dee bed. A'm no takin ony chances o dee landin on da floor, like du did on Sunday. Poor Mammie, she could hardly lift dee.'

'Aaright, aaright,' he said, 'but for God's sake hurry up.'

She wheeled him through and helped him to transfer from chair to bed. Then, picking up the empty bottle from the floor, she went to get the whisky. She'd have to work quickly, for Davie was shouting for her. Carefully she poured half the contents into the empty bottle, and topped up the new one with water from the bucket behind the door. As she went into the bedroom she pretended to open the bottle for him. He snatched it and took several noisy swallows. Then he closed his eyes as if to savour the relief he felt as the liquid burned its way down.

'Thanks, Kirsty. Du's a brick,' he murmured and took another gulp before he slumped back on the pillow.

He did not resist when she took the bottle from him. How could she take advantage of her sick brother like this? What was happening to her? Davie's breathing was fast. She put her hand on his brow. He was burning up.

'Let me look at dee legs, Davie.'

Weak with pain and fever, he made no response – only groaned as she pulled off his trousers. The dressings were filthy. She unwrapped one, easing it off gently where it was sticking. The sickly stink caught in her throat and made her gag. They couldn't afford a doctor, but something would have to be done. She could wash and clean the stumps, but she knew she needed more than water to do the job properly. Gently she pulled the covers over him and ran back along the street, this time to the chemist's shop. Sam would know what to do.

Breathless, she burst in and stood there panting, and unable to speak.

'What is it?' asked Sam hurrying out from behind the counter. 'What's wrang?'

'It's Davie's legs, Sam. Der in a terrible state. I dunna ken what ta do.' She told him about the puss and the smell.

Suspecting gangrene had set in, he asked if the stumps had looked at all black.

'No,' she said, with an attempt at a smile. 'Dey're aa colours – red, green, yellow an blue - but nae black.'

So der is hoop, thought Sam.

At this point, Mr Leask took charge of the situation.

'I think you should go with the girl and see for yourself, lad, so you can give her proper advice.' He took a bottle of iodine off the shelf. 'You'll need this, and some fresh bandages. Go now. I can manage by myself for half an hour.'

Sam threw him a grateful look.

'Thank you very much, Mr Leask. You're a proper gentleman. I'll make up the time to you and pay for…'

'Go, lad,' said Mr Leask, shaking his head and smiling.

They hurried back to Davie. Sam drew in his breath with

a little hiss when he saw the infected flesh. Ruthless cleaning was required.

'Dis'll no be easy, Kirsty. Is du sure du's up tae it?'

'A'll hae ta be, will'n I? I hae nae choice,' she said. 'Tell me what ta do.'

Davie screamed when the iodine was applied. He opened his eyes, which rolled wildly for a moment. Then he fell into a restless sleep again. Once the fresh bandages were on, Sam said, 'Du'll hae ta sponge him doon wi cowld water ta get his temperature doon. Tell dee midder ta keep doin it till da fever brakks, an she'll hae ta keep changin da dressins.'

He looked at Kirsty. 'Weel done, Kirsty. Du wid mak a fine nurse.' There was no mistaking the admiration in his eyes. 'A'll hae ta get back ta da shop noo.'

Kirsty watched him go. He was proud of her! Her heart swelled with joy, but it was bitter-sweet for she knew that his admiration would quickly fade if he found out how dishonest she had become.

When her mother returned, Kirsty told her about Davie's fever and passed on Sam's instructions.

'A'll see ta da dressins da moarn, Mammie. Could you fin an aald pillow case at we could use for bandages, an boil it ta be sure it's clean?'

'Dat sall I,' she said. 'Hit's a pity we didna keep some o yon fine moss…'

Kirsty ran all the way back. Then, looking over her shoulder to check that no-one was watching, she went straight to the wash-house and topped up Jamie's flask.

For the next two days Davie's fever raged. Ellie hardly slept – struggling to keep on top of her washing, and snatching forty winks whenever she could. Kirsty took over in the afternoons – washing, ironing, running to the drying green, nursing Davie and delivering laundry on her way back to the Jacobsons'. Feeling thoroughly despicable, she took Davie's whisky bottle. He certainly wouldn't miss it, considering the state he was in. This would earn her another couple of days, and when Davie recovered he'd probably send her for more – and she could water it down again - and she still had the quilt in reserve. The long dark tunnel didn't seem so black after all, and she realised, ruefully, that relief had tempered her sense of sin.

Jamie was holding his cards close to his chest. He felt stronger every day, but chose not to show it for he quite enjoyed being spoiled as regards his "tucker", and everyone treated him with care and consideration, afraid they might upset him. That gave him a pleasant feeling of power…but he had other reasons, and those were private. Very private. Suffice it to say it suited his plans that they should think he was still very feeble. He continued to walk unsteadily, and although the spasms rarely occurred now, he jerked his head violently from time to time.

Since her decision to become a psychiatrist, Grace was absorbed in her study, and Sam – eager to encourage her – had become her tutor and mentor. Every evening they sat at the table, poring over books together. Neither of them had time to read to Joe or tell him a bedtime story. Jean would gladly have done it, but she had strained her eyes when she was a girl, reading all hours in the flickering light of oil-lamps or candles. So she asked Kirsty, who was not a confident reader, to do it.

But before Kirsty could think of an excuse, Jamie – sensing an opportunity to win favour – butted in, offering to do it.

Each night he told Joe stories from Norse mythology – always in the kitchen before Kirsty took him up to bed. This fuelled everyone's belief that he was unable to climb the stairs. He told him about Idun and the Golden Apples, which held the secret of eternal youth; he told him about the three Norns who controlled man's fate and who were shape-changers who turned themselved into swans if they wanted to travel quickly; he told him about the World Tree and about the Bifrost, a rainbow bridge connecting heaven and earth. In spite of herself Kirsty enjoyed the stories for Jamie told them well, painting vivid pictures that caught the imagination. He was careful about his choice of subject. At no time was it at all frightening. So everyone relaxed and looked on him kindly. Later Kirsty would realise that she should have trusted her initial reaction – which was to question the motives behind his offer – for she, more than anyone, knew that spontaneous kindness was not in his nature.

The rest of that week and the beginning of the next passed uneventfully on the surface at least, for everyone was preoccupied with his or her own problems or activities – but beneath it hidden currents pulled this way and that. Only Kirsty was aware of Jamie's drinking. Living on her wits, and exploiting her brother's condition, she was managing to keep one step ahead of Jamie's "requirements", and there was only a week and a bit to go. She began to worry less about his violent streak. Maybe he was right. Maybe the alcohol did help him to sleep, and that in turn helped to keep his emotions under control. Everyone was too self-absorbed to notice the tell-tale signs that all was not well with Joe.

On the morning of the 26th as they were finishing breakfast, a boy arrived with a telegram. "Mother very poorly stop fading fast stop come soonest stop Jessie". The household was galvanised into action. Of course it was the Sale day, so everything was closed and making the necessary arrangements was difficult. Sam rushed around to Mr. Leask's house to explain the situation, and ask for a few days off as a death was expected and there would be a funeral to arrange. Next he went to the Carters' to see if he could hire a motor-car. He was worried about the cost of such a luxury, but Jean insisted it was the quickest way and her "rainy day" tin was for just such emergencies. In the event, Mr. Carter wouldn't hear of them paying for it.

'We're family, Sam. Aren't we?' he said. 'I'll be your chauffeur. I'll pick you up in an hour. Would that suit you?'

'Well, if you're sure…' Sam said, hesitantly. 'That would be a great help.'

The car would take them as far as the rough track to Grindavoe. They'd have to walk the last mile and a half. Finally he drafted a wire to his father explaining the circumstances and urging him to come to Grindavoe as soon as the ship docked. Kirsty would take it to the Post Office when they opened the following morning. Meanwhile Jean packed a carpet bag with funeral clothes for herself, Sam and Peter. She wrote out brief instructions for meals for the next few days, made out a shopping list and gave Kirsty the house-keeping purse.

'A'm sorry ta leave dee wi aa da wark ta do, but der naebody else I can ax…an I ken I can trust dee.'

Kirsty's eyes filled at the irony of this innocent remark. *If you only kent,* she thought.

'Noo, noo lass,' said Jean, misinterpreting Kirsty's tears. 'It's no great sadness for an aald wife ta meet her maker, an ta be wi her man again. We should be glad at she's geen ta a better place.' She sighed. 'Guid kens, dis world is held little joy for her since my faither an Samuel…' She sniffed and smiled, 'But if du'd kent her when she was a young wife, aye singin an gaffin. Dey were happy days, an dat's hoo A'll mind her.'

She dabbed her eyes, then went on in businesslike fashion.

'Geng ta da Sale da day, an tak Grace an Joe wi dee. Der nae need for you aa ta miss oot, an I think we should support da Red Cross an da hospital, for dey do good wark. Buy some tatties an carrots an neeps, an some kale if du can get it. Gie da bairns twartree pennies ta spend, an get some peerie thing ta deesel…an if du canna manage aa da hoosewark, never care. We'll catch up tagidder when I get back. As lang as du feeds dem, an sees at dey hae clean claes dat's aa at really maitters.'

She kissed Grace and instructed her to help Kirsty as much as she could. To Jamie she said, 'Du's no ta be upset at du's no comin wi wiz. Dee health comes first, an it's far ower far for dee ta walk ta da hoose fae da junction, an du's no able ta carry da kist. Eat whatever Kirsty sets afore dee, an keep up dee peerie walks.' She hugged him briefly, and they were off.

The three sisters took turns to sit with their mother that night. It was Jean's watch when, at first light, her breathing pattern changed. Jean wakened Sam, who was sleeping fully clothed beside the fire.

'It's time, is it?' he asked, rubbing the sleep from his eyes.

'Yea, her trials'll soon be ower. Tak da boat. It'll be quicker. Beckie can help dee ta row.'

'Beckie?'

'She can geng for Maggie o Hamar, an dey can row back. Du can come wi da doctor wi his pony an trap.' She went to wake Beckie.

'Maggie o Hamar? What do we need her for?' asked Beckie, still half asleep, as she pulled on her clothes.

'Never mine, lass. Just ax her ta come. She'll ken what it's aboot. Hurry noo.'

There was no need for Beckie to know that it was Maggie who always took charge of preparing bodies for burial in this district – especially since Granny had not yet breathed her last breath. The girl would have enough trouble coping with the loss of her grandmother without having to know about the indignities involved in laying out her mortal remains.

Just after the doctor arrived old Gracie-Ann opened her eyes and smiled.

'Osie!' she said, as if she were greeting her husband. 'Osie!' – and she tried to sit up. Then the light in her eyes faded and she fell back on the pillows with a long sighing breath, and she was at peace. Sam said a little prayer, and they sat round the fire with a cup of tea and their own private memories.

Beckie arrived back with Maggie just as the doctor was leaving.

'I'll tell the minister, and Willie Williamson,' he said,

Williamson being the carpenter-cum-undertaker. Then everyone set to the practical tasks. Jean assisted Maggie with her duties. Auntie Jessie gave the best room a thorough cleaning – it had to be spotless to receive the coffin, and the neighbours who would call for the "condolin" – to offer sympathy and say their farewells. Auntie Sarah and Beckie got up a good fire and began a mammoth baking – several batches of brand-iron bannocks and a special "brönnie" (or traditional tea-bread) for their visitors. All this was women's work so Sam kept out of the way. He had a lot of organising to do. The war was having some far-reaching effects. With his brothers, uncles and his cousins away at the war – all except Lollie, who was at the fishing – it was going to be difficult to find enough pallbearers. Usually a community could muster several "teams" who could spell one another on the long walk to the graveyard. This time he'd be hard pressed to find one. He took a walk along the beach and tried to think things through. On Saturday his father would be home, and Lollie ashore from the fishing. With the school closed, he would be able to call on the schoolmaster – and maybe a couple of the older boys. That made six, including himself. He could ask the carpenter and his men if they would be willing to help. They'd manage somehow, but the funeral would have to be on Saturday. There was no choice in the matter, for on Monday his father and Lollie would be away again, and the school would be open. Saturday it would have to be. This left only one day, Friday, for the "condolin" instead of the usual two or three, but it couldn't be he helped.

By dinnertime the undertaker arrived. He agreed with Sam's plans, and said he'd be back by tea-time with the "kist". He'd put a notice in the shop, and word would quickly spread. He was as good as his word, and before sunset Gracie-Ann was "kisted". Maggie insisted on placing a small dish of salt on her chest.

'What's she doin yon for?' Beckie asked in a whisper.

'A'm no fairly sure, jewel,' her mother replied, 'but folk in dis neighbourhood aye do it, though the reason for it is lang forgotten. I think it was maybe a kind a peace-offerin ta keep da spirits or da trows happy, so dey widna try ta hinder da "ean at's awa" fae getting ta Heevin. It's hard ta brakk awa fae da aald wyes.'

The following day there was no rest as word had flown from house to house, and there was a steady stream of visitors. Beckie marvelled at the number who had come, and at the strange mixture of grief and gossip as they hovered and sighed over her grandmother – then dabbed their eyes and settled down to pass on the news over tea and bannocks.

In the morning Sam took the pony and cart to meet his father and Cousin Lollie at the junction. When they'd paid their respects to Gracie-Ann, the lid was screwed down and the "kist" carried outdoors where it stood on two chairs, one at either end, while the mourners gathered. As it happened, there was a good turnout of men. Everyone who could come did – by boat, by pony and cart, on foot – and when they had been fortified by a plate of Auntie Sarah's soup (and a surreptitious drink from the bottle Lollie had concealed in his back pocket) – the first team of men hoisted the coffin onto their shoulders. Peter and Sam kicked the chairs over. Traditionally this ensured they were not needed for the same purpose in the near future – and Gracie-Ann took her last journey.

Jean, Sam and Peter returned home on the post-bus on Monday morning, just in time for the boat's departure for Aberdeen. Jean took one look at Kirsty's tired face.

'Early to bed for you, my lass,' she said.

So Kirsty retired at the same time as Grace. They got on their nightdresses and sat side by side at the dressing table to brush out their hair. It was then that Grace confided in her.

'I didna want ta trouble dee when Mammie was awa, du wis dat busy...'

Kirsty paused mid-stroke, and looked in the mirror at Grace's worried face.

'Go on, Grace. What is it?'

Grace was hesitant. 'A'm no fairly sure, Kirsty, but...'

'But what, Grace? What?'

Grace blurted out her story. 'I think Jamie's been goin up ta Joe in da middle o da night. I heard da stairs creakin, an I thought I heard Joe greetin. A'm heard it every night since Mammie an Sam geed.'

Kirsty laid down her hairbrush, and took Grace's hands in hers.

'Is du sure aboot dis, Grace?'

'No, dat's just it. A'm sure – an A'm no sure. Maybe I imagined it, or maybe I was dreamin.' She started to cry. 'A'm sorry. I should never a telt dee. It's likely nothin...but what would he go up yonder for? An why does he mak on at he's no able for da stairs if he is?' Her sobbing grew worse.

'Come here,' said Kirsty and took her in her arms. 'Sh,' she whispered. 'Dunna greet. It's nothin for dee ta worry aboot.'

When Grace had calmed down, she tucked her up in bed.

'Du did da right thing ta tell me,' she said, as if she were ten years older than Grace. 'Go to sleep noo. Everything's goin ta be fine.'

But alarm bells were going off in her head. Sam had been away, and Joe had been on his own in the attic bedroom. Had Jamie been up to something? She knew how devious he was, and how cruel – and she'd seen him take pleasure in scaring Joe before. She'd make it her business to find out the truth.

Chapter Eleven
Good and Evil

After tea Sam announced that he was going to see Davie.

'I have a proposition to put to him,' he said rather formally.

Everyone was curious, and waited for an explanation, but none was forthcoming.

'Dis is atween Davie an me – an Kirsty,' he added with a twinkle in his eye. 'Is du comin wi me, Kirsty?'

'Weel, I maybe could, eftir A'm done da dishes,' she said demurely, keeping her eyes lowered in case they revealed her excitement. To walk with him beside her, there and back. Just the two of them. To share a secret with him! It was more than she could have dared to hope. She turned to Jean and, looking up, added, 'if dat's aaright wi you?'

Jean nodded, 'Go while dere's still a blink o daylight.'

'Thank you,' Kirsty said, and ran to get her shawl.

'Poor lass,' Jean murmured as she watched them go, for she had read Kirsty's secret in her shining eyes. *Der little hoop for dee, my lamb. Ah, weel,* she thought, as she piled the plates into the sink. *What will be, will be.*

As Kirsty walked beside Sam she wanted to sing, to laugh, to shout, 'Look at me! A'm walkin aside him!' She wanted to skip, to dance, to jump up onto the wall and twirl round till she was dizzy! She felt more alive than she'd ever felt before, as if her whole body were radiating light. Maybe people could see it, she thought, smothering a giggle, inwardly laughing at the idea. Without even looking she was aware of his height, the way he held his shoulders, the way his left foot turned out more than his right, the way his steps were longer than hers and she had to run a little now and again to keep up with him. His voice was like music, beautiful to listen to – and he was taking her seriously, talking to her about grown-up things – about what the country owed to the soldiers and sailors. Not just to those who'd died, but to the ones who came home unable to do the jobs they did before the war.

'Du means like Davie?' she asked, looking up at him.

He smiled, and she thought her heart would melt.

'Yiss, like Davie. He canna be a cooper noo, can he?'

She shook her head.

'But his life has to go on. It has ta hae a purpose,' Sam went on. 'It's up ta wiz ta mak him see at he's still a man.'

'He's lost hert, Sam. He says he's finished.'

'So it's wir job ta persuade him at he's wrang. Will du help me?'

'Of coorse A'll help dee. I just canna see what I can do.'

Already they were at her mother's house. He turned the handle, pushed the door open and stood back to let her go first. He was treating her like a lady! She'd never felt so important before.

'Mammie,' she called. 'Sam's come ta see Davie?'

Wearily Ellie came through from the bedroom.

'I canna get him oot o his bed. He just wants ta lie yonder, starin at da waa.'

She looked at Sam and felt the same sharp pang she always felt when she saw him. His uncle had given him more than his name. He had her Samuel's looks and his bearing. Even his voice was the same. If she closed her eyes and listened to him speak it was as if her own dear Samuel had come back from the dead. *I canna help but love dis boy.*

'Maybe du'll be able ta mak him see sense,' she said as she sat down. 'I dunna ken what mair I can do.'

Kirsty and Sam went through to the bedroom. It was a dark, damp place at the best of times, with a tiny window that couldn't open and never saw sunlight. Ellie had left the stub of a candle burning. It was guttering and about to go out. Candles cost money and so did paraffin and there was no gaslight in this part of town.

'Hello, Davie,' said Sam. 'Hoo is du feelin da day?'

Davie rolled over and glared at him.

'See for deesel, man. A'm finished.' With that he rolled back to face the wall.

'We'll need mair light if A'm ta see for mesel.' Sam said, priming the Tilley lamp. He'd have to make sure they had enough fuel for it. He adjusted the flame, then hung the lamp on the hook. 'Dat's better. Noo let me tak a look at dee. Turn ower.'

'Du soonds like a doctor, man,' mumbled Davie, turning his head and shielding his eyes from the light. 'It's no a doctor A'm needin.'

'No,' said Sam, 'an dat's thanks ta Kirsty, an dee midder. Du wid a died if it wisna for dem.'

'Dey should a left me tae it,' he muttered. 'What kind o a life does du think dis is? Dey should a let me die.'

'Yon's wicked talk, Davie, an ungrateful. Der mony a poor fellow worse aff as dee.'

'Dat's easy for dee ta say.'

Sam ignored him and carried on. 'So du's lost dee legs - but du's no lost dee brain, is du? It's still in workin order? An dee eyesight is still good?'

'I suppose so,' admitted Davie, grudgingly, 'but what…?'

'I hae a proposition ta pit ta dee,' said Sam, cutting in before he had time to wallow in self-pity again.

There was a spark of interest in Davie's eyes.

'Come, Kirsty. Let's sit him up right.'

She scuttled round to the far side of the bed. They each took an arm, and on Sam's nod, they hoisted him up. She punched his pillows into shape, fetched a chair for Sam, then sat at the foot of the bed and waited, eager to hear what Sam had to say. The only sound was the hiss of the Tilley. With a story-teller's sense of timing, Sam kept them waiting just long enough to have them hanging on his every word.

'Noo listen carefully, an dunna interrupt. Hear me oot, Davie.' He lit his pipe, then began.

'Mr Leask (dat's my boss, du kens) is needin somebody ta keep da books, an he wants ta gie da job ta somebody at deserves it.' He took a long draw on his pipe and watched the smoke writhe upwards, giving time for his opening remarks to sink in. 'I pat in a good word for dee, an he's agreed ta gie dee a trial.'

'Me? What good wid I be?'

'Wheest, Davie. Did I no tell dee ta hear me oot?'

Davie nodded.

'I telt him du wis a wizard wi numbers when we wir at school, an a boannie writer too. Dy copy-book wis aye da best in da class. What idder does a book-keeper need but a good head for figures an a boannie, neat hand? Think aboot it, man.'

He puffed his pipe again and blew a perfect smoke-ring.

'I tak it du can still coont, eh?' he said, raising a quizzical eyebrow.

'Yea, but…'

'Nae buts, Davie. I aye thought it was a shame at aa yon talent should go ta waste. Noo du haes a chance ta use it. What does du say?'

'Say yiss, Davie. What harm wid it do ta gie it a try? It's a splendid chance for dee…' Eagerly Kirsty tried to persuade him.

'I ken, but A'm no sure…'

'Of coorse du can, Davie.' Kirsty and Sam laughed for they'd spoken as one.

'Weel, if you think A'm up tae it…'

'Come on, Davie. Du kens du can do it,' Kirsty urged.

After a long pause Davie agreed to give it a go.

'Good,' said Sam, 'but du'll hae ta smarten deesel up a bit… an du'll hae ta gie up da drink for du'll need a clear head. Can du do dat – gie up da drink, I mean?' Davie was silent, digesting all that had been said.

'Come on, boy,' prompted Sam. 'Gie up da drink afore it destroys dee. Get rid o yon bottle.' He nodded towards the bottle on the chest. 'Dat wid be a start.'

Davie was reluctant to take such a decisive step.

Kirsty took his hand. 'Du kens at Sam's right.'

Davie said nothing. The silence was charged with tension as Kirsty and Sam waited for his decision. When he spoke he was smiling. He knew, as they did, that this was a turning-point.

'Kirsty,' he said, 'empty it oot so A'm no tempted when da pain gets bad.'

She took the bottle and went through to the other room. Her mother was sound asleep in the chair, so she tip-toed round her and tucked it in the folds of the quilt. This certainly wasn't what Davie had in mind, and she hated deceiving him, but it would keep her safe for a few more days. She went back in time to hear Sam tell Davie to get her to bring him to the shop the following afternoon.

They closed the door behind them, leaving Ellie asleep. Pleased with the outcome of their evening's work, they strolled homeward – taking the longer route along Commercial Street and up the Nort Kirk Closs. Now and then they stopped and stood together, gazing upward – sharing their wonderment at the beauty of God's creation. Sam pointed out the stars and constellations to her, telling her their names, while she listened, spellbound – wishing this time could last for ever. It was wholly innocent, yet somehow incredibly intimate. Kirsty could hardly believe such happiness was possible. He was so handsome, and so kind-hearted – and so clever. He was everything a man should be. If only…but she knew there was no future in "if onlys".

Next morning Kirsty found herself filled with energy and optimism. She took all the rugs outside, hung them over the clothes-line and gave them a vigorous beating. Then she dusted and swept every room in the house, singing as she worked. Davie was going to work in an office! And Mammie would not have to work such long hours just to survive! In the afternoon she found Davie smartly dressed and clean-shaven. Chattering all the time, she wheeled him along to the chemist's shop. No longer gloomy and taciturn, he greeted everyone they met with a bright, 'Aye, aye' or a cheerful wave. Sam met them at the door, and promised he'd see Davie safely home at tea-time.

'Away du goes, Kirsty,' Davie dismissed her with a broad smile. 'Da men-folk haes wark ta do. We canna bide here bletherin aa day!'

She hurried back to her mother with a song in her heart. Only two more days and then Jamie would be gone, and life would return to normal – better than normal, for things were looking up, all thanks to Sam. Wonderful Sam! Her heart was brimful of love for him. If she loved him any more she would burst, and she had enough whisky to keep Jamie happy. What could possibly go wrong now?

In the evening Jean, Grace and Sam went as usual to the mid-week prayer meeting. Jamie told his story to Joe, then Kirsty took him upstairs. When she came down Jamie had retired to his room. *He's started drinkin early da night,* she thought. It was a blessing in disguise, for it meant she was spared his company by the fireside. She had just lifted the lid of the stove to put on more fuel, when she thought she heard a noise on the stairs. She stopped, peat in hand, and listened. Nothing! She was getting jumpy. She hated when the others were out. She put in the peat, replaced the lid and put the kettle on to boil for the "eight o'clocks". There it was again. She froze, cocking her ear. Could she have heard Joe calling her name? Quietly she crept upstairs, eased the door open little by little and peered through the crack.

For a split second she was turned to stone, her mind struggling to make sense of what she saw. Dear God, it couldn't be true – but it was, and the scene was burned into her mind for ever. The stark terror in Joe's eyes as he knelt before Jamie. His heart-rending look of relief when he noticed her, and his strange baby-speech as he pleaded, 'No again, Jamie. Stop him, Kirsty. Dunna let him mak me do it again.'

She had never experienced such fury. She burst in the door and flew at Jamie like a thing possessed, pushing him away with such strength that he staggered and nearly fell.

'Get awa fae da boy.' She advanced as he backed off, hammering on his chest. 'Get away, du...du animal. Du filthy evil animal.'

Jamie regained his balance and, grabbing her by the shoulders, threw her onto the bed. 'I was saving you for later,' he laughed, 'but since you're here now...'

Kirsty's blood ran cold.

'Run, Joe,' She shrieked. 'Run. Fetch Sam.'

Jamie was back by the river in France. He heard his pals' voices urging him on. 'Go on, Jamie. She's asking for it. Think how she made a fool of you...made a fool of you...made a fool of you...'

Somewhere in the distance Kirsty was screaming, 'No, Jamie. No!' and begging him to stop, but he scarcely noticed it. Kirsty and the French girl had merged into one. There was naked hatred on Jamie's face. The girls were like Joe with their angelic looks and their clean pure hearts. They were all that he was not, and never had been. He'd never known what it was to feel pure and innocent. He'd wanted to. Oh yes, he'd wanted too – a lifetime ago. Wanted to be loved and accepted the way they were – but he was different. He'd always known that. Bitches! Bitches! Their innocence infuriated him, gnawed at him, got under his skin. It had to be destroyed.

Kirsty fought – biting, scratching, kicking – but that only added to his pleasure. He knelt over her, pinning her arms above her head and he laughed that ugly laugh that she'd come to know so well.

'That's right, bitch. Fight, bite, kick for all you're worth.'

Gobs of spittle landed on her face and she smelt his stinking whisky-laden breath. Then he came forward onto her and all she knew was pain, excruciating pain and a suffocating darkness.

At last he left her and stumbled down the stairs. She lay curled up on her side, knees drawn up like an infant in the womb, swimming in darkness. One hand was stuffed in her mouth to muffle her sobs, and the other – covered in blood - was between her legs as though to protect herself from what had already happened. She heard Sam bound up the stairs two at a time. Heard his strangled cry of horror when he saw her.

'No! Oh no, sweet Jesus. No Kirsty. Please, no Kirsty.'

Jean was halfway upstairs when he ran to fetch her.

'I ken,' she said simply, and in those two words was a whole world of heartbreak. 'Bring warm water, towels, flannels, soap an disinfectant - an tell Grace ta look oot a clean nightgown. Tell her ta look eftir Joe. He can sleep in Kirsty's bed da night.'

She sat on the bed beside the weeping girl and silently gathered her into her arms. She held her and rocked her while the sobbing came wave upon wave. Then later, when the tears had subsided, she kissed her forehead, stroked her hair and wiped her bruised face. All Kirsty could say was, 'He was goin ta hurt Joe. He was goin ta hurt Joe. I wanted ta stop him.' And the weeping would start again. At length the torn and bloodstained clothing was removed. Jean sponged her and dried her gently. She smoothed soothing lotions on the cruel tears and scratches, and the clean nightdress was lowered over her head.

'Can du walk, Kirsty?'

Dumbly she nodded.

'Du'll sleep wi me da night.'

Slowly they made their way down the stairs and into Jean's room. Kirsty sat down gingerly on the bed. She gave a little cry, winced and held her breath as Jean eased her legs onto the bed. Sam knocked on the door and handed his mother a steaming cup.

'Dis'll help her sleep.'

Jean gave him a puzzled look.

'Hit's somethin fae Daddie's Saturday Bag.'

Jean nodded and took it from him.

'Kirsty,' she said, 'Drink dis. It will help.'

She held the cup and supported the girl's head while she sipped the hot bitter liquid. Soon her eyes grew heavy, and she fell asleep.

Sam sat by the stove, head in hands, trying to think things through, but he was in shock and his mind refused to function. Jean paced restlessly up and down, praying for guidance. At last she broke the silence.

'What's to be done aboot dis sorry mess, Sam? We hae ta protect Kirsty, an see she suffers nae mair hurt, an we'll hae ta see it doesna get oot, or it'll be da spaekalation o da toon. We hae ta protect her good name - an da Jacobson name too. It wid kill dy faither ta think wir family name should be at da hert o siccan a scandal. What can we do? She'll need time ta mend in body - an in her mind.'

After a long pause, Sam answered her. 'I think she should geng ta Grindavoe for a while. Auntie Jessie an Auntie Sarah wid look eftir her, an Beckie wid be a comfort ta her. Dey wir aye closs friends.'

'Hoo muckle do we need ta tell dem, does du think? Will dey need ta ken da whole story?'

'We'll hae ta tell dem she's been...raped (he could hardly bring himself to say the word) – but we dunna need ta tell dem wha did it. Naebody needs ta ken but wirsels.'

After some discussion they decided that they would put it about that Kirsty had gone to help with harvesting the potatoes. Nobody would think that odd, as Jessie's leg was still bad, and Sarah was overcome with grief at her mother's passing.

'Naebody'll ever ken,' Sam said.

'Ellie has ta ken,' Jean felt tears sting in her eyes. 'Hoo am I goin ta tell Ellie? She trusted me, an I let dis happen under my roof. Hoo can I tell her?'

'God will help you fin da words, Mammie. You ken He will.'

He went on to assure her he would make all the arrangements for Kirsty to be taken to Grindavoe, and he would take Davie to the shop in the morning. That would free Ellie to be with Kirsty until her transport arrived.

'An what aboot Jamie? He's broken my hert. Ta think a son born o my flesh could…' She blew her nose noisily. 'He's little better as a beast.' She stared at the glow of the fire. 'It's da war, Sam It changes folk – taks awa der sense o right an wrang. Jamie wid never a let his dark side tak ower if it wisna for da war.'

'I hear what you're sayin, Mammie – but A'll never be able ta forgive him or feel sorry for him. Strictly speakin, it's a matter for da law ta deal wi…'

'No, Sam!' she interrupted, her voice shrill with agitation. 'No! Du's no even ta think aboot dat. What wid it do ta dee faither? It wid be da end o him. He'd never lift up his head again. An yet, du kens as weel as I do, his conscience wid force him ta do da "right thing". He'd feel he had nae choice but ta fetch da police.' She looked at Sam and took his hands in hers. Her grip was like a vice. 'Promise me du'll see he never fins oot. Promise.'

'I promise, Mammie. You hae my word.'

Her relief was palpable. She let go of his hands and slumped in her chair.

'Thanks,' she whispered.

He remained silent for some time, then stood up purposefully. 'I'll go an tell Jamie ta bide in his room till sailin time on Friday. We dunna want Kirsty or Joe ta look on him ever again, do we?'

She shook her head. 'A'm no sure at I can bear ta look on him either.'

'Go ta bed, Mammie. We'll hae ta be up early in da mornin,'

She stood up slowly. Suddenly she was an old woman. They

held each other a long moment before she went to lie, dry-eyed and heart-sore, beside the sleeping girl.

Sam, unable to meet his brother's eyes, gave him his instructions curtly, but could not resist adding, 'Wir keepin dis quiet for Kirsty's sake, an Daddie's – no for dine.' He was shocked by the intensity of the hatred he felt for him. He didn't want God to forgive his brother – not even if he repented. *But dere's little chance o dat,* he thought bitterly. Jamie was wicked through and through. He would not pray for him. He wanted him to rot in Hell.

Chapter Twelve
Survival

Jean left Kirsty sleeping and crept through to make the breakfast. Her head was throbbing with lack of sleep and wondering what the day would bring. She had prayed long and hard through the night, asking that she might be given the wisdom and the strength to help Kirsty get through her ordeal. She knew she must remain calm, giving a lead to the rest of the family. So she went through her morning routine as if nothing had happened. She saw Grace off to school and Joe out with his sketch-book. Then she took Jamie's food to him on a tray, which she handed to him without a word. She didn't trust herself to speak.

Sam went to see to the arrangements, sending a telegram to Grindavoe asking Jessie to come at once, and he broke the news as gently as he could to Ellie and Davie. Ellie said nothing, but collapsed into her chair as though her legs had given way beneath her. She drew in her breath sharply, and held it. Then she let it out with a shuddering sigh, and whispered, 'Thanks for telling wiz, Sam.'

'Davie,' he said, 'A'll tak dee ta da shop wi me noo, dan dee midder can geng ta Kirsty.'

Ellie, having had a moment to collect herself, thanked Sam again, then put on her shawl and headed for the door.

Gradually Kirsty fought her way to consciousness, swimming

through thick grey mists of confusion. When she finally broke through the surface, the memory of what had happened hit her with an impact no less shocking and painful than an exploding shell. She gave a long howl that was barely human – a chilling sound that had within it all the loneliness and pain of a wounded animal. The hairs on the back of Jean's neck stood on end, and a shiver of horror ran down her spine. She rushed through the corridor, drying her hands on her apron, and muttering, 'Please Lord, help me do this right.'

Kirsty was distraught. 'I hooped it wis a bad dream. Tell me A'll waken up, an it'll just be a dream. Oh Auntie Jean,' she sobbed, 'dunna let it be true.'

Jean held her and patted her back, and hushed her as one would an infant. Kirsty lifted her head and looked at Jean, all her anguish written on her face.

'What's ta become o me?' she wailed, and buried her face in Jean's bosom, weeping as though she would never stop. Jean rocked her and stroked her hair while the girl's hot tears soaked into her dress. Then, speaking as calmly as she could, she began,

'Well, first du'll hae ta get washed an dressed afore dy Mammie gets here.'

Kirsty broke away from her with an expression of horror.

'No!' she gasped. 'No, Auntie Jean, I dunna want her ta see me. What'll she think o me?' She rocked back and fore in a state of distress. 'What'll she think o me?'

'Dy Mammie loves dee, Kirsty. She'll think nae less o dee da day as she did yesterday, or da day afore. She'll likely love dee even mair. Aa she'll want is what I want, an dat's ta help dee.'

'She'll think A'm a wicked, sinful lass.'

'No, Kirsty. She'll never think dat. Naebody thinks dat. Du's a lovely, boannie innocent lass. Da sin is no dine.'

She put her hand under Kirsty's chin and lifted her face so she could look into her eyes.

'The sin is not yours, believe me,' she repeated, in English this time to make it official.

Kirsty nodded and gave her a watery smile.

'Dat's better,' Jean said, handing her a mirror and a hairbrush. 'Noo do dee hair while I get some warm water.'

When she returned with a steaming ewer, Kirsty stared at her with great round eyes. Jean noted that her pupils were dilated. *She's still in shock,* she thought.

'I canna do it, Auntie Jean. I canna bear ta look in da glass. A'm faird for what I might see in my face.'

Poor lamb. Jean took the brush from her. *It's as if she thinks she'll bear a mark – like Cain. Somethin aa da world can see.* She began to brush the girl's long dark hair with smooth, rhythmic strokes.

'Du haes ta be brave, lass. Du'll need aa da courage at du can muster ta get through dis. What's done is done, an we canna alter dat...da Lord must hae His reasons...but du'll get through it, joy. Do must, an du can.'

She put the brush down. 'Noo, wash dee face while I get clean claes for dee. We hae ta be as cheery as we can for dee midder.'

When Ellie arrived Jean looked at her and there was no need to say anything. They held one another for a moment. Then Ellie went through to Kirsty, blinking back her tears. Jean left the two of them together and went to prepare Kirsty's breakfast. She was humbled by Ellie's dignified handling of the whole appalling business, knowing as she did, the agony Ellie must be feeling. She didn't apportion blame, nor did she rage and weep. She simply kissed her daughter and held her hand, talking to her about every-day things, about Grindavoe and about her love for her. When Jean brought the tray, Ellie said that Kirsty would come through to the kitchen. She led her daughter to the table and encouraged her to eat, even a little.

It was a long morning. Kirsty cried and slept, cried and slept. Jessie arrived at dinnertime, bringing Beckie with her so that Kirsty would have someone to talk to on the journey. Jean insisted that they ate before they left. It was a difficult meal. No-one knew what to say, so there were awkward silences. Of course neither Jessie nor Beckie knew about Jamie's part in what had taken place. Jean had told them that a drunken sailor had attacked Kirsty in the lane.

'A'll hae a quick word wi Jamie afore we go,' said Beckie, heading for the door.

'No, Beckie. Dunna disturb him. He needs his sleep,' said Jean, 'an it'll be better for Kirsty if she can leave right away.'

Beckie looked puzzled, but accepted her mother's advice. What was important was to look after Kirsty.

Jean and Ellie walked with them to the pony and cart. Jessie set out a box to serve as a step and Kirsty climbed stiffly in. Beckie had brought cushions to pack round her, and a blanket to put over her knees. With heavy hearts Jean and Ellie waved her goodbye.

That day - and the next – everyone was subdued and silent. They wanted to draw comfort from one another, but couldn't find the words. Besides, Grace and Joe didn't fully understand what had happened, only that it was something wicked beyond their imagining. Kirsty's absence was a tangible thing. It filled the house with a hollow sense of loss. There was no escaping it. It was as if the very fabric of the walls had absorbed her pain. At family prayers, Jean said, 'Be with Kirsty, Lord – and with us all for each and every one of us has been touched by evil…'

Jamie never emerged from his room. He knew this time he'd crossed the line.

On Friday, half an hour before the boat was due to sail, Sam went through to fetch him.

'It's time,' he said, automatically picking up Jamie's kit-bag to carry it for him.

'I dunna need dy help,' muttered Jamie through clenched teeth, and snatched the bag from him.

As they made their way down the lane, Sam reflected that this was true. Jamie didn't need help. He strode on briskly and steadily, and his head didn't twitch once. *He fooled wiz aa,* Sam thought bitterly.

Jean walked beside Sam, eyes on the ground. There was nothing any of them wanted to say. There were no hugs, no lingering goodbyes. Jamie headed straight for the gangway.

'A'll pray for dee, son,' Jean called and raised her hand to wave, but Jamie's step didn't falter. He walked out of their lives without a backward glance.

Jean was thankful that this was Peter's "away" weekend, for she wanted everyone to get their emotions under control, and their story rehearsed, before he came home. Anxious in case any of them would accidentally allow him to hear the whole truth, she schooled them so rigorously in the "drunken sailor" story that they almost believed it. It troubled her that she should deliberately deceive him and encourage her children to support her in this, but for his sake it had to be done. Apart from that, she tried to keep everything as normal as possible. The Church Social on Saturday proved to be the trickiest time, for well-meaning people asked if everything was all right. They had seen Joe's frightened face when he had burst into the Prayer Meeting on Wednesday, and had noted the Jacobsons' hasty departure.

'Thank you for askin,' Jean replied smoothly. 'Da lum was on fire, but Sam soon had it under control.' She was surprised – and a bit disconcerted – at how easily the lie had tripped off her tongue.

Somehow they got through the next week, and Kirsty returned on Friday. Everyone was delighted to see her, or wanted to be, but the girl who came back was not their Kirsty. This girl was wan and pale, with great dark circles under her eyes. She looked nervous, guilty and desperately ashamed. Convinced that they would be repulsed by her and would believe that she had unwittingly invited the attack, she kept her head down, unable to meet their eyes. At every opportunity Jean tried to reassure her and build her confidence, telling her over and over, 'It wasna dy blame. Dere's nae evil in dee.' The evil was all in her son, but she must share the blame. She'd broken Ellie's trust, and allowed unspeakable things to happen. *Hoo does ony midder cope when she kens she's brought a monster inta da world? Kirsty's shame is goin ta tak a lang time ta heal - an so is mine.*

'No,' she repeated, 'Du's a good lass, Kirsty. We aa ken dat.'

Kirsty lifted her head, tears streaming down her face.

'No, Auntie Jean, A'm done terrible things.'

Jean laughed.

'Dunna gaff, you hae nae idea what A'm had ta do.'

'What does du mean – had ta do?'

The whole sordid story came tumbling out. She told about Jamie's threats and his attack on her in the wash-house.

'He made me a thief an a liar.'

Jean listened with growing horror as Kirsty told how he'd held her face close to the boiling water. 'He said he'd scald my face, an I'd be dat ugly nae man wid have me.'

She looked up, and her agony was plain to see. 'Weel, he maybe didna mak my face ugly, but he made me ugly inside – an dat's far worse. He forced me ta tak drink inta dis hoose for him, an he said I wid hae ta tak money fae your tin ta pay for it - but I never touched it. Honest, Auntie Jean, I never touched your tin. You ken I could never do dat.' The sobbing began again with renewed vigour.

'I ken. I ken,' Jean murmured, and held her close till, exhausted, she fell asleep.

Jean felt sick with horror. She'd always known that Jamie had a dark side, but this went away beyond her worst fears. It seemed to her that the war had given free reign to his violent streak, and once it had been released there was no stopping it. She knew he'd committed a criminal offence and should be punished for it. Part of her truly wanted him to suffer for what he had done, in the hope it would bring him to his senses and make him change his ways…but she knew that punishment was not the answer. Peter's efforts to discipline him as a youngster had had the opposite effect. They'd only confirmed his belief that he wasn't loved, and had made him more resentful.

Her mind drifted back to Jamie's childhood. She knew that, under all that bravado, there was an insecure little boy who craved affection and attention. It seemed that any attention was better than none, for he had been deliberately naughty to divert her away from nursing Sam or attending to the needs of the little ones. Maybe if she'd made more time for him…if she'd tried harder to reach him, if she'd been a better mother. Perhaps it was all her fault. She convinced herself that the due course of the law would do nothing to alter Jamie's behaviour, nor would it help Kirsty. A court case would put her at the centre of a scandal, and ruin her good name. She'd always be known as the girl who was raped, and that would prevent her from getting a decent husband. Hiding the truth was the right thing to do. She repeated this argument to herself - and to Sam - over and over. If she said it often enough it might become true, and if she had Sam's approval it would strengthen her resolve.

He knew that his mother was near breaking point. She needed his love and his support – not his true opinions. The underlying motive behind all her soul-searching and all her decisions was her desire to protect Peter. He understood that, and such was his love for her that he became her willing accomplice. Jamie was the rotten apple in this family's barrel, and they were all becoming tainted. In private he prayed for forgiveness for all the family, for the lies they had told and must continue to tell. He also prayed for Jamie's future victims, for he knew that the violent behaviour would not stop here. Only imprisonment - or death – would break the pattern.

Sam brought Davie round in the evening to practise his book-keeping skills, and Ellie came with them, glad of the chance to sit by a warm fire and to be with her daughter. She looked at Davie fondly. It seemed a miracle to her to see him sitting at the table with Sam and Grace – absorbed in his studies. His life, if the truth be told, was richer than it had been when he was a cooper – and a drunk. Now he was clean, sober and hard-working. He had his dignity, and he was earning the respect of the townspeople too. Later, once Kirsty and Grace had gone to bed, she confided in Jean, 'I used to despair aboot him, but Sam sorted him oot and gied him back his self-respect. Losin his legs wisna da end o da world. I never thought I'd live ta say it, but A'm prood o my son.' She glanced at Jean a little self-consciously, 'Du'll maybe think A'm silly, Jean – but I hae da strangest feelin at Kirsty will mak somethin o her life in spite o – maybe even becaase o – dis terrible thing at's happened ta her.'

'Dat's it,' said Jean, slowly, with a look of wonderment on her face. "Mak somethin o herself", du said. Ellie du's gien me an idea.' She was suddenly animated as a plan started to form in her head. She turned to her friend, eyes bright with hope and excitement. 'Du kens at Sam aye says at everybody should hae a goal ta strive for?'

Ellie nodded and gave Jean a puzzled look.

'Weel, yon day at he geed wi Kirsty ta see ta Davie's wounds he telt me at she was a natural born nurse. He couldna stop singin her praises.'

Ellie still looked confused.

'Does du no see, Ellie? Dat's da answer. Dat's her goal – ta be a nurse. We hae ta help her ta be a nurse – an dat's wir goal!'

Ellie smiled and shook her head, 'Dat wid tak money, Jeannie – money at we dunna hae. It's a splendid idea, but it's da stuff o dreams.'

'No, Ellie. We can mak it happen. Da money will be da hardest bit – du's right dere – but I hae my "rainy day" tin – an what better use could I pit it tae? An du could help.'

'Me?! I hae nae money…'

'No, but noo at Davie's earnin du could maybe let Kirsty keep her wages, and she could save dat for her trainin.'

Ellie began to warm to the idea. 'Maybe du's right.' She laughed. 'Fancy me dependin on Davie! Yiss, Jean, it's a splendid idea.'

So Jean and Ellie drew their chairs in to the table.

'Sorry for interruptin,' Jean said, 'but we hae somethin ta tell you.'

She explained the plan, ending, 'Weel, what do you think?'

'I think it's a grand scheme,' Sam answered slowly. 'Dere's just wan thing…' He pointed out that they were getting carried away with their own enthusiasm. Had they considered that Kirsty might not want to do it? They couldn't just force it on her. 'It's her life, and she has to decide if it's what she wants, and if she's up to it.'

Crestfallen, Jean admitted that the idea of Kirsty not wanting to do it had never entered their heads.

'But A'm sure she will, when she's had time ta think it ower,' added Ellie.

'Right,' said Jean, all business-like again. 'We'll work oot what every ean o wiz can do to help and we'll write it down so we can present her wi a proper plan tomorrow night. Sam, we'll need paper and a pencil.'

He tore some sheets out of the exercise book that he was using and handed them to Davie.

'Du can be da secretary, for du haes da boanniest hand.'

As Davie prepared to write, he voiced his concerns. He was worried in case Grace's studies might be neglected in their eagerness to help Kirsty…and would they be able to find enough money to support them both?

'Maybe we'll no hae tae.'

All eyes were on Jean. 'Grace is a bright lass, an independent too. She telt me at she's goin ta try ta win a scholarship – an I believe she will.' She glanced round the table. They were all nodding in agreement.

'Right,' said Sam, smiling at his mother. 'Madam Chairman, I'd like it recorded in the minutes that I pledge to give Grace all the help she needs before giving time to Kirsty's education.'

Jean laughed, and joined in the game.

'Mr Secretary, will you see that Sam's remarks are duly recorded?'

'A'm sure if da worst comes ta da worst, we can manage atween wiz ta fin da money for baith o dem,' said Davie. 'Sam has proved ta me at onything's possible if you pit your mind tae it.'

'Yiss,' said Jean, 'an Peter will want ta help too. Noo Davy, I think we'll pit dee in charge o arithmetic an handwritin.' Davie nodded. 'An A'll work on her readin. Sam, what aboot dee?'

'A'll do anatomy an First Aid. Grace can do it wi wiz, an she can be responsible for history an geography.'

'Kirsty's goin ta be da best educated lass in Lerwick,' laughed Ellie, but tears of gratitude pricked behind her eyes. 'I wish dey wir somethin I could do ta help.'

'Dere is,' said Jean. 'A'm goin ta need help wi da cookin if A'm ta fin time for da readin, so I hae a suggestion.' She went on to ask Ellie to take over her cooking duties. 'A'm thought it aa through.'

'Noo why does dat no surprise me?' asked Sam, and they all laughed, for Jean's organisational skills were legendary. 'Go on, Mammie.'

She explained that, instead of taking their main meal in the middle of the day, they would take it at teatime, "like da grand folk do." That way Ellie could do her own work in the morning, and cook their dinner in the afternoon, and they would all eat together before the evening study session began. 'It'll save a lot o time an effort.'

Yiss, thought Sam, *It's a clever plan for it serves wir purpose, and saves Ellie money an maks sure at her an Davie are gettin right fed.*

'Do you all agree?' asked Jean in her 'official' voice. "Everyone in favour say "Aye".'

They all chorused, 'Aye,' and agreed to present their plan to Kirsty and Grace the following night.

'Then I declare this meeting closed,' she said.

Sleep didn't come easily to any of them, for their minds were busy with the implications of the plan.

Chapter Thirteen
White Lies

Jean met Peter off the boat on Saturday morning. Turning up his collar against the wind, he hurried down the gangway, eager to be home. She linked her arm through his. Smiling, he pressed it to his side and reached across to put his other hand on hers, holding her close to him. It was as near as they would ever get to a public embrace, for their passion was a precious and private thing.

'We'll tak da lang wye round, Peter, for I hae a lot ta tell dee afore we get hame.' She looked up, and he could see tha pain in her eyes.

'What is it, lass?' His voice was full of concern.

'I hardly ken hoo ta say it, but Kirsty's been...attacked. By some drunken seaman.'

He stood stock-still.

'Dear Father in Heaven!' he gasped, shocked and disbelieving. 'Did he...?'

'Yiss, he did.' She paused, blinking back her tears, then rushed on – determined to make her story convincing. He had to believe it. 'We sent her ta Grindavoe till she got ower da worst. Naebody kens but wiz – da family, I mean. We thought it best ta spare her da gossip. Her face wis badly bruised an du kens hoo fock like ta speak. We telt everybody at she was helpin dem lift da tatties. I ken it's no true, but...'

'A'm sure da Lord will forgive a peerie white lie when it's done for a good reason.'

'I hoop du's right,' Jean murmured, knowing this lie wasn't the first, and it wouldn't be the last either.

They walked a minute or so in silence, lost in their thoughts.

'Poor bairn,' whispered Peter to himself. 'Da poor bairn.' Then he asked, 'When is she comin back?'

'She cam back yesterday.'

'Did she see his face? Did she ken him?'

Jean girded herself for another lie. 'No. She'd been doon wi a message ta her midder an it was dark in da lane when she cam back. It was aye a gloomy place, an it's worse noo at da clocks are geen back. Wir no even allowed a glimmer o lamp-light fae da windows, so it's black as pitch. Did du ken at dey go roond checkin at aabody is pulled doon der blinds and closed der shutters? "Obscuration of light" dey caa it,' Jean kept her eyes lowered in case he should read the lie in them. She knew she was saying too much, but she couldn't stop herself. 'Da place was full o sailors, maist o dem foo o drink.'

'Hoo is she?'

'Shocked. She feels guilty…an soiled.'

'If I could get my hands on him…'

'No, Peter. Dunna speak like yon. It's no like dee.' She squeezed his arm, 'Onywye, wir thought o a wye ta help her.'

She explained their "education" plan to him. 'Everybody's keen ta do what dey can. Aa we need noo is for Kirsty ta agree ta it. Sam is goin ta explain it ta her da night. So what does du think?'

'It's a splendid idea, lass. I canna think hoo du managed ta dream it up. I wid like ta help, but I dunna ken what I could do – nursin an navigation dunna hae muckle in common.'

'Du could help wi da money side, Peter.'

'Yea, but what aboot Grace? A'm no made a money. I couldna manage ta pay for twa.'

'Wi ony luck du winna hae tae for Grace is tryin for a scholarship.'

He digested this, then said, 'If du thinks we can do it, I've nae doubt we can, for du has a wye a makin things happen.' His face clouded over as his thoughts turned to Kirsty. 'Du'll hae ta see at she doesna owerdo it, wi da hoosewark and da studyin forbye. It's a lot for a lass ta tak on, especially when she's been…' His voice tailed off, then he went on more brightly, 'but I suppose things'll be easier for her noo at Jamie's awa – no sae much fetchin an carryin.'

'Yea,' said Jean, conscious of the irony. 'Du's right. It's easier for her noo at he's gone.'

'Speakin o Jamie, I saa him for a minute at da train station. He didna hae muckle ta say for himsel. I think he was worryin aboot what da doctors'll say. I hoop dey let him geng back ta France since he's set his hert on it. A'm prood o his fightin spirit.'

Jean made no comment, and he continued, 'I will admit dey wir times when he was a boy at I wondered hoo he wid turn oot. Aye in trouble. I suppose it wis just youthful high spirits, an he's grown oot o it noo. Maybe I shouldna a been sae hard on him…'

After tea, when Ellie and Davie arrived, they gathered round the fire.

'Come Grace,' said Sam, 'dere 'll be nae studyin da night, for we hae somethin ta speak ower tagidder.'

Puzzled she came and joined the circle, 'Does du ken what dis is aboot, Kirsty?' She shook her head, equally mystified.

So Sam laid the scheme before them. His enthusiasm was obvious, and it was clear from their expressions that Jean, Ellie and Davie were excited about it too. Kirsty was apprehensive. What if she wasn't clever enough? What if she let them down?

'What does du say, Kirsty? Will du gie it a try?'

All eyes were on her, willing her to agree. At first she said nothing – she needed a minute to think. She had accepted what had happened to her – that couldn't be changed – and her life must go on, though she couldn't imagine what future was possible. She'd never marry. Jamie had seen to that. She didn't want to anyhow, because she knew she'd never love anyone but Sam...and even if, by some strange magic, he were to fall in love with her, it could never be. He was a good man and deserved the best that life could offer – not a woman who'd been ruined. Her girlish dreams were truly over. *A'll never be a wife or a midder,* she thought, *an if Sam thinks I wid be a good nurse...what do I hae ta lose?*

'Yiss,' she said. 'I'll try. It wid be fine ta think I could do some good in da world.'

Her shattered life now had some purpose.

For several weeks the "education plan" worked well. All Kirsty's tutors were delighted with her progress for she was an eager and apt pupil. The days flew by. Her mornings were occupied with her domestic duties, and her afternoons were spent practising her reading, and listening to extracts from Jean's favourite books. They were happy, companionable times and established Kirsty's lifelong love of literature, as well as bringing the two women even closer. She had some free time between her reading hour and their "dinner-at-teatime", and this was often spent with Joe – something Jean was keen to encourage for it was beneficial to both of them. He would sidle up to her. 'Poor Kirsty,' he'd say and stroke her hand. 'Kirsty helped Joe.' Sometimes his voice would take on a hard edge. 'Jamie hurt Kirsty,' he'd say. 'Bad, bad man.' His speech was immature in structure, but he was communicating (if only with Kirsty) – and his face, which up to now had been bland and expressionless, began to show both anger and love. Jean watched the relationship develop. Kirsty took great interest in his drawings, asking questions which he answered sometimes silently – pointing out further details in the picture – and sometimes in short, stilted sentences. Jean noted with surprise and delight that he had quite an extensive vocabulary, which he used to name objects. However, description and emotion was expressed only in the subtlety and detail of his pencil-work.

The evening meal became a lively social occasion, as each told the others about the day's events, and when it was over – and family prayers – the next study-time began. Kirsty had no time to dwell on her "trouble". Davie did number-work with her on Monday, Wednesday and Friday, and supervised her handwriting practice. On Tuesday she did Geography with Grace, and on Friday Sam introduced the girls to anatomy. On the first evening Davie suggested that, instead of working from a copy-book, she should start a diary, and keep a record of her progress. So on Monday 15th October she made her first entry.

I began my lessons today. In the afternoon I practised reading a bit from Kidnapped out loud so that I wouldn't have to stop and sound words out when I read it to Joe. Then I listened while Auntie Jean read the first bit of Pride and Prejudice to me. It is her favourite book and I think it will be mine too. After our dinner-at-teatime and prayers and Joe's story Davie started to go over the times tables with me. I did them at school but was never any good at them. We did the 2 times, 3 times, 4 times and 5 times. He made me say them until I got them right three times in a row. Then he gave me a page of sums to do. I was very tired. I hope I am gotten them right.

Next time she added a bit about the weather and her personal news.

Wednesday 17th October. The weather is terrible bad. Wind and rain and sleet. Yestarday Grace gave me a map of Shetland. There were no places marked on it. We are going to put them in. We're starting with Lerwick and Bressay. Tonight when everyone was at the Prayer Meeting Davie and me did the 6 times and the 7 times tables. It was very hard. Then we did mental. He asked me questions and I had to answer as quick as I could. It was good fun. This morning Auntie Jean asked me to go to the shop for butter for she was going to bake a special cake for my birthday. I put on my winter coat but when I got to the door I started to greet for I couldna face going out among the folk. I couldna bear them to look at me. My feet would not move. Auntie Jean was that good to me. She took me in and said she would go. I felt really bad about it especially when there was no butter or syrup or jam to be had in the town. So there will be no cake on Saturday. It does not matter. I am never had a birthday cake afore. My hand is tired with all this writing. Davie says I am holding the pencil too tight.

Her next entry included some local news.

Friday 19th October. Last night Sam started anatomy with Grace and me. He got a skeleton from a suitcase under his bed. He had it when he was going to be a doctor. He made it dance and it looked that funny that we laughed till we were greetin. Then he told us the names of some of the bones. Some of the words are boannie. I like the sound of clavicle. He said the elbow is called the humerus. It sounds like humorous. That means funny. That is why we call it our funny bone.

Beckie came in fae Grindavoe for the weekend so she can be with me on my birthday. That was a really good birthday present. She brought eggs and milk and butter so Auntie Jean baked a cake after all. Mrs Carter gave her some strawberry jam to put in the middle. Everybody gave me a present, Auntie Jean and Uncle Peter gave me a New Testament with pictures in it. Sam gave me my very own copy of Pride and Prejudice. It is my best thing ever. Mammie and Davie gave me a brooch shaped like a K and Grace and Joe gave me some crayons so I can colour my map. Beckie gave me an apron with a big pocket and she stitched my name on it in fancy letters. I am going to keep my book in it then I can read a bit whenever I have a spare minute. After the dinner-at-teatime uncle Peter played the fiddle. We pushed back the table and danced a reel. It was a good fun.

There was not much fun in Lerwick today for a Russian steamer was hit by a torpedo off the Bard o Bressay. Another boat took her in tow but she sunk anyway. I am written the Bard on my map and I put a cross on the sea where she went down. I put two crosses near the lighthouse where the boats sank last month.

On Monday 22nd she reported that 'yesterday was a terrible day', for three ships had been hit near the Bard. *Three in one day,* she wrote. *Three more crosses on my map and a lot of sailors drowned. I wonder why God lets such bad things happen. There will be mapwork with Grace tomorrow. I hope there are no more crosses to mark. I'm getting quick at my arithmetic. My hand is not so sore when I write now so I am surely getting used to it.*

So she recorded her progress and her growing confidence. Surrounded as she was by everybody's love and delight in her achievements, her self-loathing gradually faded and she felt a resurgence of hope. However, she still dreaded meeting people outwith the family circle and refused to go beyond the gate. Help came from an unexpected source, as it was little Joe who got her over this final hurdle.

'Come wi me.' he said, holding out his hand. At the harbour and he taught her about shipping and the various boats that called for water or coal, or to have their cargo inspected. He also made her more observant about the architecture of the growing town. Sometimes he took her to the seashore, where he named the birds for her, and taught her (through his drawings) to identify the various species by the shape of beak, feet and body; by their colour and markings; by size, wingspan and flight patterns. Next day they tried to identify them from their footprints in the snow. So even little Joe played a significant part in her education and recuperation.

That week Sam told them that there was a resurgence of anti-German feeling in the town, fuelled by rumours of an attack – without warning - on a convoy of merchant ships by German raiders. This was confirmed by a report in the *Shetland Times* on the 27th October. They listened, stunned, as Peter read it out. The escort ships – the HMS Mary Rose, and HMS Strongbow – had been sunk along with nine out of the twelve merchant ships. This was a shameful breach of protocol, but worse than that, the Germans had sailed away without making any effort to pick up survivors. Everyone was at first numbed with horror. Then furious and frustrated. Was there no end to German "frightfulness"?

'Wir been dat wrapped up in wir ain busy lives at wir forgotten aboot da war, an idder fock's distress,' Jean said, shame and sorrow on her face.

This was true. In fact they'd been almost happy, such was their sense of involvement and purpose, and their delight in Kirsty's progress. So they bowed their heads, and Peter led them in a prayer for the suffering world.

As she was writing up her diary on November 9th, it suddenly struck Kirsty that Joe's drawing books formed a kind of diary too, for they recorded (in pictures instead of words) what he'd seen on each day. This triggered a feeling of unease. Something was gnawing at the back of her mind. Something to do with the notebooks. What could it be? It must have been churning through her brain while she slept, for when she woke she knew what had been troubling her. She remembered Joe's agitation on the night she moved him up to the attic, how he'd insisted on going back to the parlour to collect his notebooks from under his mattress. She could see him clearly in her mind's eye, clutching them to him – the blue one he kept for pictures of ships and buildings and the green one he used for plants and birds and animals. But there had been a red one too – one she'd never seen before or since. One he never showed to anyone. What did he record in its pages? Somehow she knew it was important to find out. She'd search for it when she was cleaning the bedrooms…

She felt under his mattress. Sure enough it was there. The red notebook! She sat on the bed and began to leaf through the pages with mounting horror. Like the others, it was a kind of diary. It had no words, but spoke volumes. Clearly. Passionately. Eloquently. Yet it was chillingly objective. He was setting down the facts in pictures. The first one showed himself lying in his bed at one side of the room and Jamie in his bed at the other. Bloodcurdling images emanated from Jamie's head and hovered above him. The sequence of drawings showed how Joe had been sucked into Jamie's nightmares, learning about the atrocities he had witnesses…and perpetrated. Obviously the ghosts that haunted Jamie began to haunt Joe too.

Up till now he'd hardly ever drawn human faces. Figures were included in his pictures as "accessories" – dockers on the pier; fishermen unloading their catch; drivers of carts, gigs and the occasional motorcar – but their faces were virtually featureless. Here, in the red book, there were close-up portraits which showed in a few simple strokes the full and terrible range of human suffering. This was Joe's account of all that had happened between him and Jamie since the day he arrived. His poor young head was being crammed with images of death, decay, violence and depravity – for Jamie had revealed the truth of his war to the boy, and spared him nothing. The drawings showed water-logged trenches, with discoloured, rotting limbs embedded in their sides; men asleep on fire-steps or in dugouts – well-fed rats crawling over their faces; soldiers climbing up the ladders and out over the parapet into a hail of bullets that looked like a swarm of angry bees; soldiers dying – appearing to pirouette like dancers in the air, or lying on the ground in grotesque positions, some clutching their gaping stomachs, while their entrails spilled over their hands like glistening snakes. Other sketches showed the night sky lit by explosions or tracers – beautiful as fireworks on bonfire night – but their light revealed heart-rending silhouettes of boys entangled in the barbed wire, unable to free themselves and crawl for cover, their faces frozen in expressions of abject terror. Another page showed men huddled in a shell-hole, the living kneeling on the dead in a desperate effort to keep their heads above the rising level of the water.

Some sketches showed men rushing towards the enemy with fixed bayonets – their mouths wide open to roar their war cries, the way they had been trained to do. One portrait showed Jamie with an expression that could only be described as ecstasy, as he choked the life out of a German officer with his bare hands. And there were brothels and rape and every kind of human indignity. Kirsty turned the pages with growing revulsion, but nothing could have prepared her for the last few. These were the worst of all because they were self-portraits. Joe's contorted face revealed his terror, his pain, his anguish and his shame as he struggled to escape from Jamie who was subjecting him to acts of disgusting bestiality. Every detail was there. Here was the shocking proof of Jamie's sick mind. Kirsty flew from the room, down the stairs and to the outhouse, where she vomited violently and repeatedly.

She had believed that she had saved the boy from Jamie's cruelty. Intervened in time to prevent it. This had helped her to come to terms with her own suffering, for it had served some purpose - but suddenly she recalled Joe's voice, shrill with fear, calling out, "No! No again!" He had said, "Again", and she hadn't registered that. It wasn't the first time. Was this what Grace had heard when the others were away? *Oh Joe. Poor peerie Joe.* She wept as if her heart would break. Her ordeal was nothing to his. *Why did I no see what was goin on? I thought Joe was safe when I moved him upstair, but I should a kent at Jamie wid stop at nothin.* She crossed her arms over her stomach, hugging herself, rocking back and forth and whispering, 'A'm sorry, Joe. A'm sorry. I didna ken.' over and over again.

She was pale and tearful from time to time that day, and was unable for her study sessions. So Sam took Davie and Ellie home early. In her diary all she wrote was:

Friday 2nd November. I could not do my lessons today for all I can think about is Jamie's wickedness, and poor peerie Joe.

When Sam returned they had their "eight o'clocks". Kirsty was about to clear the cups away when Jean said, 'Lass, du looks worn oot. Du should hae an early night. A'll soon swill da cups.'

Jean gathered them up and headed for the scullery, calling, 'Bed, Kirsty,' over her shoulder. When she'd left the room Kirsty took the red notebook from her apron pocket, handed it to Sam and left the room without a word. There was nothing she could say. Puzzled, Sam flicked through the pages. He drew a sharp breath. He'd have to look at this in private. Trying to behave as if nothing was wrong, he went through to the parlour and lit the lamp. Then he learned the depths of his youngest brother's suffering.

Jean came through from the scullery and sat down heavily. Just as the world always seemed to know, and hold its breath when a storm was brewing, so she sensed that something was about to happen. Surely nothing else could go wrong. She put on her knitting belt and picked up the Fair Isle jumper she'd started a day or two before. She laid it on her lap and smoothed it with her hand, enjoying its warmth and softness as she studied the design. She preferred these natural shades to the brighter blues, reds and yellows. The natural colours were calming – creamy white instead of the harsh bleached sort; soft grey "shaela", the colour of the mists that hung like smoke on the hills in the mornings; "moorit" that reminded her of seaweed cast up on the tideline – russet-brown seaweed they used to gather by the barrowload to spread on the fields in spring; and the rich "Shetland black" that wasn't really black at all, but a dark dark brown – dark as freshly-cut peat.

She stuck the steel wire into the horse-hair pad at her right side, and anchored the growing garment firmly by tucking it into the belt at her left. Where was she? *Three white, two moorit, one white; two moorit, three white, one moorit...* soon she got into the rhythm. She sat absolutely still. No movement of elbows or shoulders. Only her fingers moved, quickly flicking the wool round the needles to form the familiar pattern. The click of the needles formed a subtle counterpoint to the clock's steady tock, tock, tock – which fell into the quiet room like raindrops into a pond. She sighed and began to feel easier. The strain of the last few weeks had caught up with her. That was all. Nothing more than that. No need for strange forebodings. She worked quickly, without looking. Her fingers knew what to do. Knitting was a simple task which she found infinitely reassuring, for she was using patterns and skills that had been passed down through generations, and which she in turn had taught to Beckie and Grace. Like the spinning, it linked her with those who had gone before. They had handled hardships with courage and fortitude, and so would she...*two white, three moorit; one white, three moorit...*

Sam burst into the room, took two unsteady steps then stopped in his tracks as though rooted to the spot. Startled, Jean looked up. Sam was clutching a red notebook, and she couldn't read the expression on his face. The moorit ball fell off her lap. They both watched it as it rolled across the floor and came to rest at his feet. Like an automaton he bent down and picked it up. Then, tucking the notebook under his arm, he wound the wool back on to the ball as he walked towards her. He placed it gently on the chair beside her and handed her the notebook. Unable to move, he stood and watched. He saw the colour drain from her face till she was as pale as peat-ash; saw her fingers tremble as she turned the pages – forcing herself to look at each and every one. At last she closed the book. Their eyes met and each saw the naked horror in the other's heart. She drew a long shuddering breath and seemed to shrink back into her chair.

'Oh, Joe,' she whispered. 'My poor peerie Joe.'

It was the first time Sam had seen his mother cry.

Chapter Fourteen

To be, or not to be

As she went about her work, Jean kept glancing at Kirsty's pale face, and the dark circles under her eyes. Over the last few days Kirsty had continued to be unwell, rushing out to the outhouse several times each morning. The truth began to dawn on Jean. This was no stomach upset. There was another reason for her sickness.

'Oh, dear Father in Heaven,' she whispered. 'Could You no have spared her dis?'

All night Jean tossed and turned, wondering if Kirsty had realised she was pregnant - and how she would cope with another hammer blow. All her energy was focused on her studies, and on Joe. Maybe that was her way of blocking it out. Jean resolved to go down the lane and discuss the matter with Ellie first thing in the morning. It broke her heart to have to share her suspicions with her friend – as if she didn't have enough problems already – but she was the lass's mother and had a right to know.

At first Ellie was silent, trying to absorb the news, containing her pain. Jean waited, giving her time. At length Ellie spoke.

'She's no the first and she'll no be the last - an I dare say she's luckier as mony a poor lass at's been turned oot in ta da streets wi no a penny in her pocket.' She stared for a long time into the distance, her eyes swimming and her lips squeezed tight together so no sob could escape. Then she pressed her clenched fist to her mouth and sniffed once or twice. 'A'll come an speak wi her – see she kens she'll be weel looked eftir, her an her bairn.'

She took her coat from the back of the door.

'Hello, Mammie. What are you doin here at dis time o day?'

With a heavy heart, Jean watched her smile of welcome fade as she saw the them exchange worried glances.

'What is it?' she asked apprehensively. 'What's happened noo?'

It was clear she hadn't seen her sickness as anything other than a "feerie", for winter vomiting was common.

Jean went quietly to her room, leaving mother and daughter alone. Through the thin walls she could hear the soft monotone of Ellie's voice. Then a sudden sharp cry, followed by, 'No! No! It canna be!' and a storm of uncontrollable weeping. She put her hands over her ears, wishing she could block it out, but she could still hear Ellie's gentle murmuring, 'So, so lass. Dunna tak on like yon. It's no da end o da world.' Then came Kirsty's shrill and desperate shouting, 'Yiss Mammie, it is. I wanted a man an bairns I could love. Noo dat'll never be…an hoo can I love dis bairn? What if it turns oot ta be like its faither? It's no fair.' The sobbing began again.

Jean knelt beside her bed and prayed, 'Dear Father, if ever we needed Thy help, it's now. Be with us. Guide us - but most of all, let Kirsty feel the power of Thy love.'

Slowly she got to her feet and, gripping the brass bedrail with both hands, she tried to compose herself for it was time to go and give what support she could.

Kirsty was slumped on the floor, her face buried in her

mother's lap. She looked up when she heard the squeak of Jean's shoes on the polished wax-cloth, and the sight of the girl's white, tear-stained face sent a shaft of pain through Jean's heart. She was right. It wasn't fair.

'Oh Auntie Jean,' she wailed. 'Everybody'll ken. A'll have brought shame on dis hoose an on my midder's hoose. I wish I could die.'

'Noo, noo lass. Yon's a wicked thing ta say,' Ellie began, but Jean interrupted urgently.

'Listen ta me, Kirsty. A'm said it afore, an A'll say it again. Da shame is not yours. Everybody at loves dee kens dat, an da Lord kens it too. So what does it maitter what idder fock think? Noo go an wash yon boannie face, an A'll mak a cup o tay afore we get on wi da wark.'

'My poor bairn,' murmured Ellie as Kirsty left the room.

'She'll be fine,' said Jean, wishing she felt as confident as she sounded. 'Da Lord will see at her back is fit for da burden.'

That evening when Kirsty was reading to Joe, Jean took Sam aside and told him. At first he said nothing, but she saw his pupils widen with shock.

'Da poor lass…has she no had enough ta contend wi?' he muttered angrily. 'It's no fair.'

'Dat's what she said,' Jean replied rather grimly, 'but life's no fair, son. Da Lord is aye testin wiz.'

'It's no fair,' he repeated dully. Then, pulling himself together, he asked, 'What can we do ta help her?'

'Aa we can do is let her ken we love her…at nothin'll ever change dat, an we'll help her aa we can.'

There was a long silence.

'A'm goin ta mairry her, Mammie.'

'Du telt me at du wid never mairry, Sam. Du said it widna be fair on ony lass, kennin dat dy life micht be cut short if dy illness comes back'.

'A'm goin ta mairry her, an if I shood die early, at least she wid hiv her guid name, dis family owes her dat. She needs a man at her side, an a faither for her bairn. It's da least at I can do.'

'Du's no dy bridder's keeper, Sam. Du doesna hae ta pay da price for his sins.' Jean spoke more sharply than she meant to, worried that Sam was making a rash and impetuous decision. 'Besides,' she continued more gently, 'du wid be doin her no favours if du mairried her oot a pity. She deserves better as dat. So dunna be in ower muckle o a hurry.'

She sighed. It was easy to forget he was so young, for in so many ways he seemed older – and wiser – than his twenty-one years. All the same, she didn't want him to marry out of a mistaken sense of duty. There had to be love. She put her hand on his.

'I ken du means weel, Sam. Du wants ta dae what's right, but sometimes it's hard ta ken what dat is. Decisions like dis shouldna be made in da heat o da moment. Mairriage is for a lifetime. Is she da wife du wants at dy side for da rest o dy days? Promise me du'll think on it carefully afore du does onything – for her sake as weel as dee ain.'

The next few days passed smoothly. No one mentioned Kirsty's pregnancy. She coped with her morning sickness calmly and without fuss, and continued with her chores and her studies as if nothing had happened. *In fact*, Jean thought, *you could nearly believe at nothin bad*. It was as if everyone was in denial, herself included. She didn't even tell Peter when he was home that weekend. There'd be plenty time for that once matters had been settled between Sam and Kirsty.

The following Sunday, when Jean and Sam were walking by the Sletts and the young ones were loitering behind, Sam brought up the subject again.

'A'm done what you said, Mammie. A'm thought aboot it every day an my mind is made up. A'm goin ta mairry Kirsty.'

She looked across the bay, towards the Bressay Light. A huge wave pulled itself up, darkening within its curve, and rushed onto the shore up, up, up over the sand.

'Does du love her?'

The sea drew back with a soft hush – as if it, like Sam, were taking a deep breath.

'I care for her a lot,' he said slowly, looking at the waves, 'an I canna help but admire da wye she's coped wi everything at's happened. A'll admit it's been hard ta think on her as a grown woman – an no da young lass at I looked on like a sister – but she is a woman, an a strong ean at dat.' He turned to his mother and she could see he was willing her to understand. Quietly he told her that they were comfortable together, and could talk easily about anything and everything. 'I aye felt better for bein in her company. Before aa dis she had such energy, an such…' he searched for words, 'an appetite for life. I miss dat, an I want ta help her get dat back. I want ta look eftir her, an see at nothin bad ever happens ta her again. So dere you have it, Mammie. A'm goin ta mairry her.'

Three times the waves surged forward and fell back before she spoke.

'Weel, son, I dare say der mony a ean has settled for less. Passion's no everything.'

Secretly she hoped that love would grow, for she wanted him to taste life to the full, and she knew Kirsty had feelings for him. 'She's a good lass, Sam. A'll no stand in dy wye.' Then she added, 'Of coorse she'll maybe no tak dee – is du thought o dat?'

She could tell by his shocked expression that the idea had never crossed his mind.

'Dunna worry, son. A'm only havin a peerie fun,' she said, and smiled reassuringly. *But aa da sam, Kirsty's a lass wi a mind o her ain...*

Monday, 19th November. In the evening Sam was restless, unable to concentrate on helping Grace. His fidgeting was disturbing Davie and Kirsty too. What was the matter with the boy?

'What's up wi dee?' Jean asked when he returned from escorting Ellie and Davie home, and they had the place to themselves. 'Du's like a cat on a windy night – canna tak paece. A'm never seen dee like dis afore.'

'You were right, Mammie. She turned me doon.'

'Ah,' said Jean, nodding her head. 'Did she gie ony reason?'

'She said she liked me ower muckle ta mairry me. What kind o daft answer is dat? Liked me ower muckle!'

'Onything else?'

'She said she wanted me ta hae a good wife, no some-ean at wis been...ruined.'

'Dat's it dan, son. She thinks she's no good enough for dee.'

'I said I wid ax her again in a week's time, when she's had time ta think it ower.'

He turned away and murmured as if to himself, 'I just want

ta hadd her in my airms an keep her safe.' Facing his Mother again, he said simply, 'I miss her, Mammie. I miss da Kirsty I kent afore.'

Jean looked at him sharply, 'Did du tell her dat?'

'No,' he said slowly. 'I said I wid try ta be a good husband ta her, an a good faither ta her bairn,' His face reddened and he went on, 'an I promised at I widna mak ony – you ken – advances. We could hae separate beds if she wanted. I thought at eftir Jamie she might no...' His voice tailed off.

'Maybe du should try tellin her hoo du really feels next time.'

Jean went into the scullery shaking her head. *Oh Sam, Sam,* she thought. *Du haes a lot ta lairn aboot women.*

All week Kirsty and Sam avoided one another's eyes. On Saturday the tension between them was so obvious that even Peter noticed.

'Sam an Kirsty seem aafil edgy,' he remarked to Jean as they were getting ready for bed. 'Dey dunna seem ta be speakin ta ean anidder. Are dey had an ootfaa?'

'No,' said Jean. 'Quite da opposite. I should a telt dee aboot it last time du wis hame, but I wis waitin till things wis settled atween dem, wan wye or da idder.' She took out her hairpins and let her hair fall onto her shoulders. She began to brush it, watching him in the mirror. 'Kirsty's goin ta hae a bairn.'

Peter looked at her. 'Oh dear Father,' he whispered. His horrified expression gave way to one of confusion. 'Surely Sam doesna blame her for dat. He does ken aboot da sailor, does'n he?'

Jean swivelled round to face him. 'Yiss, of coorse he kens.' She paused, divided her hair into three strands and began to plait it. 'He's axed her ta mairry him. He wants ta see at she's aa right.'

Peter mulled this over.

'It says a lot for him at he's willin ta tak on a stranger's bairn. He's a fine man, wir Sam – but does he ken what he's doin?'

'I telt him ta think it ower very carefully afore he axed her, an I think he truly did – but da funny thing is - she turned him doon.'

'Turned him doon?' repeated Peter, utterly astonished.

'She's aye had a notion on him, so it canna a been easy for her. She's a lass wi a conscience an she didna want him ta mairry her oot o a sense o duty – but he'll no tak "No" for an answer. He's goin ta ax her again on Monday.'

'I see,' said Peter slowly. 'If she says "Yiss" dis time, dey'll hae ta get on wi it – I mean, if dey want aabody ta think it's his bairn - an aa above board.' He lay silently staring at the ceiling. 'Tell dem dey hae my blessin, an dey should get da banns read as soon as possible.' He sighed. 'It's no da wye we wid a wanted it, Jean, but dey're twa fine young fock an we'll just hae ta laeve dem in da Lord's hands.' He turned the lamp out and took Jean in his arms. 'If she means half as much ta him as du does ta me, he'll be a lucky man.'

On Sunday Kirsty confronted Davie.

'Du's a man, Davie. A'm needin dy advice.'

Davie raised one eyebrow, and waited for her to go on.

'Sam's goin ta ax me for my answer da moarn. What does du think I should say?'

'Answer?' said Davie. 'Du'll need ta tell me da question.'

Kirsty told him the gist of the story, and poured out her misgivings to him.

'I turned him doon. I didna think it was right. I want ta mairry him. Du haes nae idea hoo much I want tae – but no like dis. I dunna want him ta mairry me oot o pity, an dan wish at he hadna. I ken he likes me, an he'd aye be kind ta me… but what if he meets somebody at he really loves an his hert is brakkin becaase he's stuck wi me? I couldna bear ta mak him suffer like dat.'

'Du's bein dramatic – makkin ower muckle o it. It's aa dis readin at du's doin.'

'No, Davie. Du haes ta tak me seriously. A'm facin da facts, an du should too. Dis is da worst thing at's happened ta me yet. Truly it is. Ta come sae near ta my secret dream, an fin it's a faersome mara.' She looked at him and her eyes said it all. 'I love him, Davie. I canna tell you hoo aften A'm dreamt o bein his wife, but aye pairt o dat dream wis at he loved me an aa – as a man should love his wife. An noo he says we could live as bridder an sister till I get ower what Jamie did, hooever lang it taks. Does dat mean he doesna want me? I keep axin mesel, could I live wi him da rest o my days lovin him da wye I do, an him no love me back? No, Davie. I dunna think I can mairry him. Nearly havin him wid be worse as no havin him ava. Aa I can think is at nae man wants ta be lumbered wi a ruined wife an anidder man's bairn.'

'Noo see here, Kirsty,' he began, 'I hae just twa things ta say ta dee, so listen weel. Du kens A'm no a man o words. Da first is – du'll never get a better man as Sam; da second is – he loves dee. He maybe doesna ken it yet, but du'll see. An anidder thing – it's no up ta dee ta decide what's best for him. He's da only wan at can do dat.'

'Dat's three things, Davie.' She sniffed and gave him an almost mischievous smile.

'Aye, an here's anidder. Is du ever spared a thought for what du can do for him?'

She opened her mouth to protest, but he held up his hand to stop her.

'No, Kirsty. Let me finish. Du kens he's no strong an da consumption can come back. He'll need somebody ta look eftir him. Wid du no like ta be dat body? Pit it like dis – could du bear no ta be? I ken A'm no pittin dis very weel, but life is no like it is in storybooks. Naebody kens dat better as me.'

Kirsty looked crestfallen and ashamed. 'A'm sorry, Davie. I wis never thinkin aboot dy hoops an dreams. Hoo could I be dat selfish? What is happenin ta me?' Her lip trembled.

'Wheest, lass. Let me go on while I hae da words. A'm settled for da best I can be, an A'm happy. Dat's thanks ta Sam. Look, lass,' he took her hands in his, 'wir no sae different, dee an me. Wir baith suffered cruel blows, but we hae ta mak da best o it. So could du no settle for a kindly helpmate an a good father for da bairn? Wha's ta say at things'll no turn oot a whole lot better as du thinks?' His eyes held hers. 'Hang on ta dy dream, Kirsty. I do, an maybe some day A'll fin a lass at will accept me da wye I am. Coont deesel lucky, lass, an mairry da man.'

'Oh Davie,' she cried, jumping to her feet and planting a kiss on his forehead. 'Naebody could hae a better bridder as dee!'

'A'm goin ta walk Ellie an Davie hame noo,' said Sam once Monday's lesson was finished. 'Is du comin wi me, Kirsty?' He needed a chance to talk to her in private.

When Ellie and Davie were safely indoors and the door had clicked behind them they were alone.

'We could wander oot ta da Sooth End, if du likes?' he said.

Side by side they walked, not quite touching. Each was acutely aware of the other, and of the fact that what took place between them in the next few minutes would alter the course of their lives for ever. The moon lit their path, silvering the flagstones, which glittered with frost. Through the gaps between the shops and houses they could glimse the sea, which lay like crumpled metal – catching the light on its irregular, shifting planes. They stopped by the sea-wall above Bain's Beach to watch it.

They turned to face one another, and he took her hands in his.

'Kirsty,' he began, then hesitated. Suddenly he was at a loss for words.

'Yiss,' she said. 'Da answer is "yiss".'

'Did du say "Yiss"?' asked Sam. 'Does du mean at du will mairry me?'

'Dat's what I said.' He couldn't quite read her expression. Calm certainly, but there was a hint of something else... determination?

'I hae wan condition.'

Ah, he thought, *I kent dere wid be somethin.*

'I will mairry dee, Sam, but we'll do what du said – live like bridder an sister till eftir da bairn is born. If du can hadd da bairn in dee airms, an think on him as dy bairn - wir bairn - an if du thinks at du could come ta love me, dan we could think aboot bein man an wife. If no, du can go free, for da marriage'll no have been a real mairriage accordin ta da laa.' She looked directly at him. 'I ken, for A'm been ta da Readin Room, an I looked it up in a book.'

Sam looked at her face, milk-white in the moonlight – and her earnest grey eyes. She never ceased to amaze him. She was only sixteen, had been cruelly blackmailed, brutally violated and now, pregnant with the child of a man she reviled, she was laying down conditions to protect *his* rights. He longed to sweep her into his arms and tell her he loved her. Loved her? The thought had sprung into his mind unbidden, taking him by surprise. But it was true. He did love her, and not as a brother. He really loved her. He loved her seriousness, he loved her sincerity, he loved her courage – and that determined lift of her chin. He loved her imagination, her curiosity and her sense of fun too, and it would be his mission to get all these things to surface again – to get his Kirsty back and make her love him. He wanted her. God how he ached for her. Excitement seemed to crackle in the air around them, but it would have to be contained till after the bairn. He fumbled in his pocket and took out a little heart-shaped box.

'If I agree ta dy condition, will du wear my ring?'

She nodded.

'Gie me dee hand.' He threaded the ring onto her finger. 'Some fock say at pearls are for tears, but no aa tears are sad, are dey? Dere can be happy tears.'

She looked at the ring, at the pure translucency of the single pearl.

'It's like da moon,' she whispered. 'Du's gien me da moon.'

Her breath caught in her throat - half-laugh, half-sob. Droplets glistened on her lashes. Gently, so gently he kissed her eyelids, and when their lips met to seal the bargain, she tasted the salt of her own tears.

PART TWO

Chapter Fifteen
Plans

Jean was full of suspense because she knew that Sam would have put the question to Kirsty the previous evening. *What wis her answer?* she wondered. Nothing was said at breakfast-time. Nothing was said at their mid-day meal. During the afternoon reading session she searched the girl's face for clues, but her expression gave nothing away. *If he says nothin at dinnertime, A'll ax him straight oot,* she vowed.

When Sam came home from work, Kirsty was setting the table calmly, concentrating on the job in hand. They were still avoiding one another's eyes. *I canna bear dis,* Jean thought. *If he doesna say somethin in da next five minutes, it'll mean she's turned him doon again...but he doesna look broken-herted. What is goin on?*

Ellie set a steaming tureen on the table, and they bowed their heads while Sam said the grace.

'Father, we thank Thee for the food Thou hast provided, and for the love and fellowship we share at this table. We would also ask Thy blessing on the marriage that is to take place between Kirsty and me, for she has agreed to be my wife.' All eyes flew open but his and Kirsty's. 'We ask this humbly in the name of Thy Son, Jesus Christ, our Lord. Amen.'

There was instant pandemonium. Everyone leapt to their feet and the couple were enveloped in a flurry of kisses and congratulations. Kirsty, suddenly shy and blushing, produced the ring (which she'd secreted in her apron pocket) and put it on. There were gasps of admiration as she held out her hand for everybody to see. Ellie kissed her again.

'My dear, dear lass,' she murmured with a tremor in her voice. 'Du couldna get a better man, an I thank da Good Lord at he's brought you tagidder.'

Her relief was obvious, and her delight, but as she turned away Jean saw tears, and her expression was one of wistful longing. She knew that Ellie was remembering her own beloved Samuel, thinking of what might have been, and praying that her daughter would find the kind of love that she'd had, and lost.

'And my Sam couldna get a better wife,' Jean said swiftly, to mask Ellie's unguarded moment. She held out her arms to Kirsty. 'Come here, lass an let me gie dee a hug. A'm loved dee like my ain since du first cam here wi dee midder when du wis a peerie lass, an noo du truly will be my dowter.'

'An du'll be my sister!' Grace seized her round the waist and birled her round, laughing, till they were both breathless and dizzy.

Davie wheeled his chair over to sit beside Kirsty, who had flopped into a chair, and was fanning her face with her hand.

'Thanks, Davie,' Kirsty whispered in his ear. 'Du gied me da courage ta say "Yiss".'

The initial excitement over, they all drifted back to the table.

'Sister,' said Joe, as Kirsty took her place beside him.

'Dis soup must be ston cowld noo,' said Ellie in mock annoyance. 'A'm goin ta hae ta pit it back on da stove for twartree minutes.'

'Let's hae a toast while wir waitin,' said Jean, getting a bottle of Ginger Cordial out of the cupboard. 'Bring da glesses please, Grace. Davie, will du do da honours?'

'Please be upstandin – everybody at can,' he laughed, 'an toast a couple at wis made for ean anidder.' He lifted his glass. 'Kirsty an Sam – long life an happiness.'

There was an air of festivity as they clinked glasses and echoed Davie's words.

'We should drink ta dat, Kirsty,' Sam said softly, 'Long life and happiness.'

Please God, let it be true, Kirsty prayed as their glasses touched, and his eyes met hers.

'Nae lessons da night,' declared Sam when they'd finished their meal. 'Naebody's in da mood for study.'

So they pushed back the table and pulled in their chairs to form a wide circle round the stove. Sam lit his pipe.

'We'll no be able ta mak ony arrangements till wir spoken ta Daddie. It widna be right for da whole a Lerwick ta ken wir news afore him.'

'He kens, an he gies you his blessin,' said Jean confident that he would have read her thoughts across the miles, now that their lines of communication were open again. Not being able to reach him was one of the things that had hurt her the most during the dark days of their grief, but now they could see into each other's hearts, together or apart. It was a gift that no-one questioned, but accepted as completely natural.

'Right,' said Sam. 'The first thing we hae ta do is set the date. What does du think, Kirsty? It'll hae ta be a Saturday when Daddie's hame.'

Kirsty consulted the calendar on the wall. Peter's "home" weekends were clearly marked.

'Dis is da 27th o November. He'll be hame on da eighth o December, an again on da 22nd.'

'Da eighth is ower soon. No enough time for da Banns ta be read,' said Jean. 'Dey hae ta be read on three Sundays.'

'It'll hae ta be da 22nd dan,' said Kirsty, 'if dat's aa right wi dee, Sam?'

Sam smiled. 'We'll go an see da minister da moarn's eftirnoon, when du's done dee readin, for it's my half-day.'

Kirsty nodded, and turned to her mother.

'What else do we hae ta do, Mammie?'

'You'll hae ta decide whaar it's goin ta be, an wha's goin ta be dere.'

'Weel, whaar can it be? I dunna want a lot o fock starin at me.'

Sam noted there was a hint of panic.

'It could be in da kirk, of coorse, or in da manse, or…'

'I'd like it in da manse,' said Kirsty firmly. 'Please.'

'Dat's settled, dan,' he said, giving her a reassuring smile.

'We'll hae da meal here in da kitchen – just da fock at you want ta be dere – an we'll clear da front room for da dancin,' said Jean.

Sam said that would be splendid. Then, noticing that Kirsty was a bit overwhelmed, suggested that they'd probably done enough arranging for one night. He took his father's fiddle off the wall and handed it to Davie.

'What about geein wiz a tune, boy?'

Davie protested that he hadn't played for years – but, after some encouragement from his mother, tuned up. The first few notes were tentative, but he soon had their toes tapping to a selection of reels and polkas.

Jean was proud of the way that Sam had handled things. He was sensitive to Kirsty's anxieties, and he'd steered the evening to a cheerful conclusion. *They'll be fine,* she thought, and she knew by the way Ellie was looking at them that she was thinking the same.

Kirsty and Sam went to see the Reverend Wemyss the following day. Having assured himself that they were fully aware of the sanctity of marriage, he entered their details in his diary.

'Ten thirty then, on the 22nd of December,' he said as he wrote. Then glancing up, 'You're sure you don't want to be married in church?'

'No thank you,' Sam said firmly. 'We want a quiet family wedding.'

'I'd like Beckie ta be my bridesmaid,' Kirsty volunteered, as they walked home, for she's my very best friend. Wha does du want for dy best man?'

'I wish it could a been Robert,' he replied sadly 'but Davie's come ta be like a bridder ta me. A'm goin ta ax him.'

'Oh Sam, dat's just perfect.' She gave a little skip. 'I thought it wid be Jake, since he's dy best friend.' She named the young policeman, who was his sparring partner at the Debating Society, and who had often taken walks with him during his recuperation. She'd seen them on many occasions, lost in earnest conversation, and knew that they were close. 'No at I dunna like Jake, du understands, but it will be special ta hae wir Davie.'

'I thought it wid be fine ta keep it in da family.'

'Perfect!' she repeated.

'Da night, eftir du's done dee writin an dee arithmetic, we'll mak a list o da fock at we'd like ta be dere.' She nodded. 'Noo we'll better hurry or we'll be late for wir dinner.'

He crooked his elbow, offering her his arm. A little self-conscious, she glanced round to see if anyone was looking.

'Du's my fiancée noo, an I want everybody ta ken!'

So she linked her arm through his and, after the first few steps, felt quite at ease. It was almost like a real engagement, she thought, ruefully. If it wasn't for the seed that was swelling in her belly, she would have been the happiest girl in the world.

The guest list was soon compiled in consultation with Jean and Ellie their closest relatives, plus the Leasks, the Carters and Jake.

'A'll write ta Geordie, of coorse, but I dunna suppose it'll do much good.' Ellie sighed. 'He had a pal at used ta read his letters ta him – an write for him noo an again – but it's mair as twa year since I heard fae him. I think his pal must a been killed. Poor Geordie, for aa his brash talk, he was aye ashamed at he couldna read an write.'

'It wid be fine if he could be at his dowter's weddin,' said Jean, though secretly she added, *but only if he's sober an no in fightin mood.* She did a quick calculation. *Dat'll be twinty – mair if da boys get hame.* It was unlikely that Isaac and Osie would get leave, but Henry might. *It'll be a tight squeeze, but we'll manage.*

Over the next two weeks Jean and Ellie threw themselves into the domestic arrangements. It was going to be difficult to provide a proper wedding feast when food was so scarce, *but A'm sure I can depend on da Grindavoe fock ta help oot. If everybody brings what dey can, it'll mak a fine spread.*

Soon Mrs Carter was involved too, offering the use of her fine tableware to augment Jean's best china. She also said she had a store of bottled fruit waiting for a special occasion, and would like to make jellies for them in her fancy moulds.

'They always look so festive,' she said, 'and we'll have no more of this "Mrs Carter" nonsense. We're related by marriage, aren't we? And surely we're friends? You must call me Charlotte.'

Jean knew instinctively that Mrs Carter - Charlotte – needed her friendship, and wanted to confide in her.

'You know, Jean – I can call you Jean? – I miss Catherine so much, and I worry about her all the time. We never know where she is, or what she's doing – only that it's dangerous, and she doesn't care tuppence for her own safety. How she can bear to be apart from Roberta, I'll never understand' She blew her nose and cleared her throat. 'You've lost your lovely son, Jean, and I've lost my lovely daughter. Oh I know she's not dead – but she's lost to me…and to her child. I try to keep cheery for Alexander's sake and for the little one, but it's hard. Folk give me such disapproving looks when I take her out. No-one can forgive a mother who deserts her child.'

Dey shouldna be sae quick ta judge, Jean said to herself. *We aa do things we never thought we could, when wir pushed far enough - especially when it's done for love.* Aloud she sympathised, 'I know. I heard them whispering when our two got married. Didn't think our son was good enough for your daughter.' She glanced at her new friend. 'I dare say you hoped she'd do better for herself too…'

'No,' Charlotte interupted, 'You mustn't think that. We loved Robert. He was a good, honest worker. Alex intended to take him into the business after the war. Said he had a good head on him - but something tells me that Robert would have wanted to make his own way. He was an independent young man, and Catherine would have backed him all the way. We brought her up to have a mind of her own, and Robert was her choice. They were well suited. Both free spirits. So young. So happy. So full of dreams.' She bit her lip as if she might burst into tears.

Hoping she wasn't presuming too much, Jean followed her instinct and put her arms round Charlotte. 'Come now. We have to put the past behind us. There's a wedding to arrange, and we want to make it as happy for them as we can.' After a moment she stood back and Charlotte gave her a grateful smile. Then she went on.

'They're not having an easy start, you know.'

Charlotte raised her eyebrows in a questioning look.

'I might as well tell you, since you're family and I know it won't go any further. Kirsty's going to have a baby…and it's not Sam's. She was raped one night on the way back from her mother's. She doesn't know who it was – only that he was a sailor, and very drunk.'

Charlotte gasped and her hand flew to her mouth. 'Oh my dear…the poor girl. Her mother must be heart-broken, and you and the Captain. I don't know what to say. What a sacrifice for Sam to make! I had no idea. They seemed to be so right for each other.'

'And so they are,' said Jean firmly. 'It's been a shock and a trial for us all, but I'm proud of my Sam for standing by her, and I'm proud of her too for the way she's come through it. Of course it's not how we would have wished it – but they're strong-minded, both of them and they're fond of each other. We're hoping, of course, that everyone will think the baby is Sam's, come before it's time. That way the whole ugly story will never come out, and they'll keep their good names.'

There was only a week to go till the wedding when Jean overheard Kirsty say to her mother that she had nothing "special" to wear.

'Dy Sunday frock is lovely, jewel,' Ellie assured her. 'I wish I could afford ta get dee a right weddin ootfit, but...'

'A'm no complainin, Mammie. You're no ta think dat. It's just at I want ta look my best for Sam.'

Jean gave no indication that she'd heard the little conversation, but she was immediately working out a plan. *A'll ax Charlotte. Dat's what A'll do.* She put on her hat and coat and set off for the Carters.

'A'll no be lang,' she called. 'I hae a peerie message ta do.'

She rang the doorbell and the maid showed her into the morning-room. She was a bit nervous. Maybe she was asking too much of their friendship.

'This is a nice surprise,' said Charlotte, with a welcoming smile. 'You'll have a cup of tea?'

Without waiting for a reply, she pressed the bell and the maid reappeared.

'Will you bring a pot of tea, please, Daisy. And some biscuits.' She waited till the maid had left the room. 'I don't suppose you came to talk about the weather or the price of tea - so out with it. How can I help you?'

'You'll maybe think this is terribly cheeky, Charlotte – but Kirsty has nothing "special" to wear and it struck me that she's the same size as Catherine, and I wondered if…oh dear, I wish I'd never come. I'm sorry Charlotte. It was a mistake. I don't know what you must think of me.' She stood up to go. 'Please forgive me.'

'Sit down, Jean. Please. It's a wonderful idea. I'm ashamed I didn't think of it myself.'

The maid returned with a silver tray. Charlotte poured the tea.

'When we've finished this, I'll go and look out Catherine's wedding things while you go and fetch Kirsty – and Ellie too, if she's not too busy. Now, do have a biscuit.'

Within half an hour the three of them – Jean, Kirsty and Ellie – were on the Carters' doorstep. Charlotte opened the door herself, and her eyes were sparkling.

'This is so exciting,' she said as she led them up the wide staircase, past the tall arched window on the landing, and up to the room that had been Catherine's.

Kirsty's eyes were like saucers. Jean knew she'd never been in such a grand house before, never seen such beautiful furnishings – and, of course, she had no idea why she was there. She stared, wide-eyed, at the flower-sprigged curtains and matching eider-down; at the marble-topped wash-stand with its rose-pink ewer and basin. China. Gold-edged. Not the white enamel she was used to. She looked at the carved wooden bedstead, and its matching dressing-table and wardrobe with beautiful mirrored doors.

'It's a room for a princess,' she whispered.

'Yes,' replied Charlotte, rather wistfully. 'In a way it was, for our princess...' Then she went on more briskly, 'but I'm going to have it done up for Roberta after Christmas. It's time she had a proper nursery.'

She walked over to the bed, where the wedding things were laid out.

'Now, my dear. What do you think of this?' She held up the gown that Catherine had worn on her wedding day almost exactly two years before. It was dove-grey. Pure silk, with a row of tiny buttons from neck to waist. The neckline and cuffs were trimmed with delicate lace.

'Try it on, Kirsty.'

As if in a dream, Kirsty allowed them to pull off her dress and lower the silk gown over her head.

'What do you think?' Charlotte asked her, fastening the last of the tiny buttons and turning her to face the mirror. 'Here! Hold these.' She handed Kirsty a posy of velvet daisies.

'I made these myself, for Catherine was like you – a December bride – and there were no fresh flowers to be had.'

Kirsty gazed at her reflection. She could hardly speak.

'It's da boanniest dress A'm seen in my whole life.'

'A beautiful dress for a beautiful girl. He's a lucky man, isn't he?'

Charlotte turned to Ellie and Jean for confirmation. Neither of them could do anything but nod, for they were so overcome as Kirsty turned to face them, her eyes shining like stars.

'I wanted ta be boannie for Sam. He's been dat good

ta me. Thank you, Mrs Carter, fae da boddam o my hert. I dunna ken what ta say but “Thank you”. You’re made me feel like a real bride.’

‘I canna wait ta see Sam’s face when he sees dee in it.’ Ellie’s voice was husky. *Hoo could he help but love her?*

Chapter Sixteen
Preparations

The tension of the war was temporarily forgotten in the Jacobson house – swept aside by the excitement, which grew and gathered momentum like a snowball rolling down a hill. Everyone got involved in the preparations for the wedding, eager to make the day special for Kirsty – as if, somehow, that could cancel out the pain that had brought it about.

Ellie arrived just after breakfast on the day before the wedding, and helped Jean to give the house a thorough going over. Everything had to look its best. Beckie arrived in the afternoon, bent double under the weight of the kishie which she carried on her back in the country fashion. Red-faced and puffing, she dropped it on the floor with a dull thud, declaring she'd never be able to straighten up again – it was so heavy with the Grindavoe contribution to the feast. The main culprit was a huge roast of pork, for they'd killed a pig in honour of the occasion, but in addition to that there was butter, milk and a sweet bannock - with carraway seeds in it - that Auntie Sarah had made. She said it would not do if Kirsty didn't have a traditional "Bride's Bonn", even if she was a "toon" lass!

Ellie quickly made a cup of tea to revive her, then the two girls – excused from any further tasks – washed each other's hair, and chattered nineteen to the dozen as young girls will, while they dried it in front of the fire, which Sam had lit in the parlour before he went back to work. He said it was to air the room, which hadn't been used since Jamie left, but Jean and Ellie reckoned it was so the men would have a place of refuge, once the women took over the kitchen and started cooking in earnest! Meanwhile, they polished glasses and cutlery and got out the best china, which they washed and stacked in readiness. Then they prepared a huge meal of salt fish, potatoes and extravagant lashings of Grindavoe butter.

Cousin Lollie arrived with his wife, Ina, as Sam and Davie came home from work. Then just when Jean and Ellie were about to serve the meal, Henry burst in stamping his feet, and shaking hailstones off his coat.

'Henry! Oh Henry, du's come!' exclaimed Jean, rushing to take his coat from him.

'You didna think I wid miss wir Sam's weddin, did you?' He enveloped his mother in an affectionate bear hug. Then he pumped his father's hand up and down.

'It's good to be here,' he said, beaming at everyone.

'Come on, noo. Move up an mak room for Henry,' said Jean, and they shuffled along with a scraping of chairs.

Henry gave Sam a friendly punch on the shoulder as he squeezed in beside him.

'Du's a dark horse, I must say! Dee an peerie Kirsty! I never even kent at you wir coortin - but is it no grand ta hae a happy event in da middle o aa dis gloom? I dunna mind tellin you at it'll be a relief ta forget aboot yon U-boat at lies at da back o Bressay for a peerie start. Wir nae sooner gotten a passage cleared as he creeps in again an lays mair o yon haethenish mines. It's a never-endin job.'

'Du's right, boy. We should forget aboot it for noo. Wir real gled at du's made it. It means a lot ta wiz, does'n it, Kirsty?' said Sam, diverting the conversation back to the wedding.

She nodded and smiled, rather shyly, for she was still a bit awkward about meeting people who hadn't seen her since her ordeal.

'Say the grace, Sam, an let wiz eat afore it gets cowld.'

They'd hardly had time to clear the table before the Carters arrived with little Roberta. Daisy and Mrs Peterson, their house-keeper were close behind laden with baskets containing crockery and cutlery, shining copper jelly moulds and who-knows-what besides. Mr Carter was carrying a large box with as much care as he'd have given the Crown Jewels, for it contained the wedding cake, which his wife had made. Everyone crowded round to admire it.

'I'm afraid its not up to my usual standard,' said Charlotte, 'but with sugar in short supply I could only ice the top, and make do with a ribbon round the sides, but it is a proper fruit cake.'

'It's just perfect, Mrs Carter - Charlotte, I mean - I never thought we wid hae a right weddin cake, wi da war on.' She looked more closely. 'It's got wir names on it…' she broke off, not knowing how to respond to such unexpected kindness.

'Yes, my dear – tied with a lovers' knot.'

'You're been dat good ta wiz. I dunna ken what ta say.'

'Say nothing at all, dear. It was my pleasure to make it for such a lovely couple.'

'That's enough of this emotional stuff,' interrupted her husband, clearing his throat. 'Surely you women have things to do?' He turned to the men. 'We should go and fetch the extra chairs from our house.'

'The Leasks are lending some as well,' said Sam.

'Gracious, it's going to take us all night! We'll need all hands to the plough. Are you coming?'

By the time they returned with the second load of chairs Charlotte had made the jellies and put them in the pantry to set overnight, and the kitchen was filled with tantalising cooking smells. Mrs Peterson and Daisy had asked Mrs Carter if they could stay and prepare the vegetables, so everything was ready ahead of schedule.

'Let's have a cup of tea before we clew up for the night,' said Jean.

'We'll make it,' offered Mrs Peterson, 'if that's all right with you, Mrs Jacobson?'

'That sounds like a good idea,' said Charlotte. 'Shall we go and join the others? Mrs Peterson and Daisy will bring it through.'

Somewhat embarrassed, Jean allowed herself to be escorted through to the parlour, and as they squeezed past the stacks of chairs, Charlotte added, 'By the way, Jean, they've asked permission to come and serve the meal for you tomorrow, and do the washing up. They're quite caught up in this wedding, and want to be part of it. I said it was a splendid idea. I hope you don't mind?'

For once Jean didn't know what to say.

'Good,' said Charlotte. 'That's settled. You and Ellie will be able to enjoy the fruits of your labour without having to dance attendance on everyone else. That's as it should be at your children's wedding.'

Jean didn't want to take advantage of the Carters' generosity, nor did she want to exploit their servants, but clearly this was something they wanted to do. It would be churlish not to accept.

'Thank you,' she said simply. 'You're such a good friend, Charlotte. Kind and thoughtful.'

Charlotte rewarded her with a radiant smile. It was as if Jean had given her a gift – and perhaps she had. The gift of friendship. It wasn't only the servants who were caught up in the wedding, Jean thought. Being involved made Charlotte feel as though she were part of the family - and this made her feel closer to her daughter. Jean understood that. So if it made Charlotte feel good, she would allow herself to be waited on at her own table by uniformed servants - something that went against her principles of equality. In this instance, she reflected, perhaps it was more blessed for her to receive Charlotte's bounty graciously, than it was to give. This new friendship, which crossed the boundaries of social class, was fraught with confusion – but what was important was to reach out and be a comfort to one another. When they'd finished their belated "eight o'clocks", Kirsty and Beckie said their goodnights, and set off with the Carters, who had insisted that the girls spend the night at their house. It was bad luck, Charlotte informed them, for the groom to look on the bride on the wedding day until they were standing side by side ready to make their vows. 'We'll take no chances,' she said.

There were many "Oohs" and "Aahs" from Beckie as Mrs Carter showed them into Catherine's room, and many more when Kirsty showed her the dress she was going to wear.

'You could try this one if you like,' said Mrs Carter quickly, taking a deep lilac dress from a carved chest at the foot of the bed and handing it to Beckie – for she had seen the look of resignation on the girl's face when she shook out her own best dress, and draped it over the back of a chair, next to the beautiful silk one.

'Oh, it's lovely,' Beckie gasped, holding it up against her and twirling around. 'Noo A'll be really boannie an aa!' Forgetting herself in her excitement, she gave a surprised and delighted Mrs Carter an impetuous hug.

'Into bed with you,' she said, laughing. 'I'll send Daisy up with some hot milk for you. Now try not to talk all night,' she said with a twinkle in her eyes. 'You have a big day ahead of you tomorrow.'

'Fancy wiz sleepin in a room like dis,' whispered Beckie as Mrs Carter closed the door. She sat on the bed, discovering she could bounce up and down. Patting the bed, she invited Kirsty to join her, and their giggles of delight made Mrs Carter smile as she went downstairs. *Children, she thought. They're little more than children.*

'It's like a palace, is'n it Kirsty? I dunna think da queen's room could be ony boannier.' Beckie flew around the room examining all the furnishings, running her hand over the polished wood. 'Wir a pair o Cinderellas goin ta da ball' She held her dress in front of her and waltzed around the room. 'Come on, Kirsty. Dance!'

So Kirsty entered into the game, and they spun round in dizzy circles until the maid knocked at the door with their hot drinks.

'Come in,' they chorused, sitting demurely on the bed and trying to suppress their laughter.

Daisy set the tray on the night-stand and closed the curtains for them.

'Will you be needing anything else?' she asked.

'No, thank you,' said Kirsty. 'We have everything we need.'

Wide-eyed, they watched her leave the room, then climbed onto the canopied bed.

'It's a different world,' said Beckie, suddenly serious, as they sipped their milk. 'No really for da likes o wiz, is it?'

'No,' replied Kirsty. 'An I canna say A'm sorry. I like it better when everybody's da sam. I mean, my Mammy was dy Mammie's servant, but she never felt...oh, I dunna ken what A'm tryin ta say...'

'As if she wasna as good a person as my Mammy?'

'Yiss, dat's it. Dey wir aye good friends an equals, an though A'm – or I was – dy Mammy's maid, wir like sisters, dee an me.' Kirsty looked at Beckie for confirmation.

'Dat's true – an we'll really be sisters da moarn.' She sighed. 'Dee an Sam! Du's aye been sweet on him, is'n du? An noo du's mairryin him, an du'll hae him here wi dee – no awa at da war, an dee aye wonderin if he'll ever come back. Du's dat lucky, Kirsty. I wish at I was dee.' With that, she burst into tears.

'What's up wi dee, Beckie? What is it? Tell me, du kens du can tell me – whatever it is.'

'Promise du'll no let on, Kirsty, but I...I really like Johnnie Anderson.'

'Johnnie Anderson? Does du mean my cousin, Johnnie Anderson?'

Beckie sniffed, and brightened up.

'Yiss, da very sam! I danced wi him at da Johnsmas Foy. He can fairly dance, nearly birled me aff me feet, an he has siccan sparklin een - full o fun. I could tell at he really liked me. I saa him again when Granny died. He cam wi his boss – dat's Willie Williamson, da undertaker – when dey brought da kist, an dan when dey cam ta help wi da funeral. He's lairnin ta be a carpenter.' Her face clouded over. 'He'll be eighteen soon, an he's goin ta join da Navy. He axed me if I wid write ta him, an he made me promise at I widna dance wi ony idder body while he's awa.' She beamed at Kirsty, 'Mr Williamson is goin ta keep his job open for him for when he comes back. He says he's goin ta do up his grandfaither's hoose at's lyin empty. So we'll hae wir ain peerie hoose when we get mairried.' She started to cry again. 'A'm dat scared at onything happens ta him, an he doesna come back. It's aa at I can think aboot – him an me…' She glanced at Kirsty 'Dat's why I wish I was dee. Mairryin da man at du loves, an havin him safe wi dee – for always. It's romantic, dat's what it is.'

'Oh Beckie, I canna keep it fae dee ony mair. Der nothin romantic aboot dis weddin. It's true I love Sam, but he doesna ken, an he doesna love me – no like dy Johnnie loves dee. I only wish he did.'

'So why…?'

'Why is he mairryin me? Oot o da goodness o his hert.'

'What does du mean? I dunna understand.'

Kirsty drew a deep breath. 'Du minds da reason I cam ta bide at Grindavoe?'

Beckie nodded.

'A'm goin ta hae a bairn, Beckie, an Sam is mairryin me so A'm no on my ain, an so da bairn haes a faither. He doesna want me ta loss my good name. Is he no da best and kindest man in da world?'

'Yea, he is dat. Der no mony like him, but he's aye been fond o dee, Kirsty. Du kens he loves dee.'

Kirsty sighed. 'Yiss, like a bridder - an dat's what wir goin ta be till eftir da bairn is boarn. Bridder an sister. I made him promise dat.'

Beckie stared at her in astonishment. 'Why?' she asked. 'What on earth did du do dat for?'

Kirsty tried to explain the reason why she'd made him agree to her condition – that it was for *his* sake. 'I dunna want him ta regret mairryin me, an come ta resent me an da bairn. I wid rather struggle on on my ain, an leave him free ta fin a wife he can really love as see him miserable, an tied ta me.'

'Du's dat brave.' Beckie looked at her in admiration. 'I wid tak him on ony terms if it was me, just ta keep him near me. It *is* romantic, for if he bides wi dee du'll ken for sure at he loves dee wi his whole hert. It's like in a book…'

'No, it's just playin fair. I dunna want him ever ta feel he's been trapped – by me, or by his conscience. Ta tell da truth, I envy dee. Everything is straightforward. Du loves him an he loves dee, an you'll get mairried an live happily ever eftir. Noo dat's romantic, like a story book – an he will come back ta dee. I ken he will. Noo I think we should say wir prayers an try ta sleep.'

They jumped out of bed and knelt side by side.

'A'll pray at he comes back ta dee, Beckie. Will du pray for me?'

Beckie nodded, and they bowed their heads for a few minutes, then scrambled back to bed. Soon Beckie was asleep, but Kirsty lay in the darkness wondering what Sam was thinking. Was he having misgivings – regretting already that he'd asked her to marry him?

Chapter Seventeen

A Quiet Wedding

The morning dawned windy and cold. To the east, over Bressay, the sun rose surrounded by angry-looking clouds that seemed to boil up – swirling, filling the sky with a fiery glow. *Not a good sign,* thought Jean, glancing at it and shaking her head. But, as everyone had to have an early breakfast and Kirsty wasn't there to help her, she had no time to worry about it and, before long, the wind had died away and the heavens had turned an impossible, innocent cloudless blue. The day was set fair.

Soon Peter arrived with a cheery, 'Hello-o, A'm hame!' and was set to work, helping Lollie to carve the cold meats and arrange them on two platters – one for the Grindavoe pork, and one for boiled mutton. Sam went to fetch Davie and Ellie, and Jean began to lay the table.

'Grace,' she called, 'wid du fetch da 'Bride's Bonn' fae da pantry, an brak it inta peerie bits?'

Seeing her puzzled look, Jean explained that it was an old country tradition. The pieces were thrown over the crowd of people who came to see the bride when she returned home after the wedding, and everyone scrambled to get a bit, which they would put under their pillow that night.

'It's supposed to bring them happy dreams an good luck. We'll ax Mrs Leask ta do it, for she's da aaldest.'

Grace laughed, 'You dunna really believe it brings good luck, do you, Mammie?'

'No, no really – but what harm can it do? It's a bit o fun, an what's wrang wi dat? We can aa do wi a bit o fun, can we no?' *An a bit o good luck widna go amiss either,* she added silently. 'Noo geng an wrap da pieces in a cloth, ready for Mrs Leask.'

Ellie arrived ahead of Sam and Davie, and proceeded to put on her apron.

'Ellie Johnson!' exclaimed Jean in mock horror. 'Tak yon peenie aff. Du's da bride's midder, an dy place is wi her. Away du goes up ta da Carters'. I hae Grace ta help me.'

'And me!' said Cousin Ina, taking the apron from her and putting it on.

'Du sees?' said Jean, pushing a laughing Ellie out the door. 'Noo for da jellies. A'm been dreadin dis. What if dey dunna come oot in wan piece? Bring da kettle, Grace, an poor da water inta da basin. Noo dan, wish me luck.'

They held their breath while she lowered the mould into the steaming water and held it there for a few seconds. Then, taking it out, she placed a plate over it, and deftly inverted it. Anxiously they watched as she removed the mould. Grace clapped her hands as the fancy dessert was revealed in all its glory.

'It's lovely, Mammie. Naebody'll want ta eat it. Dey'll just want ta look at it!'

'Noo, let wiz see if I can do it again.'

She repeated the process with the second one, and carried them through – one red and one green – and set them on the dresser at either side of the wedding cake. Then they stood back to admire the glistening, castle-shaped creations.

'Charlotte was right,' said Jean, delighted. 'Dey do look festive.'

'Dey certainly do,' agreed Sam as he wheeled Davie in. 'It's a grand feast. You're done wiz prood. Thanks Mammie.' He gave her a hug, and added softly, 'You ken hoo much it means ta me. I really want Kirsty ta feel it's a special day.'

'You deserve it, son – baith o you.' She went on more seriously, 'She's a fine young woman, Sam, an I believe you were meant ta be tagidder. God works in mysterious wyes sometimes. Noo, awa an get deesel smartened up. It's nearly time for dee ta geng ta da manse.'

Meanwhile, in the Carter villa, Kirsty and Beckie were being pampered. Their breakfast was brought to them on a tray. Then Daisy ran a bath for Kirsty – a deep, hot bath with rose-scented salts in it, and gave her a huge soft towel to dry herself with afterwards. She'd never experienced such luxury – never had a proper bath in a proper bathroom before. Beckie had washed and dressed while Kirsty bathed. Now she took charge of her friend. She laced her into her corset and eased the borrowed wedding dress carefully over her head. With trembling fingers Kirsty began to do up the row of pearl buttons.

'Here, let me do that,' said Beckie. 'Stand still.'

When that was done she ordered the bride to sit at the dressing table. Obediently Kirsty did as she was told, while Beckie brushed her hair till it was gleaming, then pinned it up for her. *Can that really be me?* Kirsty wondered, as she watched her image change from an apprehensive girl to a poised and confident young woman.

'Thanks Beckie, I…' but before she could say more, there was a knock at the door.

'Your mother is here, Kirsty,' called Mrs Carter. 'May we come in?'

Beckie ran and opened the door.

'Are you ever seen onybody sae boannie?' she asked, standing back so they could see the bride.

'No,' said Ellie, trying to swallow the lump in her throat. 'Never – an dat's da truth.'

'You look beautiful, truly beautiful.' Mrs Carter echoed her sentiments. 'Here, I want you to have these.' She produced a pair of mother-of-pearl combs. 'They were my mother's. I wore them on special occasions when I was young, but they're lost in my white hair now. They need someone young and dark-haired to show them off.'

'I canna tak dem, Mrs Carter. No somethin as special as yon…'

'Nonsense, my dear. I want you to have them,' She slid them into Kirsty's shining dark hair. 'They're just the right finishing touch. Besides you must have something old – you know the rhyme? Something old…'

Kirsty and Beckie nodded and completed the saying, chanting it together,

'Something new, something borrowed and something blue.'

'Well then,' said Mrs Carter, 'these are your "something old". Have you got something new?'

'I hae my ring.' Kirsty looked at it with misty eyes. 'What could be better as dis?'

'Perfect,' said Ellie, 'an da dress is borrowed. So aa du needs is…'

'Dis!' Beckie handed her a handkerchief with tiny blue hearts embroidered round the edges. 'I made it for dee. So du's ready noo.'

'Yiss,' Kirsty echoed. 'A'm ready noo.' She picked up the posy of daisies.

Ellie took her daughter in her arms and held her as if she'd never let her go.

'Du's a grown woman noo,' she whispered, 'no my peerie lass ony mair. I pray at life will treat dee kindly fae dis day on.'

'Come, Ellie,' said Mrs Carter gently. 'Time we were off.'

The two women, each wrapped in her own thoughts, hurried to the Jacobsons', with Mrs Peterson, Daisy and Roberta hot on their heels.

Mr Carter brought the car to the door.

'In you get, ladies.' He held the door open for Kirsty, then went to the other side and did the same for Beckie.

The girls held hands as he drove them the short distance to the manse. Then he helped them down as if they truly were gentle-folk, and escorted them – one on each arm – down the path. He rang the bell and, when the maid appeared to show them in, he kissed Kirsty on the cheek. With that he doffed his hat and turned away.

Kirsty was suddenly overwhelmed by the enormity of what she was about to do.

'Oh Beckie, does du think I should go through wi it? It's a terrible thing A'm doin ta Sam.' But before she had time to reply, Mr Wemyss came to greet them. The door to his study was open and they could see Sam, tall and straight, standing beside Davie's wheeled chair. As she approached he turned, and the look in his eyes was full of tender longing.

'He loves dee,' whispered Beckie. 'Did du no see da wye at he looked at dee? He loves dee. Truly he does.'

Could it be possible? Taking her place by his side, Kirsty breathed a silent prayer. *Please, Lord, let it be so.*

When they came out, Mr Carter helped Beckie push Davie's chair up the path, while Sam led the way with Kirsty on his arm.

'You drive the ladies, Sam, and I'll take Davie. Oh, I almost forgot...' Mr Carter smiled broadly, 'May I be the first to congratulate you, Mr and Mrs Jacobson.'

He kissed Kirsty and shook Sam's hand.

Mrs Jacobson! I am Mrs Jacobson, thought Kirsty as she climbed into the car. *For better or worse, for richer for poorer, in sickness and in health...*

The car bucked violently as Sam tried to move off, making the girls laugh.

'Sorry,' he said. 'A'm oot o practice – havena done dis since I was in Edinburgh.' The car moved forward in a series of jerks, then more smoothly. 'Dere,' he said. 'A'm getting da hang o it noo.'

There was a loud bang and the engine stalled. Eventually, after several attempts to start the car, Sam got out and used the starting handle. Mr Carter and Davie caught up with them.

'We'll be dere afore you,' shouted Davie, wiping tears of laughter with the back of his hand.

This time the car ran smoothly and they arrived in style. Everyone had gathered at the top of the lane to greet them. Mr Carter lifted the bonnet of the car and put a rug over the engine.

'That should help her to start quickly when we need her again.'

Mrs Leask threw the morsels of "Bride's Bonn" over the crowd and everyone tried to get one – laughing and pushing each other in mock fights. Then Peter led them to the house playing a lively march on his fiddle, and they all milled round waiting their chance to congratulate the bride and groom.

Mr Leask set up his camera in the front room and, disappearing under a thick brown cloth, prepared to take pictures of the wedding party. After he'd finished, he handed Sam an envelope.

'This is our gift, lad. Open it later...you might need time to think about it.' Sam thanked him, somewhat puzzled. It seemed very mysterious, but he had no time to consider it further as Daisy came in and announced that the meal was ready.

It was a great success and when everyone had eaten his fill, there were the usual toasts. Finally, Peter stood up and welcomed Kirsty into the family. Everyone clapped, and nodded in agreement. Then he went on... 'We hae a surprise for you. Geng an change inta warm claes. You'll fin a bag packed for each o you in your rooms.'

They looked at him, and at each other, in astonishment.

'You're goin ta Grindavoe for your honeymoon. You'll hae da place ta yoursels, for Jessie an Sarah are bidin here. Just be back for your Christmas dinner.'

'Honeymoon?' gasped Sam, 'but hoo will we get dere? An...'

'It's all arranged,' said Mr Carter, laughing at their confusion. 'You're going to take my car. It's a good job you've had some practice.'

Amid much hilarity, Davie told the company about the problems Sam had had in the morning.

'What aboot petrol?' asked Sam, well aware that it was in short supply.

'The tank is full. Think of it as a wedding gift.'

Auntie Jessie gave the rest of the instructions. They were to leave the car at the junction and transfer to the horse and cart. 'We left it dere at Charlie an Lizzie's. Da horse is in der stable,' she said. 'Everything's arranged.'

'An we got in da water an plenty o peats, an dere's a pot o soup in da scullery. Da fire should still be lyin in, so da hoose will soon warm up.' Auntie Sarah was clearly thrilled to have been part of the conspiracy.

Jean smiled. 'Away you go an get ready. You want ta get dere afore it's black dark.'

Can dis really be happenin? Kirsty wondered. She glanced at Sam as he drove – smoothly and competently this time. Was there nothing he couldn't do? And he was so handsome – like a hero in a book. Her own Mr Darcy...but much kinder. No darkness in him. She loved to study him when he wasn't looking, loved his clean-cut profile, as he concentrated on the road ahead. She marvelled at his skill as he changed gear – co-ordinating the operation of the steering wheel with one hand, the gear-stick with the other, and the pedals with his feet – double de-clutching with ease, and all the while naming the landmarks for her. He knew all the little townships, every loch, burn and hill. She settled back into the leather seat with a soft sigh. She wasn't afraid of the future any more. How could she be, with Sam beside her? He was a man, not a boy. A man with a good and gentle heart.

She remembered the way he had looked at her when

she arrived at the manse. Was it possible that he loved her? For the space of a heartbeat she had believed so, but she knew she shouldn't read too much into it. Maybe he'd been bewitched by the fine silk dress and the beautiful combs in her hair. She glanced sideways at him again, and caught him looking at her with undisguised tenderness. Her heart fluttered and she felt her cheeks burn. She could still feel the touch of his lips on hers when she had accepted his ring. The kiss that had sealed their bargain. She wished that she hadn't made him agree to it, for she wanted to throw herself into his arms - now this minute – to hear him say he loved her, to tell him she felt the same - and had done for as long as she could remember - but she realised that if he knew, it would only make her seem more vulnerable to him. It would be another tooth in the trap, which his sense of right and duty had fastened around him. No! Loving words would have no meaning if he said them out of pity. She had done the right thing in making him agree to her conditions. He owed her nothing, and for that reason she owed him the promise of freedom. This was the reality that she must not allow herself to forget. And for a moment the dark cloud that was Jamie weighed down upon her. She began to feel a growing resentment towards the child, which had drawn them together - and might yet push them apart. Instinctively she laid her hand on her stomach – she must not blame the bairn. It was entirely innocent – a person in its own right. A flicker of love took her by surprise, almost made her laugh – it was so unexpected. *I love dee, peerie baby,* she told it. *I wondered if I wid care...*

'Did you say somethin?' asked Sam.

'I just axed if we were nearly dere.'

'Yea, it's no far noo.'

A few minutes later they arrived at the junction of road and rough track. Daylight was fading into a glorious sunset. Sam fetched the horse, hitched it up, put their bags in the cart and helped Kirsty to sit up beside him, spreading a warm blanket over her knees.

'Du haes ta wrap da car up too, Sam. Mind what Mr Carter said? It'll no start if du doesna keep it warm.'

'Mercy me!' he exclaimed. 'I clean forgot. It's a good job I hae dee ta keep me right. Wir goin ta mak a good team, dee an me.'

He jumped down and attended to the car while the horse moved restlessly, eager to be off. Soon they were on their way again, the horse plodding steadily along the familiar path. Before long they could see the black outline of the "but and ben" silhouetted against the red, gold and purple sky. To their right the sea lay gleamimg, streaked with colour borrowed from the setting sun. Their breath was forming little clouds in the now-frosty air, and there was a timeless, dreamlike quality to the afternoon. Kirsty wished it could last for ever.

'Whoa,' said Sam, pulling the horse to a standstill and jumping down. 'Here we are – Grindavoe. What does du think?'

'It's like a painted picter,' she replied.

'An so is du,' said Sam, smiling as he lifted her down. 'Kirsty…' He kept his hands on her waist and his expression grew serious. 'I want dee ta ken at, whatever da Lord haes in store for wiz, A'm never been happier as I am right noo…an A'm prood ta hae dee for my wife.'

Her heart almost burst with joy, but she made no response. She dared not look at him for she knew she would not be able to hide her feelings. Everything she felt would show in her eyes, and he must not know. Not yet. Maybe never.

'In du goes,' he said, opening the door. 'Mak deesel at home. A'll see ta da animals.'

She stepped into the porch, which served as a scullery, and looked around. There was a bucket of clean water on the shelf. She lifted the corner of a crisp white cloth and found a plate of bannocks. Under another was a dish of fresh butter beside a plate of smoked mutton. The aunts had left everything in readiness for them. She took off her coat and hat and hung them on the back of the door. The unmistakeable smell of peat met her as she went into the living room – she'd smelt it in the air outside, but it was stronger here. Homely and reassuring. Shivering, she bent over the fire, and moved the peats gently with the tongs, letting the air in. They responded immediately with a burst of flame. Sitting on a little wooden stool, she held out her hands to it for a few minutes, then rubbed them together to restore the circulation for her fingers were numb with cold. She knew she would not be able to manipulate a match or taper to light the lamps till the feeling came back, so she sat a little longer, warming herself. Glancing around in the half-light, she felt as if she'd been transported back to another time. No gas mantles here, no stove to cook on – only oil lamps and the open fire, with a chain and crook hanging down from inside the chimney. She'd never seen such an arrangement before, but she'd heard all about it from her mother. So she knew to hook the kettle on to the chain, just above the flames so it would boil quickly.

By the time Sam came in, stamping his feet and blowing on his fingers, the lamps were lit, the supper laid out on the table and the kettle singing. Conversation was stilted as they waited for it to boil, for they were feeling a bit awkward. Somehow the easy "brother and sister" relationship was no longer possible, for Kirsty's pact had made them aware of something which had, till now, been spontaneous – a thing they'd taken for granted. Now there was a barrier of self-consciousness between them.

Once they had commented on everyone's kindness to them, they fell silent. Sam said grace, and they ate their simple meal. When it was cleared away they sat by the fire again.

'I was wonderin...' Kirsty began, staring into the flames,

'Go on,' Sam prompted gently. 'What was du wonderin?'

'It doesna maitter,' she said.

'Yiss, it does. What was it? We shouldna hae secrets noo wir man an wife.'

'Weel...I was wonderin if A'll hae ta stop my lessons, for I canna be a nurse noo A'm a mairried wife. So dere wid be nae point tae it.'

'Bein mairried is nae reason ta stop lairnin, Kirsty. God gied dee a good brain, an A'm sure at he wants dee ta use it. Besides, every wan o dy "teachers" enjoyed da lessons, so I think du can tak it at dey'll carry on wi dem as lang as du wants dem tae.'

'A'm thankful for dat.' She smiled at him. 'My lessons are like meat an drink ta me.'

'Yea, da thirst for lairnin is somethin at's never satisfied. Da mair we lairn, da mair we realise hoo little we ken aboot da world. If everybody wid pit dir energy inta lairnin aboot it instead o destroyin it...'

'Everybody's no meanin ta destroy it, Sam. Der plenty o good folk aboot.'

'Du's fairly right. Of coorse du is. A'm sorry, Kirsty, but I just get carried awa sometimes. I hate dis war an what it does ta folk. Of coorse dere's good, kind folk aboot – which minds me, I better open Mr Leask's envelope. I was forgotten aboot it, wi aa da excitement.'

Kirsty watched as he slit it open with his pocket knife. She saw his eyes widen and his cheeks redden as he read it.

'What is it? Is somethin wrang?'

'Nothin's wrang, joy. Just da opposite. Read it for deesel.'

He handed her the letter. She read it slowly, mouthing the words.

Dear Sam,

I do not find it easy to say these things, but you have become like a son to me and Mrs Leask. We have watched with admiration and respect the way you have coped with your illness, and how you have tackled your work with me, showing yourself to be a hard-working young man with intelligence and integrity. You have all the qualities I would look for in a partner, and indeed in a son.

By the time you read this you will be a married man with responsibilities, and will have to think seriously about your future. With this in mind, I have a proposal to put to you. When you have finished your apprenticeship, I would like to make you my partner and my heir. I am getting old now and will soon be considering retirement. I want to leave the business in good hands, and can think of none better than yours. I have discussed the matter fully with Mrs Leask and she is in complete agreement. What I am saying, my boy, is that one day the business will be yours, and our house. That is, if you want it. We shall discuss this in the New Year and, if you accept, have the legal documents drawn up. Think about it, and talk it over with your wife.

Mrs Leask joins me in wishing you every happiness in your married life.

Yrs sincerely,
Andrew A Leask

'Weel,' she said, handing the letter back to him. 'Weel, I dunna ken what ta say.'

'Neither do I,' said Sam, overwhelmed by Mr Leask's generosity – and by his praise. 'I never dreamed onything like dis could ever happen ta me. Ta wiz. We surely do hae a guardian angel... I canna tak it in! Does du see what dis means? A'll be able ta look eftir dee an da bairn da wye at I should...an some day – no ower soon I hoop, for we want dem ta live tae a ripe aald age – but some day yon lovely hoose will be wirs.'

'We'll be fine aside dy folk,' Kirsty murmured, quite unable to picture herself as mistress of such a fine house.

'I ken dat, joy, for eenoo...but we'll need a bigger place when we hae bairns o wir ain.'

'Bairns o wir ain!' Kirsty could not allow herself to imagine that. 'Du's movin ower fast, Sam. Du's forgettin wir bargain. Du canna let deesel think o a future for wiz till we ken at we hae ean – eftir da bairn comes. Du's movin ower fast.'

'I suppose I am,' he agreed reluctantly. He tapped his pipe against the palm of his hand and threw the dottle in the fire.

They watched the sparks fly up the chimney. 'Come an see if da Merry Dancers are oot. Dis is da right kind o night – still an frosty.'

She put on Auntie Jessie's shawl, which was draped over the back of the chair, and went to stand beside him on the doorstep. The stars were diamond-bright. Blinking. Looking down on them. Wishing them well, Kirsty thought. Suddenly the Merry Dancers began to sweep across the heavens. In his excitement, Sam reached out to put his arm around her shoulders. A week or so ago this would have been completely natural, but now it seemed in breach of their agreement. So he let his hand fall to his side.

'Aurora Borealis,' he said. 'Dat's der right name.'

'Aurora Borealis,' she repeated, trying it out. 'It soonds fine, but I like "Merry Dancers" best.'

She gave no sign that she had noticed his impulse, and his holding back. It twisted her heart, but the pain was sweet and gave her hope. It was going to be a long seven months. Then the child conceived in cruelty would decide whether her future would be joy or heartbreak.

'Du's gettin cowld,' Sam said, for he had seen her involuntary shiver. 'Go inta da hoose. A'll bide here an hae a smoke while du gets ready for bed. Du can tak aff dee claes afore da fire.'

She knew he was trying to make things easy for her.

'A'll be in in twartree minutes,' he added. 'Du can sleep "but" in Granny's bed, an A'll geng "ben" in Auntie Jessie's ean.'

'No Sam. It's freezin "ben". Bide wi me an get da good o da fire.'

She knew she could trust him to honour their pact. They would spend this night – and many more – side by side, without touching.

Chapter Eighteen
The Darkest Hour

During the night Sam wakened to find Kirsty doubled up in pain.

'What is it, joy? What ails dee?'

'A'm bleedin, Sam. It's da bairn.' She started to cry quietly. 'I dunna ken what ta do. I dunna want ta loss it.'

'Lie still. Don't move. A'll geng an get Maggie o Hamar,' said Sam, jumping out of bed, 'She'll ken what ta do.' He lit the lamp and pulled on his trousers. 'Try ta keep calm,' he told her, though he felt far from calm himself. He reesled the fire into life and hooked on the kettle. All he knew about situations like this was that hot water was needed.

'Hurry, Sam,' she whispered, drawing up her knees to ride out another painful spasm.

'A'll be as quick as I can,' he assured her, putting on as many layers of clothing as he could fit beneath his heavy winter coat. He leaned in over the bed to kiss her forehead. In the lamplight he could see the terror in her face.

She gripped his hand. 'Hurry back,' she said.

'Chin up, lass. Du'll be fine.' He mustered a smile, and tried to sound confident.

He lit the hurricane lamp that hung behind the porch door, then went out into the night. He glanced at the sky. Banks of clouds, heavy with snow, were building up – at times obscuring the moon. How was he going to find his way? He led the horse out of the stable and hitched it to the cart. He'd noticed a second lamp in the byre. Rushing into the byre, he grabbed it - and a length of rope. That was it! He'd fix the two of them to the cart, one at each side like the carriage lamps they used in the town. His fingers were all thumbs as he struggled to fix the lamps in place, but at last the job was done.

'Come on, Lightning,' he exhorted the horse. 'Try ta live up ta dee name for wance.' But Lightning knew only one speed, and had no sense of urgency. He was wasting his breath. He tried to calm himself, but his heart was pounding with fear. Over and over he prayed, *Dunna let onything come at my peerie Kirsty. Keep her safe, Lord. Please keep her safe. I love her mair as I ever thought a man could love a wife...*

The wind was picking up as he rounded the head of the voe, a biting wind that cut through all his layers of clothing and chilled him to the bone. For a moment he contemplated abandoning the cart and taking the motor, but he knew there was over a mile of rough track from the end of the road to Maggie's place. He'd have to stick with Lightning. Oblivious to the seriousness of the situation, the horse plodded on. Head down and imperturbable. At times the lamps flickered and Sam feared they might go out, leaving him in darkness. There was little moonlight now.

At last he reached Hamar. He tried to untie one of the lamps to light his way to the door, but it was impossible – his fingers were so numb. He fumbled for his knife, and was about to try to cut the rope, when there was a break in the clouds, and the moon obligingly bathed the path in silvery light. Gratefully he stumbled to the door and battered on it with both fists.

'Maggie!' he shouted at the top of his voice. 'Open da door.' He was close to tears. 'For da love o God, woman. Open da door. Maggie, come on. My Kirsty needs dee.'

His words were carried away in the wind, but he continued to shout and bang on the door. When it opened, he fell across the threshold practically knocking the surprised and sleepy woman over, and sending the candle flying out of her hand.

'Thank Goodness,' he gasped, gripping her by the shoulders. 'Come wi me ta Grindavoe, Maggie. My Kirsty needs dee. She'd bleedin. She says she's lossin da bairn.' Distraught, he tried to pull the astonished woman out in her nightdress.

'Steady on, noo,' she said freeing herself, and bending down to retrieve the candle, which – miraculously – was still alight. Holding it up, she cast her eye over him. *Gracie-Anne's grandson – da quiet ean.* What was he doing here in the heart of winter? *Oh weel, A'll fin dat oot soon enough.* He was here now, shivering...and his eyes were full of fear.

She nodded, 'A'll come. Warm deesel at da fire while I get ready. Mak a cup o tay – da kettle's still hot. I had a cup afore I geed ta bed.' She headed for the other room, talking as she went. 'Da wife at Southerhoose had her bairn da night. Took her time aboot it too.'

Sam wished she would stop prattling.

'Der nae time for cups o tay, Maggie. Kirsty needs dee noo.' He was pacing up and down.

She turned to face him. 'Du'll do what I say, boy,' she said sternly, 'or A'll no come. So du'll tak a cup o tay whether du wants it or no – an wi somethin in it too – or du'll be nae use ta onybody.'

Sam sat down wearily. 'Du's right, Maggie. A cup o tay wid be fine.' He could see the sense in it, but was anxious about further delay.

The journey back was a nightmare. The wind was in their backs when they set out, and the lamps burned steadily, lighting their way – but the snow had started to fall by the time they reached the head of the voe, and was a full blizzard as they made their way along the other side, on the home stretch. They could no longer keep their eyes open – not that it mattered, because the lamps were thickly covered with snow – and they had to pull their scarves up over their noses and mouths in order to breathe. All they could do was put their trust in Lightning, who plodded on unperturbed, never missing a step, and who seemed to know the way.

At last they were there.

'Dis is women's business, boy. Go an see ta da horse – an keep oot o da wye for a peerie while.'

Maggie stumbled through the snow and went indoors. She threw off her coat and kilted up her sleeves.

'So du's Kirsty?' she asked, opening the doors of the box-bed wide, and peering into the shadows. 'Ellie Johnson's lass?'

Kirsty nodded wanly. 'We got mairried yesterday, Sam an me.'

'Let me tak a look at dee.'

She held up the lamp. One look was all she needed. It was over. Everything had come away. The lass had lost a lot of blood and an eight-week foetus. All she could do was clean her up and help her get over the shock. She was very pale. Little more than a bairn herself. Who would have thought that a fine young man like Sam Jacobson would have got her in the family way before there was a ring on her finger?

'Du's lucky…'

'Lucky? Hoo can du say dat?'

'Well, naebody need ever ken, for du widna be shaa-in yet – an dey'll no hear it fae me. It's no my place ta judge fock.'

'Du doesna understand, Maggie. Naebody does.' Kirsty's voice was full of despair, and the ghost of Jamie was back.

'I ken, lass. I ken. Du's feelin weak an sore, an mournin for da bairn at never was. But du's young an strong. Tak my word for it, it'll no be lang till der anidder ean on da wye.'

Kirsty sighed. 'If only du kent, Maggie. It's no as easy as dat.'

'Believe me, du'll feel different in twartree days, when du gets up dy strength. Noo, come an we'll get dee ower ta da fire while I change da bed. Dere'll be plenty o clean sheets ben in da kist, an A'll fin dee a clean goonie.'

She helped Kirsty over to the rocking chair and bustled away to find the linen.

'Here we are, dan. Hands up!'

'Dat's what my Mammie used ta say when I was a bairn,' Kirsty protested half laughing. But she held her hands up and let Maggie take off the soiled garment and put on the clean one. Next Maggie attended to the bed.

'In you get,' she said, plumping up the pillows, 'and see if du can manage a peerie smile for yon man o dine. He deserves it eftir aa he's been through da night. A'm goin ta heat up some milk for wiz aa, for wir used up nearly aa da water – der just enough in da kettle for a cup o tay in da mornin.'

Maggie was in the porch when Sam came in. She eyed him sharply. He was shivering uncontrollably and on the point of collapse. Even his lips were white.

'Tak a sup o dis,' she said, producing a bottle from her carpet bag. 'Medicinal purposes. Da Lord'll no had it against dee.'

He took a gulp, and then another – grateful for the burning of it as it went down his throat, and the warmth that spread within him.

'Hoo's Kirsty? Is she…?'

'She's fine, Sam. Nothin at rest an kindness canna cure.'

'Thank God,' he murmured. 'I dunna ken what I wid do if onything happened ta her. Da bairn? What aboot da bairn?'

Maggie shook her head. Sam went over to comfort Kirsty, but she was fast asleep. He stroked her hair gently.

'Come an drink dis.' Maggie handed him a cup of hot milk. 'Sleep is what she needs. Da moarn du'll hae ta let her rest. She'll likely no hae muckle ta say, an der'll be tears. Be patient wi her. It's no an easy thing for a wife, lossin a bairn.' She stared into the fire. Then she stood up briskly. 'I pat a hot ston in my bed, an it should be fine an warm. So A'll bid dee goodnight.'

She stopped at the door. 'A'm been thinkin…what I usually do when I hae ta bide da night at dis side o da voe, is spread a blanket on da green in da mornin as a signal. Dan some-ean comes ower wi a boat ta fetch me.' She gave him a sharp look. 'Dis time I think it wid be better if du rowed me ower at first light – if da gale is blawn itsel oot. Dat wye naebody need ever ken aboot dis night's on-goins.'

'Thanks, Maggie. Du haes a good hert.' Sam wondered how he'd ever thought of her as cold and unfeeling.

It was still dark when he woke. Maggie was warming herself by the fire. He climbed out of bed carefully, so as not to wake Kirsty.

'Da wind is faan awa, an da sea is flat calm. We should mak a move afore da Hamar fock are up an doin.'

He dressed quickly and shrugged into his still-wet coat. They waded through the deep drifts of snow down to the "noost" where the boat was drawn up. Taking a side each, they pulled it to the sea's edge, climbed in and brushed the snow off the seats. It took little more than fifteen minutes to cross the voe, the oars dipping steadily into the glassy water.

'Thanks, Maggie,' he said as she climbed out onto the rocky promontory. 'A'll never forget dis.'

'Wheest wi dee, boy. What are we here for if it's no ta help ean anidder? Hame wi dee noo, an see at du gies Kirsty a good brakkfast.' She clambered over the slippery rocks. 'Mind an tak ta deesel an aa,' she called, turning back to give him a wave.

He pushed the boat off and, sculling with one oar, turned it round. For a minute or two he watched Maggie's shadowy figure move like a ghost through the snow-covered hillocks, and disappear from sight. The salt of the earth, she was – and he hadn't known it till now.

Kirsty stirred when he came in, but didn't wake. He busied himself fetching water, feeding the animals, milking the cow. Then he boiled eggs for their breakfast.

'Here,' he said, shaking her gently. 'Maggie says du haes ta keep up dee strength.'

She smiled half-heartedly and ate her food. Then she turned her face to the wall and appeared to fall asleep again.

At mid-day he heated some of Auntie Sarah's soup, and when Kirsty sat up to take it, he saw that her face was swollen and tearstained.

'A'm sorry, I…'

'It's aa right. Maggie warned me du wid be a bit 'greety' for twartree days. I understand.'

'No, Sam. It's no what du thinks.'

'What does du mean?'

'It's no lossin da bairn…weel it is, an it's no.'

Sam laughed. 'Du's no makkin a lot a sense, joy. Come on. Tell me straight. Hoo can I help, if I dunna ken what's troublin dee?'

She took a deep breath. 'Does du no see? Der nae baby noo.' She turned her head so he wouldn't see her distress, and said softly, almost as though speaking to herself, 'Da baby's geen, so der nae reason for dee ta bide wi me.'

She turned back and looked at him with that determined lift of her chin that had always touched his heart. 'Du mairried me so I widna hae da shame o a faitherless bairn…but der nae baby noo,' she repeated, 'so A'll no had dee tae it. Dat was wir bargain.' Her voice was firm.

'Oh Kirsty, my Kirsty. Surely du kens at I love dee? I could never leave dee. Never. Du's everything ta me. If du only kent da faer at gripped my hert dastreen, when I thought…' His feelings welled up, and he was unable to finish his sentence. He climbed into the bed and took her in his arms. 'It's true I didna love dee like dis da first time at I axed dee ta mairry me, but I was faan for dee hook, line an sinker by da time I axed dee again.'

There was a look of incredulous disbelief on her face. She

wanted to believe him. How she wanted to believe him – but could it be true?

'A'm loved dee aa my life, Sam – an I never thought at du could love me. Is it true? Does du really mean it?'

'I really mean it,' he said, laughing. Then suddenly serious, he looked into her eyes. 'I love dee, Kirsty, an I always will.' He kissed her, gently at first – then more urgently.

'Oh Sam,' she said breathlessly. 'I never kent a body could be sae happy. Say da words, Sam. Please.'

'What words? A'm telt dee I love dee…'

'No, Sam. Say da weddin words – "I, Samuel Jacobson take thee, Kirsty Johnson" – for when we said dem afore I didna ken at du really meant dem.'

Solemnly they repeated their vows, then fell asleep in each other's arms. Exhaustion – both mental and physical – had taken its toll and Nature was giving them healing time. They didn't wake till almost noon on Monday.

Rain had fallen in the night, and continued relentlessly all day bringing a dramatic thaw. Sam rose, built up a blazing fire, and heated some more of Auntie Sarah's soup, which they took in bed. Soon it was dark. They lay watching the flickering blue and gold of the flames licking up the chimney, their light casting dancing patterns on walls and ceiling. They both knew that Kirsty's body needed time to heal before they could be fully man and wife. So they gave themselves up to the delicious, tantalising torment of anticipation – touching, caressing, exploring and holding each other close. They couldn't stop smiling, and every time their eyes met they mouthed, "I love dee."

Kirsty woke first on Christmas Day. The room was chilly, for the fire had gone out. Sleep had caught them unawares the previous night, before Sam had got round to doing the bedtime chores. She smiled, remembering, as she lit the fire. When it was hot enough, she baked some bannocks on the grid-iron while the kettle boiled.

'Happy Christmas,' she said as she handed him his breakfast. 'I didna hae da hert ta waken dee earlier, but we'll hae ta laeve soon if wir goin ta be in time for da Christmas dinner.'

'Happy Christmas, hjarta,' he said, using the traditional endearment, and pulled her down to him for a kiss.

'Careful, or du'll spill da tay,' she laughed. 'Noo, eat up an get up – du haes da beasts ta see tae, an I hae da washin ta do. I want ta leave everything boannie an clean for dem comin back – dey're been dat good ta wiz.'

'I see I mairried a bossy wife,' he said in mock seriousness, but he did as he was told.

By the time he'd done his chores and got the horse and cart ready, Kirsty had hung the sheets on the line, banked the fire and had their bags packed.

He lifted her up onto the seat at the front of the cart, then got up beside her. A flick of the reins and they were off. Both were silent. For a few precious days their world had been bounded by the walls of the little croft house. Nothing had existed but the two of them. There they'd gone through Hell, and then it had become their private Heaven - which they were reluctant to leave.

'A'm sad aboot da baby, Sam. It was pairt o me…an, in spite o everything, I ken I wid a loved it,' she paused and glanced at him, 'an A'm grateful ta it, for withoot it I widna hae dee.'

He took the reins in one hand and put the other round her shoulders, drawing her close.

'Well, maybe no sae soon, hjarta – but some day sooner or later I wid a come ta my senses, an seen at du was da only lass in da world for me.'

Soon they were at the junction. He stabled the horse and she got in the car which, amazingly, wheezed into life at the first turn of the starting handle. The homeward journey passed more quickly than the outward one had done, for they had so much to talk about. Now they could share their dreams about the future – Sam's promotion to partner, the prospect of owning the business…and the house one day, and filling it with children!

'Wir dat lucky, Sam,' Kirsty said, full of wonder, as he stopped the car at the top of the lane.

'Yea,' he agreed, 'Dat's true.' And his heart swelled with admiration for the young girl who was his wife, and who had the strength of spirit to put her hurt behind her, and face the future without a trace of bitterness. She had such faith in him that he vowed he'd never let her down.

'Come, Mrs Jacobson,' he said, offering her his arm.

Everyone greeted them with hugs and kisses and cries of "Happy Christmas."

'Dere's anidder surprise for you,' said Grace, unable to contain her excitement. 'Come an see what da boys – an Mr an Mrs Carter - are done for you.'

She skipped along the passage to the parlour. 'See!' She flung the door open and stood back

'Oh my!' said Kirsty, overcome with emotion.

'Oh my!' echoed Sam, equally moved, for the room had been redecorated. It was a bedroom again, furnished with the suite that had once been Catherine's – the beautiful canopied bed, the marble-topped wash-stand complete with the pink ewer and basin…even the rose-sprigged curtains and eiderdown.

'It's too much! You're…' he broke off, unable to find the words.

'Dinnertime,' called a beaming Jean, saving him from stuttering. 'We hae ta get on. Lizzie an Charlie are comin for Sarah an Jessie at two o'clock'.

'Only Sarah an Jessie? Does dat mean at Beckie's bidin here?' asked Kirsty eagerly.

'Dat she is,' replied Auntie Jessie. 'We can manage fine at Grindavoe noo.'

'An,' added Jean, 'she can get her ain bed back, noo at du's no needin it.'

Kirsty blushed, and smiled shyly at Sam. She hadn't got accustomed to being accepted as his wife.

'An anidder thing – du canna caa me "Auntie Jean" ony mair, an du certainly canna caa me "Mrs Jacobson".'

'An du canna caa her "Mammie", for dat's me,' interrupted Ellie, laughing.

After a moment's thought, Kirsty announced, 'A'll caa you "Mammie Jea".'

'So you'll hae ta be "Daddie Peter", no "da Captain" ony mair,' said Sam, smiling at his father.

'Right,' said Peter. 'Noo dat's settled A'll say grace.'

Later, as she was helping to clear away the meal, Kirsty told her mother and Jean about the miscarriage.

'It's funny, but I hae siccan mixed-up feelins aboot it. A'm glad in wan wye, for it pat an end ta da bad times, but A'm sad as weel. Da bairn was done nothin wrang an it didna deserve ta die. A'm grateful tae it – even ta Jamie ...'

'Grateful!? Hoo can du say dat?' Ellie's expression was one of astonishment mixed with horror.

'Weel Mammie, if it wasna for Jamie an his bairn I widna be mairried ta Sam.' She lifted her head. Her eyes were shining, and her words came out in a joyful tumble. 'He loves me, Mammie. Can you believe it? He really loves me.'

'I aye kent you twa were meant for ean anidder,' said Jean. 'A'm only thankful at you baith ken it an aa. A'm said it afore an A'll say it again: "God works in mysterious ways His wonders to perform".'

'Whaar's Beckie?' asked Kirsty.

'She's geen ta see Auntie Jessie an Auntie Sarah aff. Charlie an Lizzie will be waitin for dem at da Hillhead.'

'A'll geng an wave ta dem an aa,' Kirsty called over her shoulder as she ran to get her coat.

When they'd watched the horse and cart disappear from sight, Kirsty linked arms with Beckie, and told her about the loss of her baby.

'I hae somethin else ta tell dee...'

'Du doesna need ta say a word,' Beckie broke in, squeezing her arm affectionately. 'Sam's in love wi dee. A blind man could see dat.'

Serious now, Kirsty nodded and said, 'Aa we need noo is for dis wicked war ta end, an dy Johnnie ta come hame. Dan du'll be as happy as me.'

'Du shouldna a said yon oot lood, Kirsty. Du's temptin Fate.' Beckie smiled, but she felt uneasy for life's uncertainties had made her superstitious. She prayed, oh how she prayed, 'Let him come back, Lord. Dunna let him die,' as she knelt by her bed at night...but she also crossed her fingers, avoided stepping on cracks, and turned a sixpence when she saw the new moon.

Chapter Nineteen
A Bleak Mid-winter

Boxing Day was bright and sunny with a cold northerly breeze. In the afternoon Kirsty and Beckie wrapped up warmly and went for a walk. Sam declined their invitation to join them, saying he would stay in and read his book. When they returned he was huddled over the fire, his hands wrapped round a cup of Bovril. Immediately he sat up straight as though nothing was wrong and tried to greet them, but he was stricken by a little cough that caught at the back of his throat and wouldn't let him speak. On and on it went till his eyes were watering and he was worn out and breathless.

'It's just a tickle,' he gasped, trying to smile. 'Nothin ta worry aboot.'

'Aa da sam,' said Kirsty cheerfully, hiding her twinge of anxiety, 'Du should geng ta dee bed an keep warm. A'll bring dee a hot water bottle.'

'Aye aye, Captain. Whatever du says.' He gave a mock salute, making her laugh as he'd intended, but another spell of coughing took hold of him as he went through the corridor. Kirsty held her breath, and waited till it was over.

'He was chilled ta da bon when he geed ta fetch Maggie da night I lost da bairn, an he was soaked through. Even his inside claes was sabbin. Dey had ta fight der wye through a blizzard – a real "moorie caavie". It's nae wonder he's gotten da cowld.'

She must keep calm. He wouldn't want a fuss. After all,

it was just a touch of cold. She said it aloud, as though that would make it true. 'He's gotten da cowld. Dat's aa. He'll be fine.'

'Of coorse he will,' said Beckie, but she had a bad feeling about it, and a voice inside her head kept saying, *Du tempted Fate, Kirsty. I telt dee du shouldna tempt Fate.*

The next day Sam's cough worsened, and settled on his chest. Dr. Robertson came and examined him, gave him some linctus and suggested a mustard poultice to relieve the congestion, and instructed them, 'Call me at once if he becomes fevered, or has difficulty breathing.'

In the small hours of the 28th December, Kirsty woke to find Sam tossing and turning, and muttering deliriously in the grip of a high fever. His pyjamas, her nightdress - and even the sheets – were saturated with his sweat. Heat seemed to radiate off him. Fear traced an icy path from her gullet to the pit of her stomach. She leapt out of bed, had several attempts to strike a match – her fingers were trembling so much. She lit the lamp and held it up to see him better. There were circles of colour on his cheekbones – unnatural and clown-like, as if someone had painted on daubs of rouge. Suddenly his body was wracked with coughing. She thought he'd never catch his breath.

'Sorry,' he gasped, and gave a weak smile.

'Sh, sh. Dunna try ta speak. Du's goin ta be fine,' she said, hoping she sounded firm and confident. She set down the lamp, flew over to the wash-stand, grabbed a damp flannel and ran back to wipe his face and hands. Her brain was churning, making a list of things she must do. First she must calm herself.

I must try ta be like Mammie Jean. I hae ta be strong, for he'll need ta draa strength fae me. She took a few deep breaths, and asked the Lord to be with her. Suddenly a strange stillness settled over her. He would not die. She would not let him.

Da Doctor – dat's da first thing, she told herself. She pulled a shawl round her shoulders. Her nightdress clung to her, clammy and icy cold. Taking the lamp, she hurried barefoot across the linoleum to Jean and Peter's room, and tapped on the door.

'Mammie Jean. Mammie Jean,' she called urgently as she crossed the floor amd shook her mother-in-law more roughly than she meant to, for her calmness had momentarily deserted her. 'Come on, Mammie Jean. Sam's terrible ill. He needs da Doctor.'

Hearing the panic in Kirsty's voice, Jean was instantly alert. She sat up, her long silver pigtail over her shoulder, and looked at Kirsty. The lamplight accentuated the planes and shadows on her face, making her look like a ghost in her white gown.

'Peter will go for him,' she said, rousing him with a sharp nudge of her elbow. 'Da Doctor, Peter. Sam needs da Doctor.' She flung back the quilt. 'Go an get dressed, lass, or du'll catch dee death.'

The word hung in the air between them. Death...death... death...

'Sam's not goin ta die,' Kirsty said, calm again, 'for A'll no let him.'

She left the room reciting her list of things to do under her breath. *Get dressed, see ta da stove, pit on da kettle, light a fire in da bedroom, fin clean sheets an pyjamas...*

Peter threw on his clothes. Fastening his buttons in the wrong holes, pushing his bare feet into his shoes and pulling his cheese-cutter over his uncombed hair, he set off at a run to fetch Dr Robertson.

'Hurry noo,' Jean called rather superfluously, 'an tie dee laces or du'll faa...' She closed the door and went to see Sam.

Kirsty was kneeling in front of the grate arranging the paper and the sticks. She glanced at Jean.

'A'll get him changed when da fire taks up.'

She had a smudge of soot on her nose, which made her look so young and vulnerable. *Like a street urchin...*Jean found it difficult not to rush in and take charge. *A'll hae ta be careful,* she reminded herself. *He's my son, but he's her man first. A'll hae ta mind dat. I canna come atween man an wife – no if A'm ta keep dem closs.*

'Kirsty?' Sam's voice was barely a whisper.

'A'm here, love – an sae is Mammie Jean. She'll bide wi dee while I wash my hands.'

Jean felt a glow of gratitude. Kirsty wasn't going to push her aside. *I should a kent dat. She's a lass wi a generous hert.*

'Kirsty?' muttered Sam, turning his head from side to side. 'Kirsty?' Agitated, he tried to sit up.

'Easy, son. She'll be back in a minute.' Jean sponged his face. Her gentle expression told nothing of her frantic intercessions. *Dear sweet Jesus, You canna tak him noo – just when he haes a chance o real happiness. Spare him wan mair time. Tak me instead o him.*

Kirsty returned with an armful of clean linen which she dropped with a soft thud on the chair by the window. Their senses were on edge. They heard every little sound with a new clarity, as if for the first time. She fetched a jug of warm water and poured it into the enamel ewer, its crystal cascade vying with the crackle of the sticks as they took light. She took a pair of fresh pyjamas from the chest of drawers – the rattle of its brass handles forming another little motif. It seemed as if all these commonplace domestic sounds were conspiring to accentuate the ugly rasp of Sam's erratic breathing. Jean noticed Kirsty's quiet efficiency, and the worried little frown lines, which disappeared when she looked down at Sam. Her expression changed to one of undisguised tenderness. Adoration even. Jean felt a little shock of recognition. She was an intruder, for she had seen into Kirsty's private heart. This child loved her son with all the power a woman can, *as much as I love my Peter.* It was as simple as that. What more could any mother want for her son? *Please God,* she reiterated, *dunna tak him noo. Let dem hae some joy on dis earth afore You tak him tae You.*

'Will you help me?' Kirsty asked.

Together they turned back the bed-clothes and eased off the sweat-soaked pyjamas. Naked and compliant, Sam slept while Kirsty washed him – every stroke of the flannel was a caress. Jean noted how desperately thin he was – collar-bones prominent, and each rib clearly defined. She wanted to weep for them both, for the fragility of life. Kirsty rinsed the cloth, applied more soap, and wiped the hollow of his stomach. Completely unembarrassed, she worked down his body – loins, thighs, calves and feet, which she bathed with humility and tenderness. Then she kissed the upturned palm of each hand before nodding to Jean to help dress him. They had just finished when Peter returned with the Doctor. Jean was about to leave the room, when Kirsty whispered, 'No, Mammie Jean. I want you ta bide wi me.'

'So what have we here, then?' Dr Robertson said – a little too heartily – as he approached the bed, and studied his patient. 'Pneumonia, I fear. I can hear it in his breathing.' He got out his stethoscope and listened to Sam's chest, back and front, while Kirsty supported him and held up his pyjama jacket. 'As I thought, double pneumonia,' he said as he straightened up. 'I can't pretend it's not serious, but you're doing all the right things, Mrs Jacobson – Kirsty, isn't it?' She nodded dumbly. 'Keep sponging him down, and give him sips of water. Your husband is a fighter, my dear. We've seen that before, and there's no reason to suppose he won't win through again. If anyone can beat this thing, he can. I'll give you something to loosen the cough, but the illness will have to run its course. Quite honestly, he's in God's hands.' He picked up his bag. 'I'll look in again in the evening.'

'A'll see you ta da door, Doctor,' said Jean.

'You've got a fine little nurse there, Jean,' he said as he put on his hat. 'We'll just have to pray this doesn't trigger his old trouble.'

'God forbid,' murmured Jean, as she closed the door behind him.

Everyone walked on tip-toe, and spoke in whispers. With every breath they prayed for Sam's recovery. In his delirium he called for Kirsty constantly. She never left his side. Day and night she was there attending to his every need. She kissed him, bathed him, gave him water, sang to him and spoke to him – telling him about her girlish dreams. 'Dat's aa dey wir, Sam. Dreams. I never thought dey could come true.' She told him about her joyful disbelief when he said he loved her, lifting her from a deep well of hopelessness to a world filled with light. 'Nothin can ever come atween wiz noo,' she whispered, taking his hand in hers. For several days his skin was burning to the touch and his breathing fast and shallow, and on New Year's E'en the crisis came. For an hour he struggled to hold on to life, trying to clear his lungs of the yellow froth that was drowning him. His eyes were open, seeing nothing. Kirsty worked to get his fever down, urging him not to leave her, calling him back. 'Dunna slip dee grip, Sam. Hadd on. Bide wi me, bide wi me. Du canna leave me noo.' Her tears dripped unchecked onto his face.

At last his breathing settled, became slower, less laboured. His chest stopped heaving, and the heat from his body was less intense. Kirsty stumbled through to tell Jean.

'Come,' she said, tugging her arm. 'Come an see for yoursel.'

Together they looked down at him, sleeping peacefully.

'Da worst is past,' said Jean. 'Thanks be to God.'

'Thanks be to God,' Kirsty echoed. Then, in a stupor of exhaustion, she slumped into the chair and was instantly asleep. Gently Jean tucked a blanket around her and tip-toed away.

An hour or so later she returned with a light supper for Kirsty. She found Sam awake. He smiled at her weakly, and looked at Kirsty with such adoration that Jean had to turn away. No-one but Kirsty should see that look. It was for her alone.

'She brought me back, Mammie. I felt mesel goin awa, but I heard her voice tellin me ta bide wi her. She brought me back. You hae nae idea hoo much I love her.'

'Yiss, son. I do,' she said simply. 'You twa hae somethin very rare an precious. See at you treasure it.'

So 1917 came to an end, and 1918 crept unnoticed into the Jacobson house. January was dominated by the bitter weather – the coldest in thirty years. Gas supplies failed, so they were back to candles and oil-lamps. Heavy and persistent snowfall blocked the roads. Nothing moved. No cars, lorries or bicycles Not even horse-drawn vehicles. The schools were closed – partly due to the snow, and partly due to the epidemic of whooping cough that raged through the town. The only sound to be heard was the shrieking of the children who had escaped the illness, and spent their unscheduled holiday sledging down Willy Goylet's Brae.

Food was in very short supply. Butcher shops were closed, and a new rationing scheme was introduced – two meatless days per week. Housewives had to use all their skill and ingenuity to feed their families. Reserves of flour and oatmeal ran low. Even potatoes were scarce, because the stocks which crofters had stored in shallow pits were affected by the severity of the frosts. At last, on January 19th there was a sudden thaw. Wheels began to turn again, and basic foodstuffs reappeared on the shelves. The whooping cough had run its course, and the schools reopened with some poignantly empty desks. Life returned to a kind of normality, but still the war dragged on.

Beckie took over Kirsty's household duties so she was free to devote herself entirely to Sam. At first she fed him and washed him as if he were a child, but soon he began to do little things for himself. Visitors called – the Leasks, the Carters, friends and relations, people from the kirk, people from the various clubs he belonged to, folk from the library, and even customers who missed his friendly banter at the shop. He'd never known he had so many friends! But best of all he enjoyed the companionable hours he spent with Kirsty reading and talking by the fireside. Their love lapped round them, warm and gentle as the summer sea. They floated on it, immersed themselves in it. At times it sparkled as though lit by the sun, at times it lay languid – deep and still.

It was a time of discovery. Their love was a miracle, but strangely chaste, for their marriage had not yet been consummated. First her illness and then his had made it impossible, but he was growing stronger each day. By the end of February he was taking short walks, and by mid-March he was able to go back to work for half-days.

This was when it happened. Their normal affectionate embrace became unexpectedly charged with an urgency that demanded to be satisfied. Their breathing quickened, pulses raced and any inhibitions they might have had were washed away. Their bodies dictated what to do and, after so much waiting, there was no holding back. Their passion, their desire had all the energy of an Atlantic breaker, which seemed to curl over them, crash down on them, and carry them with it, rolling them over and over in an ecstasy of giving and taking… and just when they thought it was finished with them, it would lift them up again – kissing, tasting; clutching, holding; writhing, thrusting; crying out again and again, until at last they were sated and slept, naked, in each other's arms. Nothing could have prepared them for the power of it. Kirsty laced her fingers through his. 'Nae dee. Nae me. Noo wir truly wan.'

Sam smiled. To think he'd worried so much about how it would be for her, after Jamie… but his brother's brutality had simply been swept away. It was no match for their love.

'Come here.' He pulled her back into his arms. 'Does du hae ony idea hoo much I love dee?'

'Yiss,' she said, her voice muffled against his chest, 'aboot as much as I love dee.'

She lifted her head. Her eyes shone and her skin was pink and glowing. 'Naebody in da history o da world is ever loved like dis.'

March passed, and April. Sam began to work full days, and Kirsty's lessons were resumed. Their happiness was infectious, touching everyone. Despite the war, the house rang with laughter and song, and soon there was another reason to be joyful. Kirsty was blooming, expecting Sam's child.

PART THREE

Chapter Twenty
Back to the Front
October 1917

By the time Jamie reached the hospital he had already locked in the deep recesses of his mind everything that had taken place at home in Lerwick. After all, it was of no importance to him. All he could think about was getting back to France. He knew what he had to do. He had to convince the medics that he was fit for action - both in body and in mind - and he set about it with a single-minded sense of purpose. He ate well, gaining a little weight, and he worked hard at regaining his physical fitness – firstly by walking daily, steadily increasing the distance and the amount he carried with him. At the same time, he showed that he was emotionally stable by being cheerful and helpful to the staff, and sympathetic and encouraging to his fellow patients. He helped to feed and shave them, read their letters to them and wheeled them round the hospital grounds in their wheelchairs. An "all-round good fellow" and "patriotic to the core" was the verdict of those around him.

However, when the assessment team met at the end of October - and again at the end of November – to discuss the readiness of patients for drafting back to the front, they found that Jamie's physical condition was not up to the required standard. Furious, and not a little offended, Jamie set about proving them wrong. He designed a strenuous programme of exercise for himself, until he was putting himself through the same gruelling routine that he'd imposed on his men back in France. At the December meeting, they noted that Sergeant Jacobson had made a good recovery largely down to his own determination and fighting spirit. 'We could do with more chaps like him,' said the Senior Medical Officer.

'I'm not so sure,' said Benson, a young psychologist, relatively new to the team. 'I had misgivings about the diagnosis when he came here first…'

'Are you suggesting he wasn't shell-shocked? Do you think he was malingering?'

'No, sir. He was shell-shocked all right, and he is certainly not malingering. He is undoubtedly eager to get back to France. Definitely no shirker. But there's more to it. I'm sure of that.'

'What do you mean, man? Spit it out. We have a lot of cases to get through.' He looked at his watch pointedly.

'Haven't you noticed how meticulous he is about his routines? How he drives himself? It's more than is healthy. These are obsessive behaviours.'

'Nonsense. It's just good old-fashioned military discipline.'

There was a murmur of agreement round the table, but young Benson refused to be intimidated, and persisted with his argument.

'To my mind there's something else going on here.' He looked round at his superior officers. 'I believe he could possibly be psychotic.'

'Psychotic? Don't be ridiculous. We can't afford to be namby-pamby about this. The army needs replacements, and it's our job to see they get them. Every man who is fit must go, and in my opinion this man is fit for service.' The SMO prepared to stamp Jamie's form accordingly.

'All I'm saying is that if I'm right - and he is psychotic – he'll be a danger to himself and to his men. A man without fear is a man to be feared.'

'Do you mean he has a death wish?' asked the SMO. Laughter spread among the officers seated round the table. 'Listen to me Doctor Benson, a man without fear is a man of courage – just the sort we need.' And the stamp went down firmly. A3. Fit for active service. 'Next?' He looked at his watch again. This case had taken up too much time. He really mustn't be late. He'd promised Millicent he'd be home in time to take her to the theatre, and there would be the devil to pay if he let her down.

When Jamie was informed of their decision, he saluted, did a neat about turn and marched smartly out of the room. In the corridor, he threw back his head and laughed gales of hysterical laughter. He'd done it! He'd proved them wrong. He laughed till the tears were running down his cheeks, but no-one paid any heed. They were used to eccentric behaviour here.

The first two weeks of 1918 were passed in a state of nervous excitement, waiting for news of discharge from hospital. At last he got his draft leave. This he spent in London, mainly in pubs or music halls. He avoided the brothels and the invitations of street women, and took care not to drink too much. He didn't want to miss his draft by being sent to the pox hospital or by ending up in the clink for fighting. Nothing must stop him from getting to France. Next he was sent to Warminster to wait till his draft was due to sail. Progress toward the battlefield was painfully slow. Jamie found it hard to maintain his outward image of calm and steady devotion to duty, as another fortnight crawled by, but at least they were kept busy. They practised building and repairing trenches; they carried out various mock stunts where they attacked "enemy" lines; they went on long marches carrying a ridiculous amount of equipment, and they had bayonet practice – where Jamie was able to give vent to his frustration, as he thrust his blade through sacks of straw while giving blood-curdling roars and shouting hate-words. At last they were issued with their kit, and the final day was taken up with checking that their gas masks were in working order, and seeing that they knew how to use them. Several respirators were found to be faulty, and the unlucky souls who had been allocated these emerged choking and gasping for breath from the gas-filled chamber. Their streaming eyes were so painful that their draft had to be cancelled. Some men looked on them with envy, but Jamie was thankful that his mask had been fault-free. Another delay would have been more than he could bear.

The following day they entrained for Shorecliffe, and an hour's march to a rest camp close to Folkestone. There another few days were wasted, waiting. Tension was mounting; most men were trying to steel themselves for action. Many were "old" men in their twenties, experienced soldiers disenchanted by the war and secretly feeling that their luck was sure to run out this time. Some were young boys of eighteen (or under) who had no idea of the reality of life in the trenches and were eager for action…and there was Jamie who had his own agenda.

At last they boarded a decrepit paddle-steamer, more suited to genteel pleasure jaunts than ploughing through the leaden waves of the English Channel. "Old hands" lay stretched out on the filthy deck, heads on haversacks, and slept, while others hunkered down or stood crushed together, arms pinned to their sides. Their degree of comfort depended on how aggressive they had been in securing a space for themselves. They dozed when they could, or hung over the rails spewing into the wind. Some were so sea-sick – and so afraid of losing their place - that they threw up where they were. They arrived in Boulogne on a miserable grey morning, and, without having a chance to clean themselves up, marched through the rough country roads or the cobbled streets of little villages towards their first camp. On the way they passed lines of weary grey-faced soldiers trudging toward the Channel ports and a ship home for leave. They also passed numerous lorries loaded with the wounded en route for hospitals. This was the first indication to the young recruits that they were not embarking on an exciting game of soldiers. Their next stop was the "bull-ring", where seasoned SMs put the newcomers through gruelling drills and fatigues designed to change them from raw and innocent country boys to fighting men in a week, or perhaps two. They barked out orders, shouted and swore at their charges and humiliated them over and over again, until instant obedience was a conditioned reflex – something that might save their lives some day soon.

Jamie rejoined his old Division at a camp near Doullens, and found that a good number of his former comrades had "bought it", or were nursing their wounds in some hospital. Here he spent his days – and sometimes his nights – staggering through water-logged trenches laden like a pack-mule with bales of barbed wire, pickets, sheets of corrugated iron or planks of wood; alternatively, he was repairing the revetements or digging latrines. This wasn't what he'd come to France for, but he knew he had to toe the line and his chance would come. And come it did, for on March 21st the Germans launched their offensive (known as Operation Michael) on the British Troops in the Arras/St Quentin area of the Somme. General Ludendorff wanted to exploit the German superiority in numbers – 63 divisions to the British 26 – before the Americans arrived to even things out. Also he thought he could make use of the fact that the British and French had different priorities. The British would be more concerned with protecting the Channel ports, and the French were unlikely to offer them full support for their chief concern was the defence of Paris. Jamie's Division along with other Australians were sent to strengthen the British 5th Army. The Tommies were, reportedly, "windy" and ready to retreat from relentless German attacks with gas and artillery shells.

This was more like it. Jamie's adrenaline was flowing, and it pleased him to think that the Aussies would succeed where the Brits had failed. They had no sooner consolidated their position, than they were rushed to the small town of Hebuterne to plug another gap there. Jamie was in his element for this involved a good deal of hand to hand fighting in the streets, and much use of the bayonet. He made several successful attacks, the most notable being when he stepped in to save a young private. The boy stood rooted to the spot, unable to react, while a German Officer rushed towards him, his bayonet ready to strike. Jamie thrust the boy aside and, without hesitation, stuck his blade into the German's stomach, and gave it a vicious twist before pulling it out dripping with blood. The boy watched mesmerised as Jamie's victim sank to his knees and keeled over. 'No time for that son,' yelled Jamie as two more enemy soldiers appeared directly in front of them. 'You take the left, and I'll take the right.' The numbed boy automatically followed his hero, and made his first kill. Jamie's skill and fearlessness was noted by the lieutenant, who complimented him on his bravery and leadership skills. Jamie resolved to make use of his good opinion as soon as a suitable occasion arose.

Next they marched to Albert to rectify another British blunder. Due to some misunderstanding, the British had withdrawn leaving the town undefended, which in turn left the way clear to the town of Amiens, an important strategic town on account of its roads and railways. They were too late to prevent the enemy from taking Albert, and Jamie's Division was then sent to halt the German attack on Villers-Bretonneux, another village which played a crucial role in blocking the German advance to Amiens. Orders were given that they must hold the line "at all costs". On April 4th a dramatic bayonet charge halted German advance, and drove the demoralised Hun back over two miles. Jamie's blood was up. This was real warfare! By now the Australians held the front from south of Villers-Bretonneux as far as Albert.

During this period the Aussies became renowned for a series of night raids, where small groups of men crept through

No Man's Land and attacked enemy listening posts, or gun emplacements. Their main weapon was their sheer audacity and the element of surprise. "Peaceful Penetration" was the name given to these stealthy attacks. Several Australian soldiers were decorated for their imaginative and daring "stunts", and Jamie resolved to achieve the same. His chance came when the Germans, in an attempt to demoralise the enemy, launched a devastating attack of mustard gas shells. This cost the Australians dearly. They urgently needed to prevent further gas attacks, and clear the way for the men to advance. However, the gun emplacement responsible for launching the shells was protected by carefully placed sniper fire. Intelligence had informed them that the snipers were concealed in two shellholes, close to the enemy front line, one on either side of the gun. They would have to be removed before any attack could be made on the gun.

Jamie saw this as his golden opportunity. He approached his Lieutenant and told him his plan.

'Sir, I'd like to have a go at the blighter. If you give me one good man to go with me, I believe I can take out the snipers, capture the gun, then launch a grenade attack on the trench.'

'Tell me more, Jacobson. How do you intend to surprise the snipers?'

'We'll crawl out at night and circle round them, attacking from behind...'

'The soldiers in the trenches...what about them?'

'They won't see us, sir. Too complacent, you see. They're depending on the snipers to give them good warning.' Jamie laughed. 'They won't know what's hit them.'

Lieutenant Smiley, considered the proposal briefly. Jacobson was a good man, and the plan had some merit. It would be a feather in the Division's cap if he could pull it off.

'Right, Jacobson. Choose your man, and get him up to speed. There's only an hour till its dark.'

'Thank you, sir. You won't regret it, I promise you.'

'You're sure you only need one man?'

'Yes, only the one. Less chance of being spotted.'

An hour later Jamie climbed out "over the bags", cut the wire and wriggled through, then beckoned to his chosen partner to follow. They spaced themselves out, about thirty feet between them, and moved steadily across the rough moonscape of No Man's Land. Forbes was to his right. His right-hand man! He was good at close combat. Jamie had seen him in action - killing a Tommy with his bare hands in a street brawl, then melting into the shadows. Word had it that he was good with a knife too. Jamie was depending on that. The two of them would circle out giving the snipers a wide berth, then they'd move in again behind the shell-holes. They pulled themselves along on their elbows, close to the ground. Whenever the flares lit the sky, they froze, moulding their bodies to the ground. Still as stones they lay, but their eyes were scanning the terrain ahead, charting and memorising their route through the broken ground – the route they would take in the brief spell of darkness before the next flare.

This wasn't a job to be rushed. Slow but sure. That was the ticket. He cursed under his breath whenever his hands were cut with the debris of shrapnel that littered the ground, or when his elbow sunk into a soft spongy mass of rotting flesh that gave off a stench that caught in the throat. He hadn't realised the smell would be so bad – as bad as the gas had been the previous day, and it made his eyes sting too. He looked for Forbes but couldn't see him. Couldn't see anything. Wait for the next flare. Another twenty yards or so and they'd be in position. That was the most dangerous time, and the most exciting, for they'd have to wait there, Gerry in front and behind them until the next flare went up. They had to see one another in order to synchronise their attacks. The cheek of it made him want to laugh. Lying so close to Fritz, who had no idea they were so near to their final breath! Jamie's sense of power was pure joy.

The flare lit the sky. He held up his hand indicating five seconds. Forbes nodded. Darkness. One. Two. Three. Four. Five - and they were off. Over the rim of the crater, left arm round to cover the mouth, one slick stroke of the knife-blade to sever the jugular, a spurt of blood, the hint of a gurgle, a sighing breath and the deed was done. Another flare and he watched for Forbes' nod to indicate his attack had been successful. Jamie crept to the left, to the gun emplacement, while Forbes moved closer to the trench. Two gunners! Only two! That was a stroke of luck. The poor bastards didn't have time to register what was happening before Jamie's revolver coughed twice, putting a bullet neatly in each forehead. Jamie patted the barrel of the gun –a 15cm heavy field howitzer. *Not exactly 'Big Bertha', but you'll do. A good stock of ammunition too.* He nodded, satisfied, then he calmly relieved one of the gunners of his Luger. He held up his hand in the light of the next flare, indicating that it was time for the Mills bombs. He heard a soft click as Forbes pulled the pin, and waited a few seconds for the detonation. Another bomb, and another. Down now to the trench where Forbes was rounding up the dazed survivors. It took only a few minutes to clear the trench, leaving a tangle of dead and dismembered soldiers. Jamie, only a step behind Forbes shot him in the back with the Luger at point blank range, and, without compunction, kicked his body into the trench to lie with the dead (or dying) Huns.

'Sorry mate,' he breathed. 'Can't have you taking any of the credit for this. It's my show.' Then, single-handed, he marched their prisoners back across No Man's Land.

In a state of euphoria, he accepted the congratulations of the Lieutenant and the extra tot of rum.

'I'm going to recommend you for a medal, Jacobson. Well done, lad. I'm proud of you. Tomorrow at first light we'll push forward and attack the German reserves with their own gun.'

As the adrenaline rush faded and exhaustion took over, Jamie realised he was breathless and had severe chest pains. His eyes were burning. It had been hard going, every muscle screaming out as they had crossed No Man's Land, and his eyes were strained with peering into the darkness. He'd feel better tomorrow…

The following day there was no improvement. Barely aware of what was happening, he was loaded onto a stretcher and carried down the line to a Field Hospital. There he was diagnosed with mustard gas poisoning. He should have realised the stench that was choking him as he crawled out from the parapet was not just death and putrifaction. The MO explained that, although the gas from the previous day's bombardment had dispersed, some of the liquid had seeped into the ground, where its effects could persist for some time. If he'd been standing up he'd have been all right, but with his face only inches fron the ground... He was taken by ambulance to another hospital where they injected morphine under his eye-lids, and he got some relief. From there he was shipped off to Blighty. His war was over, for the effects of the gassing lingered. He was moved from one hospital to another. From time to time he felt better, but he had frequent bouts of weakness and vomiting; head-aches and breathlessness; fevers and erratic heartbeat.

In May Peter and Jean received an envelope which contained a cutting from the *Anzac Bulletin*, giving an account of Jamie's "stunt". *News has just come in*, it said, *of a daring night raid which Sergeant James Jacobson carried out virtually single handed.* It went on giving details of the raid – and Forbes' tragic death at the hand of a German. Thanks to Sergeant Jacobson's selfless courage his unit was able to advance, occupy the German trench and drive back their reserve line, using their own artillery shells. Sergeant Jacobson has been recommended for a gallantry medal.

Peter was so proud of his son that he, who rarely put pen to paper, wrote to Jamie telling him so. *You are a hero,* he wrote, *and I thank the Good Lord for giving you the strength of mind and heart. You were ready to risk your life for your men, and I have not the words to tell you how sorry I am that*

I ever doubted you. He signed it *Yr affectionate father, Peter Jacobson.*

Jamie read his father's large childish hand with satisfaction, but made no reply other than a curt note saying he'd been recommended for a military medal. He knew the news would fly around the town like wildfire, and would undoubtedly appear in the local press. "James Jacobson – Hero". He pictured the headline. That would make them all sit up and take notice.

In October, as a 1914 recruit, he was among the first to be repatriated to Australia. There he received a hero's welcome. He knew he would never be fit for service again, and, strangely, his wish to die a hero's death had deserted him. As a celebrity, he was fêted everywhere he went, and a frequent house-guest of the rich and famous. He had everything he wanted here – feasting, drinking, gaming and women. No need to go to Valhalla.

PART FOUR

Chapter Twenty-One
Armistice and Aftermath

At last the guns were silent. The cease-fire was effective from the eleventh hour of the eleventh day of the eleventh month – a day which would resonate down the years. It brought with it a confused tangle of emotions – relief, elation, sorrow and guilt in equal parts. However, the initial reaction was joy. It seemed that every church bell and every carillon rang out across the country. In London and in all the big cities the townspeople spilled out onto the streets singing and dancing, waving flags. Hearts pounded and eyes glistened. Sexual energy made every nerve tingle in anticipation of passionate reunions. They embraced friends, relations and strangers alike – bonded by the relief that there would be no more killing and their lovers and husbands would soon be home - and by the mistaken belief that things would return to normal. They no longer had to contain the fear that had been with them every minute of every day – the fear that their own "dear boy" would not come back. It rushed away like a river in spate carrying all their caution with it. The dam had burst and there was no holding back. It became a night of excesses and indiscretions, and there wouldn't be another like it for many years to come.

The news reached Lerwick initially through Rear Admiral Greatorex, who had it by wireless. He immediately informed the *Shetland Times*, which placed a placard in their window in Commercial Street. People appeared at once, as if by telepathy, to read the good news. When the official news came through the Central News Agency, the newspaper printed handbills. 'The Prime Minister makes the following announcement: The Armistice was signed at 5 o'clock this morning, and hostilities cease on all fronts at 11a.m. today.' Schoolboys were released from school to distribute the leaflets to every house. It was official! The news was greeted with "unspeakable pleasure" by all, but as the *Shetland Times* reported, 'There were no indications of hilarity. The strain had been too great, the tension too strong to permit of levity. There was no presence of what is known as "popular" rejoicings. It was with subdued feelings, a sensation that ran too deep for words, that the people met each other, and with genuine hand-clasps congratulated each other that the maiming and killing of the boys was at an end.'

At first the church bells rang out, and vessels in the harbour sounded their sirens, and soon – as if by magic – bunting appeared on public buildings and ships were "dressed". During the afternoon flags appeared on shops and private dwellings. Early evening saw the young people parade the streets proudly carrying the Union Jack, the French Tricolour and the Stars and Stripes of America. The Brass Band took up its position at the Market Cross and played a lively selection of marches and patriotic tunes. Kirsty and Sam, Beckie and Grace joined the growing throng. Joe, who could not cope with crowds and noise, remained at home with his mother - who did not feel in celebratory mood.

She sat by the fire, her heart full of conflicting emotions. She gave heartfelt thanks that Peter and their sea-faring sons would no longer have to face the danger of torpedoes, mines or attack by enemy warships…but the sorrow at the loss of her much-loved boys – which she had managed to hold in check – came back as sharply painful as it had been the days she heard that they were dead. Tears flowed, unstoppable, while the celebrations went on. Eventually the pain settled to a permanent dull ache. Ironically she came to welcome it, for it meant that Robert and Andrew were always with her.

She knew of course that there were many like her, for whom the end of the war was a hollow joy – who found the festivities meaningless. Parents who had lost sons could think only of the waste of unlived lives, and the glaring, agonising gaps in their own. Widows found their personal grief compounded by the fear and anxiety they felt at the prospect of bringing up fatherless children alone. Lovers - destined to spend tortured nights throbbing with longing for the strong arms that would never hold them again – now tasted remembered kisses, and wept at the thought of a lifetime of loneliness. Chaste sweethearts, who had been "keeping themselves" for the marriage bed once the war was over, now reproached themselves for the sins they had not committed, and the comfort they had not given, or received, and resigned themselves to a life of barren spinsterhood. All these people remained indoors, trying to stop their ears to the sounds of celebration; trying not to envy their friends and neighbours whose boys would come home soon; trying to ward off the terrible "why me?" and to kill off the seeds of bitterness before they took root and choked their spirit.

Later in the evening vessels sounded their sirens again, and signal rockets were fired. As the *Shetland Times* later reported – 'their long lances of fire pierced the sky and burst in glowing colours.'

Sam noticed that Kirsty, now heavily pregnant, was looking pale and tired.

'I think we'll geng hame, an leave dem tae it,' he said, anxious lest she might be jostled or pushed, for the mood of the crowd was growing more and more exuberant.

Kirsty nodded, relieved that he didn't want to stay. The war for her meant Jamie, and thinking of it was bringing back unwanted memories. She smiled at Sam, and held tight to his arm as they eased their way through the crowd. Their life together was her celebration. As they walked home, they stopped from time to time to gaze at the aurora that had suddenly appeared in the northern sky, sending rippling ribbons of colour above and beyond the exploding fireworks. It seemed as if the natural world wanted to play its part in the human expression of joy and relief.

Jean put on a cheerful front when they came in, and bustled around seeing that Kirsty was comfortable and making the inevitable cup of tea. At ease with one another they sat in silence, allowing each other space to think their own thoughts. Sam looked at his young wife, and admitted to himself that the prospect of fatherhood had altered his attitude to war. He was grateful – passionately so – to those who had fought, creating a peaceful world for his child to grow up in. *Wid I a wanted ta fight if dis bairn was already been born?* He asked himself. *Maybe…maybe I wid…Strange hoo wir principles change accordin ta wir situation.* Of course he wouldn't have been allowed to fight, so the question was purely hypothetical, but the notion that deep-held principles can be modified - or even abandoned – to suit one's circumstances was disturbing. The idea that the "Thou shalts" and "Thou shalt nots" - which had always informed his behaviour and attitudes – were not permanently fixed was deeply disconcerting. However, he reassured himself, there were lines that he would never cross, no matter what. He was certain of that. Jean finished her tea, and coming out of her reverie, took their cups from them.

'It's time ta look forward noo. A lot o fock will need help.'

Over the next few weeks she threw herself into doing what she could. She visited the bereaved and tried to console them. Her empathy was genuine, and they could sense that, so her visits always left them feeling that they were not alone in their suffering. Strong bonds were formed and her positive attitude gave them heart to face life, one small step at a time. She made them realise that getting through each day was an achievement.

Town Officials had envisaged arranging a grand welcome for returning service-men, whom they imagined arriving en masse and marching through the streets to bands playing, and greeted by flag-waving, cheering crowds. The reality was somewhat different. They returned in dribs and drabs – wounded, exhausted and broken men.

Jean offered practical help – bringing food or a few peats for the fire; showing wives how to dress wounds and teaching them the importance of hygiene. Peter accompanied her when he was home, offering his comforting remedies.

Influenza raged and though it was not the devastating "Spanish" 'flu, it was still serious and life-threatening. So much so that the *Times* published advice on how best to avoid it, or to cope if suffering from it. However, many of the most needful either did not see the paper, or were unable to read and understand it. Jean tried to explain in simple terms what they should do, but became incensed at the ignorance of the official line which tried to impress the need for "good food, and plenty of it" on those who had no money to buy it, or the need for "careful ventilation" on those whose windows could not open. Meanwhile she mixed up disinfectant gargles for them, and relieved the exhausted wives from their nursing duties to allow them to snatch a few hours' sleep. Nothing was too much trouble for her, but the family urged her not to drive herself so hard. They could see she was stretching herself to the limit. She grew thinner and whiter, more lined...and she frequently fell asleep in her chair.

Even the fittest, most positive men found it difficult to adapt to life at home. The bonds they'd formed with their chums in the trenches were the strongest they'd ever experienced, and they were lost without them. They could no longer share their thoughts or memories – which were often unspeakable – with wives or sweethearts, who felt pushed aside. They had become changed men. Their experiences had turned good-natured, easy-going fellows into spiteful, demanding strangers - or into silent withdrawn old men with unfocused eyes. Children were afraid of the fathers they barely knew. Relationships disintegrated, and love-making – if it were possible – was no longer tender or passionate, but mechanical or violent.

Beckie found herself to be a victim of war damage. Her Johnnie came home, physically unscathed. Her excitement knew no bounds, she was ready to give herself to him the minute they could be alone – but his passion did not match hers. Distraught, she asked him, 'Does du no love me ony mair? Is du fun somebody else?'

Always the answer was the same. He loved her, and only her, but the wedding was repeatedly deferred. She was confused, hurt and felt cheapened by his rejection. Gradually the troubled boy tried to explain that he wanted to marry her, but he couldn't allow himself to be happy when so many of his pals had been killed or wounded. It wouldn't be right. He felt guilty for being alive.

'I ken A'm hurtin dee an it's brakkin my hert, but I canna help it.'

A second strand to his problem was his self-loathing, and he was unable to explain this to her. He couldn't come to terms with the brutal acts he'd carried out, and the horrors he'd witnessed. *A'm a killer an a murderer. Hoo can I touch an innocent, lovely lass like her.* He believed he was contaminated by evil, and if he allowed her to get close to him she would become contaminated too. How could he do that to her? His love for her was almost unbearable.

Beckie confided in Kirsty.

'I thought everything wid be aa right if only he cam hame safe, but A'm lost him just as surely as if he was dead. Da worst is at der nothin I can dae ta help him. Naebody can. He says it's easier for wiz baith if we dunna see ean anidder again. Bein near me is like a knife in his hert, he says.' She took a deep trembling breath and looked at Kirsty. 'No bein near him is like a knife in mine.'

Then came the pent-up tears. Kirsty held her while she wept. After a while Kirsty said, 'You ken, Beckie, I can understand some o what he said.'

'What does du mean?'

'Weel,' she began, stroking her swollen belly, 'it hurts me ta be sae happy when things are turned oot like dis for dee. It maks me feel kinda guilty.'

'No, Kirsty. Never! Du's no ta feel like dat,' said Beckie, horrified that her unhappiness should affect her friend. 'Du'll just hae ta be happy enough for baith o wiz.' She wiped her reddened, bloodshot eyes.

'So what is Johnnie goin ta do?'

'He's goin back ta da Wast Side, ta his aald job, an he's goin ta bide in his grandfaither's hoose.' She gave a little sniff, and glanced at Kirsty. 'Da ean at we were goin ta bide in when we got mairried.'

'I see,' said Kirsty. 'An what is du goin ta do?' She knew that Beckie would have something at the back of her mind, for she was pragmatic. Kirsty was confident that she had the strength to rise above anything that life meted out to her.

After a moment's thought, Beckie confessed that she'd always had a desire to have her own dress-making business.

'Du kens hoo I like needle-wark, an fock'll be wantin some boannie new claes wance da murnin time is by. Maybe noo is da time ta start.' Ideally she'd like a machine, but she could put money aside for that if she got steady work hand-sewing to begin with. Soon her mind was a-whirl, working out how this dream could be made reality.

'Nae faer o dee, Beckie,' said Kirsty, giving her an affectionate hug. 'I can see it noo – a fine peerie shop wi dy name abon da door, an a lang list o customers waitin for a "Beckie Jacobson" ootfit. Du'll do it, Beckie. I ken du will.'

Kirsty was pleased that her "sister" had crossed the first hurdle, and could begin to look ahead.

A month after the Armistice Jean fell ill with influenza, which was not entirely surprising as she had been exposing herself to it on a daily basis for some weeks. She was so worn out that she was in no fit state to withstand the disease. Kirsty was immediately dispatched to the Carters' to minimise the risk to her and the unborn child. Reluctantly she agreed. Word was sent to Peter by wireless, but the Fates were conspiring against him and a combination of fog and stormy weather delayed the boat, so that he didn't get home to say his goodbyes.

For three days Jean lay, shivering till her teeth chattered, or burning up with fever. Her throat was so painful she could hardly speak or swallow. Beckie nursed her with Ellie's help, as she grew steadily weaker. On the third day she rallied slightly and indicated thet she needed to speak to Sam – alone. Fear clutching at his heart, he sat beside her holding her hand till she was ready to speak. With enormous effort she began in a breathless, husky whisper – the fractured sentences punctuated by long pauses, as she summoned up the strength to continue.

'I want dee ta promise me twa things. First, at du will see ta it at dee faither never fins oot aboot Kirsty an Joe. He's dat prood o Jamie. It wid be fine ta keep it like dat...' She was silent so long that Sam thought he might never hear her second request. Then she spoke again. 'Da second promise is aboot peerie Joe. I need ta be sure at he'll be right lookit eftir. So will du tak care o him, dee an Kirsty?'

Sam nodded. 'Of coorse we will, Mammie.'

She seemed satisfied for she smiled and appeared to fall asleep.

Suddenly she opened her eyes and looked at Sam with unnerving clarity. 'It's no easy…ta say dis, but du kens as weel as I do at dy life might be cut short. So du'll hae ta tell dy bridders everything, for if onything should happen ta dee ean o dem will hae ta tak him on, an dey canna understand him…if dey dunna ken - what he's been through.' Her breathing became more distressed. She had made a major effort to tell him this much, but she wasn't finished. 'Du'll hae ta mak dem gie dee der word at dey…' she faltered, but went on, 'at dey will keep it fae dee faither. Mak dem swear apo da bible.'

Sam nodded and squeezed her hand.

'If du looks in da tap drawer,' She glanced at the tall-boy. 'du'll fin a bundle o letters. Der fae Uncle Tom. Tak dem, Sam, for I dunna want dee faither ta see dem.'

She watched as he opened the drawer and put the letters in his pocket, then came back to her bedside and took her hand in his.

Her eyes began to glaze over. 'Du's been a good son. I couldna a had better.' The pauses between her utterances had become longer, and her voice had faded to the softest whisper. Her eyes flickered and a faint smile touched her lips.

'Look eftir peerie Kirsty noo, an keep an eye on dee father for me.' With that her grip on his hand loosened, and she slipped away.

Sam sat – how long he did not know – looking at her dear sweet face, young now in repose. He had neither words nor thoughts. All he felt was love. She had been his life-line and his strength, and now she was gone. He couldn't imagine the world without her. At last he tucked her hand under the bed-clothes, as if to make it warm again. Then he closed her eyes with a gentle caress, kissed her brow, and went to tell the others. The doctor came and signed the Death Certificate. He was clearly moved by her passing.

'She was a good woman,' he said. 'You have my deepest sympathy. She'll be sadly missed by the people of the town.'

Before he went to bed, Sam went to look at her again. The years – and her suffering – had fallen away. Her face was peaceful and serene, unlined and youthful in repose, so beautiful it made him catch his breath.

'Goodnight, Mammie,' he whispered, and kissed her cold cheek. Then he tiptoed away, as if afraid he'd wake her.

The following day he met his father at the pier to tell him he was too late.

'I ken,' he said

'Wha telt you?' asked Sam.

'Naebody,' Peter replied. 'I saa it in a veesion. A'm aye seen her life-force like a candle, burnin bright, wi a steady flame. On Monday it started ta flicker as if it might geng oot, but it burnt low wi a feeble light for three days. Dan it geed oot, an I was left in da black dark.' He looked up, and Sam could see the loneliness in his eyes. 'Dat's when I kent at she was geen.'

Chapter Twenty-Two

Secrets and Solidarity

The women watched as the men carried the coffin out of the house, raised it to their shoulders, and made their way slowly down the garden path to the high wooden gate. *She wid a been prood o dem,* Kirsty thought. *Good men, tall an handsome every wan.*

Peter was at the head - his face a smooth, white, expressionless mask. The thought crossed Kirsty's mind that if she were to touch his cheek, it would feel cold – ice-cold and hard as stone, like Mammie Jean's had been when she kissed her goodbye.

Behind him, at either side, were Osie (who had been granted special leave) and Henry. Then came Sam and Lollie, followed by Cousins Albert and Andrew, newly home from the war. Isaac, as the eldest son, brought up the rear. Kirsty looked at Sam's taut, shuttered face. She wanted to run to him and hold him, as if by touching she could draw the suffering from his body into her own and bear it for him. He stared ahead, and did not look her way. She knew that had he seen the heartbreak in her eyes, it would have been harder for him to conduct himself with dignity, and that was what it was about. Dignity. No public displays of inner torment. This was how they showed their respect for a woman who had been at the hub of the family – giving them support, guidance and unconditional love for as long as they could remember. Burying the dead was men's business. Women wept in the gloomy half-light of rooms with lowered blinds, knowing they must put on a brave face when their men returned, for life must go on.

The road was lined with mourners who stood with bowed, uncovered heads as the little procession passed slowly by, and the church was full to overflowing for the whole community – rich and poor alike - wanted to pay their respects to a woman who had touched their hearts. Relatives and friends were invited to the house for refreshments which the women had prepared, and the day dragged on with hand-shakes and embraces, and touching personal anecdotes mixed with desultory small-talk. Sam wished they would all go home and leave the family in peace, for he was growing more and more tense. When was he going to get an opportunity to carry out his promise to his mother? Isaac and Osie – who had not yet received their discharge papers - were travelling back the next day to rejoin their ships, so it had to be tonight. How was he going to get them alone?

No one had any appetite at dinnertime, but they sat round the table and went through the motions. Afterwards, finding solace in familiar routines, Peter did the bible reading – Jean's favourite, the Beatitudes, at Sam's request. Then he solemnly entered the date of her death on the front page, blotted the ink, and closed the book with a soft thud. This had such an air of finality about it that it brought raw feelings to the surface. The girls, after seeing that Joe was settled for the night, retired to their rooms to shed their private tears. Peter followed soon after, saying they'd have to excuse him, but he needed some time to himself. This was the moment Sam had been waiting for.

'A'm glad we hae da place ta wirsels, boys,' he said, 'for I hae somethin important ta tell you - a promise at I made ta Mammie just afore she died.' He drew his chair in to the fire, and indicated that they should do the same. 'It's hard ta ken whaar ta start…' He began to light his pipe, while he collected his thoughts.

'Get on wi it, Sam,' Isaac urged him. Patience was not his strongest virtue. 'It canna be dat bad.'

So Sam told them about their mother's need for assurance that Joe would be well cared for, and that he and Kirsty had agreed to take him on.

'So whaar do we come in,' asked Osie.

He explained that, given his medical history, it was on the cards that he might die before his time, and in that case the responsibility would fall to them – either singly or jointly.

'It's no sae easy for wiz when wir at sea,' Isaac said, thoughtfully, 'but I've nae doot we could work somethin oot.'

The others nodded in agreement

'Dere's mair tae it,' said Sam. 'Somethin you hae ta ken aboot Joe, if you're goin ta look efter him right. You need ta understand what he's been through, an dan you'll see at he needs special care.'

Trying to remain objective, he told them the whole sordid story about what Jamie had done to Joe, and to Kirsty. Speechless, they looked at him in disbelief.

'I ken it's hard ta accept at what A'm tellin you is true, so I want you aa ta look at dis.' He handed Isaac Joe's red book.

'Dis is Joe's diary. You'll hae na doots, wance you're seen it.' He went to the door and stood in the fresh air, trying to clear his head - and giving them time to digest the contents.

When he went back in, there was no mistaking their expressions of horror. At first they said nothing - they couldn't find the words. Gradually horror turned to outrage. Why had Jamie not been sent to prison? How was it possible to get off with such crimes? Their questions came thick and fast, as their fury grew.

'Dere's somethin far wrang wi da laa o dis land, if he can get aff wi yon. Hangin's ower good for da likes o him,' said Isaac.

Then Henry asked, quietly, 'What wye are we no heard aboot it till noo, Sam. Dat's what's puzzlin me. A scandal like yon must a been da talk o da toon.'

The others fell silent. This was food for thought.

Sam knocked out his pipe, lifted the lid of the stove and threw the dottle into the fire before he dropped the bombshell.

'We never sent for da police.'

'You never sent for da police?' repeated an incredulous Isaac, and a clamour of outraged questions were directed at Sam again. Then Isaac rounded on him, 'Du should a seen ta it at da police took him in. Du was da man o da hoose...'

'Whoa! Hadd on a minute,' said Sam, holding up his hand to stop the flow. 'Hear me oot.'

He explained that their mother had forbidden him to call in the law, and tried to explain her reasoning. It was to protect Kirsty and Joe. 'Fock wid be pointin da finger at dem,' she said, 'an you ken what dey'd be sayin. Bringin in da police wid only add ta der suffering.'

The brothers reluctantly conceded that there was some truth in what she said. Quickly Sam got on with the story, that greater even than her need to protect Kirsty and Joe was her need to protect their father. They looked mystified, and urged him to go on.

Sam drew a long breath and looked at each in turn.

'I dunna think you hae ony idea just hoo low Daddie was eftir Robert an Andrew's deaths.' He told them how withdrawn their father had become, how his depression had put their marriage under strain, and how their mother couldn't bear that to happen again. She didn't think he'd be able to cope with the knowledge that a son of his flesh was a rapist and a child molester. What father could? And if it became public knowledge, he'd never lift up his head again. And he was vulnerable. She had to protect him.

'Yea, I can see dat,' said Henry, and the others mumbled their agreement.

Sam continued. She feared that, if Daddie knew what had happened, his unswerving sense of right and wrong would oblige him to report the crime and face the consequences. It would finish him one way or the other. She simply would not allow that to happen to the man she loved with all her heart. Sam looked at his brothers, willing them to understand. 'Her love for him,' he said, 'was sae powerful dat it swept away her love o justice an truth. Can you understand dat?'

They struggled to come to terms with this, for they could hardly imagine their mother straying in any way from the teachings of the Good Book. At length they said they could see her reasons, so Sam continued.

'She made wiz promise dat Daddie wid never hear aboot it, an we aa began ta live a lie.' He looked at them urgently. 'She axed me ta get you ta promise da sam as wiz.' He got the bible from the shelf. 'You're ta swear apo da Good Book.'

Solemnly they did as their mother had asked.

Isaac stood by the window with his back to them, clenching and unclenching his fists as he tried to grasp the enormity of all Sam had said. When at last he turned round, his face was dark with fury – but his voice was calm and cold as ice. He had reached his conclusions.

'We hae ta honour wir promise,' he said. They all murmured their assent. 'But justice must be done.' He spoke slowly, emphasising every word. 'Dat's a matter o honour. Jamie has ta pay for what he's done. Do you no agree?'

They looked at him, their expressions unreadable.

'Aye,' said Osie, 'but how? We canna go ta da police or Daddie will ken.'

'Justice has ta be done,' Isaac reiterated. 'He has ta be punished.'

'What can we do?' Osie's heart was thumping, for he had an inkling of what was in Isaac's mind.

'If it canna be done officially, through proper channels…'

'No, Isaac! No! Think what du's sayin, man.' There was a tone of alarm in Henry's voice, 'We canna…'

'What choice do we hae?' Isaac's mind was made up.

There was a tense silence while they tried to accept what he had said.

'Can I just get dis clear?' asked Sam in horror. 'Is du suggestin at we…'

'Kill him.' Isaac finished his sentence for him. 'Dat's what A'm sayin. "If thine eye offend thee, pluck it out." Dat's what it says in da bible. Weel, he's certainly offended wiz. His behaviour wid offend ony decent man. It's da right thing ta do.'

Silence.

Henry spoke first. 'He has ta be punished, wir aa agreed on dat, but…'

'Yiss, but ta turn wirsels inta murderers.' Sam was appalled.

'As lang as he's livin, innocent fock will be in danger, Sam. Surely du can see dat?'

Sam made no reply. This couldn't be happening. It was a horrible nightmare.

Isaac was unstoppable. 'A man at's done what he's done will do it again. Dere'll be nae haddin him back.'

They discussed the subject for some time, wondering why some men were driven to behave like Jamie.

'It's in der nature,' said Henry. 'Some fock seem ta get a thrill fae hurtin idder fock – usually eans at's weaker as demsels. Jamie was aye like dat, right fae he was a peerie boy. Aye da big man. Aye a bully.'

Isaac nodded. 'Da war gied men like Jamie a chance ta satisfy der need for violence. Dey got praised for doin things at wid a been condemned in peacetime. Dat made dem think at it was acceptable - an noo at da war is ower dey canna stop, for der gotten a taste for it.'

'An if dey didna hae a taste for it ta begin wi, der trainin pat it in dem.' Osie had seen men on their way to the front full of blood-lust, with hatred gleaming in their eyes.

'Yiss,' said Henry with a heavy sigh. 'You're baith right. Da war brought oot da best in men, but it brought oot da worst an aa.'

'So are we agreed on what has ta be done?' asked Isaac, trying to get the conversation back on track. 'Mind at wir doin it sae he's punished for what he did, an ta see at he canna do it again, an wir doin it in da only wye at it can be done wi'oot Daddie learnin aboot it – da only wye at we can keep wir promise ta Mammie.'

He looked at Osie. 'What does du say?'

'I dunna like it, but I suppose du's right.'

'Henry?'

He nodded.

'Sam?'

Sam gave no answer. How had it come to this? How could they contemplate breaking the most serious commandment – "Thou shalt not kill"?

'Sam,' Isaac prompted. 'Ax deesel dis. Does du want him ta get aff scot-free? Does du want him ta hurt idder fock?'

Sam shook his head.

'Does du want wiz ta go ta da police?'

'No.' His voice was barely audible.

'Dan du's in, agreed?'

Sam nodded, tears streaming down his face. He was trapped by his promise to his mother…and by family solidarity.

'Whaar do we go fae here, dan?' asked Henry.

Isaac said they should all consider where, when, and how the deed would be done, and then they could pool their ideas next time they were home on leave. 'Der nae need ta hurry,' he said. 'We need ta get it right.'

Sam went outside and was violently sick before he went to

bed. Staring into the darkness, all he could think was that his unborn child would have a murderer for a father.

Two days before Christmas, on the anniversary of her miscarriage, Kirsty gave birth to a healthy little girl.

'We'll caa her Jeanette,' she said. 'Peerie Jean.'

Sam held his daughter in his arms. Her little crumpled face was the most beautiful thing he'd ever seen. So fragile, so vulnerable. He knew he would do anything to protect her from harm. Heart full, he handed her back to her mother. Kirsty, exhausted but radiant, had a Madonna-like serenity about her. He loved them both so much he wanted to weep for the joy of it. He clung to that feeling as long as he could, because he knew he'd never experience such perfection again. The shadow of what must be done was with him day and night. The evil in Jamie had reached out and touched him too. He felt, rather as Beckie's young man had done, unworthy…and afraid that his touch would, in turn, contaminate those he loved.

Christmas passed quietly in the Jacobson house. A life had been taken, and a new life given. Peerie Jean, or Netta as she came to be known, became the focus of all their hope and love. Kirsty, however, was troubled. Sam had changed, and the change in him appeared to co-incide with his mother's death. It had undoubtedly been a devastating blow to him, and she didn't mean to underestimate that – but she'd always thought of Sam as strong and resilient. She felt he was cooling towards her. Was it solely due to his grieving? Was he wishing that he hadn't married her? Surely not. Not now they had their own beautiful baby – a perfect child, conceived in love. She must do as Mammie Jean had done when Daddie Peter had had his dark days. She would be steadfast in her love, and pray that the Lord would help him weather whatever storm it was that he was going through.

Chapter Twenty-Three

Where? When? How?

January 1919

During the early months of the year, Kirsty watched Sam lose his zest for life. He seemed exhausted, physically and mentally, and his eyes lacked their usual lustre. Occasionally she caught him looking at her, and baby Netta, with a mixture of sadness and longing. He loved her – she knew that – but something was preventing him from expressing it. It was more than bereavement; she was convinced of that. Was he finding the responsibilities of being a father too much of a strain? Or was studying for his pharmaceutical exams too much for him? Or was it a combination of all three. She tried not to show her anxiety, for that would only add to his burden.

Her own grieving centred round her deep sadness that Mammie Jean wasn't there to share her delight in little Netta – to marvel at the perfect little fingers and toes, at the first smiles, the contented gurgles, even at the lusty crying as she demanded to be fed. *I wish at you were here ta sing ta her, Mammie Jean*, she thought, as she rocked the cradle. In fact she sometimes fancied she heard Jean's voice singing gently, "Dan come boannie angels ta wir bairn noo." She knew then that Mammie Jean was watching over them.

Ellie was there, of course, and adored her little grandchild. She still did the cooking for them although it wasn't strictly necessary with Beckie at home, but everyone wanted the arrangement to continue. She was mourning a life-long friend, but Jean's absence brought mother and daughter closer than ever before. Kirsty began to confide in her, and Ellie tried to allay her daughter's worries about Sam.

'Gie him time lass, an space ta work things through. Grievin canna be rushed. It taks its ain time.' In her secret heart she agreed with Kirsty. There was more to it.

Isaac and Osie were both due leave in March, and Sam grew more nervous and preoccupied as the time approached. On the evening of their arrival, when the women withdrew and left them to "men's talk", they sat round the fire. Their father bade them a good night and retired to bed. Alone now, Isaac took charge and controlled the discussion as if it were an official meeting – business-like and objective, with a clear agenda. He didn't want their misgivings about the morality of their proposed actions to deflect them from their agreed purpose. The decision had been taken - and that, at far as he was concerned, was that.

The first issue for consideration was secrecy.

'For da sake o wir ain safety,' he said, 'naebody ootside this room can ever ken what wir plannin ta do, an naebody can ever ken aboot it when da deed is done. So we'll hae ta tak an oath on it – swear an oath o silence.'

Each of them solemnly said, 'I swear.'

The second issue was the question of who would carry out the deed. Should they hire someone to do it on their behalf?

Sam felt he was being drawn into a world of fantasy where normal rules no longer applied - a kind of *Boys' Own* adventure, where swash-buckling heroes would stop at nothing to right wrongs and defeat evil-doers. The reality was that here were his brothers, all good God-fearing men, seriously discussing murder as if they were a gang of common criminals - and he was part of it.

He heard Osie say, as if from a distance, 'In my opinion it wid be fine ta get somebody else ta pull da trigger, for nane o wiz wants ta tak dat step - but dat wid mean at somebody besides wirsels wid ken aboot it. He might let da cat oot o da bag, even by mistak.' He reminded them of their oath.

'Du's fairly right,' said Isaac. 'Safer if we do it wirsels. Dat brings wiz ta da next point. Du said "pull da trigger" sammas we wir decided at he wid be shot. I think we'll hae ta be a lot smarter as dat. A bullet in a body points ta murder, an an investigation. Dat we dunna want.'

Osie and Henry made murmurs of assent.

Isaac continued, 'We want a wye o killin at maks it look like 'natural causes'. Wid you agree?'

Sam found himself nodding with the others.

Then Henry found his voice. 'Afore we get inta discussin da "how", I think we need ta think aboot da "whaar?" Eftir aa, he's in Australia. Are we aa goin ta cross da world ta do it, or will ean o wiz geng? Ta my mind dat's pittin ower muckle responsibility on wan body…an hoo do we decide wha dat body should be? Mind, wir in dis tagidder.'

As usual Henry had given them something to think about. For the next few minutes they threw ideas into the melting pot, getting nowhere.

Finally Isaac said, 'It's late, boys, an wir no thinkin clearly.

Wir done enough for da night.' What they needed to do was go away and put their minds to the two main problems. Firstly, since they couldn't go to Australia, Jamie would have to come home...and how were they going to arrange that? Secondly they'd need to consider how the deed was to be accomplished. Everyone would have to come up with ideas, which they would weigh up at their next meeting. That was unlikely to be before June, but, as he'd said before, there was no need to rush. Slow but sure was the best approach.

In June Henry's mine-sweeper was decommissioned, and it reverted to being a trawler again – after being fitted with the latest equipment. Things were getting back to a kind of normality. At the next meeting, no-one had come up with any ideas for attracting Jamie back to Shetland, so discussion focussed on comparing the relative merits of different methods of killing.

Sam listened while they thrashed out the pros and cons. First they considered drowning. Shetland was surrounded by the sea, which dominated the lives of its people. Accidental drownings were all too common. Jamie could "fall" off a cliff or a pier, or go overboard on a fishing expedition. There were numerous possibilities, but as Henry pointed out, they would never be able to rule out the possibility of witnesses. There was always someone combing the beaches, or looking out over the sea with a telescope. It was too dangerous. So drowning was eliminated.

They decided stabbing, garotting, or strangling with their bare hands were just too repugnant. None of them would have the stomach for it. In addition, like shooting, all these methods pointed immediately to foul play and would bring in the police. Smothering didn't seem quite so barbaric, but there would always be feathers in the nostrils or throat or some other physical evidence. That left poisoning.

Everyone was tasked with finding out what they could about various poisons – how they worked, what evidence they left - and to continue trying to come up with a way of enticing Jamie home.

'Du's no had much ta say for deesel da night, Sam. I hoop du'll mak up for it next time - eftir aa, du's in da ideal job for it.'

Isaac's remarks were like a body-blow to Sam. He'd sat on the side-lines till now, but he wouldn't get off with that any more. Things were getting worse by the day, and he felt he was getting near breaking point.

In August Osie came home for good, and went to the fishing with Cousin Lollie, so meetings took place whenever Isaac could get home. It was September before they met again. Without beating about the bush, Isaac got straight to the point, and asked Sam to report on his findings. Sam said that, although he worked in a chemist's shop, and had done a year's medical study in Edinburgh, it hardly made him an expert on poisons. However, he had gone along with Isaac's request, and done some research.

'Let's hear it dan. What's du fun oot?' asked Isaac.

Sam told them that many of the poisons which were available – meaning those that could be purchased over the counter – were unsuitable for their purpose for any number of reasons - either because they took too long to act, or did not guarantee death, or were difficult to administer. In addition to that, Mr Leask was obliged to keep a Poisons Register, noting all sales of toxic substances together with the name of the purchaser and the date of purchase.

'A lot o fock use arsenic or strychnine ta kill aff rats, do dey no?' countered Osie, 'an naebody suspects dem o murder.'

'An do dey no use cyanide ta kill aff bugs on der flooers? An what aboot weed killers?' added Isaac. 'Fock can easy get der hands on dem.'

'Dat's true.' Sam answered., 'but my point is dat dey can be traced back ta da body at bought it. A slim risk, maybe…but a risk we shouldna tak.' He sighed. 'It's goin ta be a lang an complicated business, makin sure we pick da right wan.'

They were silent for a while, pondering this. Isaac paced the room, and Osie drummed his fingers on the table. Henry closed his eyes in thought, and finally said, 'I think we need to decide what kind o poison we need. I mean, what, em…' he searched for words 'properties it should have. We ken at it has ta be quick-actin, an it must be somethin at'll leave nae clues, an he has ta look as if it's been a natural death.'

'Yea, as if he was had a hert attack. *We* ken, an we can mak sure at everybody else kens, at he has a weak hert,' added Isaac. 'Dat wye his death'll no come as sae much o a shock, an naebody'll suspect at der ony, em, foul play.'

Then Henry suggested that they should leave it to Sam to make a list of poisons and all their properties – at their next meeting, they could study the information together, and eliminate everything that didn't fit the bill. 'Dat wye,' he said, 'we'll soon whittle it doon.'

'Good idea,' said Isaac, and the meeting ended there.

Towards the end of the month Grace, with a scholarship in place, set off to University. She looked so young, Sam thought, but her enthusiasm and her commitment would stand her in good stead, and she had got lodgings in Leith, beside homely Shetland folk so she'd still hear the home tongue. That would help her not to feel homesick. It was a big step, leaving the islands for the first time. Sam remembered that well. Her first term flew, and when she came home for Christmas she looked more grown-up and, though she was excited to be with them, she could talk about nothing but psychiatry, and how much good it would do in the world.

Osie came home for Christmas too, but Isaac didn't, so there was no "meeting" – which was a blessed relief to Sam. He could almost convince himself that the "Justice Scheme" – as they'd come to call it - had gone away, and he began to feel more light-hearted. Everyone was silent and subdued on the anniversary of Jean's death. Thinking about that day prompted Sam to read Uncle Tom's letters, which had lain forgotten all year. Each epistle was little more than a catalogue of Jamie's misdeeds and brushes with the law – brawling, gambling and thieving…and whispers of violence toward women. It angered him to think that his mother had known this, and kept it to herself. Jamie certainly hadn't mended his ways when he began his new life, thought Sam. His brothers were right. Jamie would never change. As long as he lived he would continue to exploit the vulnerable. This went a little way to helping Sam to justify what they were about to do, but the pain of it was still like a bleeding wound in his conscience.

"Peerie Jean's" first birthday gave them an excuse for a little family celebration, and raised their spirits again. Everyone gave her a little gift, the most special being a beautiful dress that Beckie had made. It was lace-trimmed, and had a hand-smocked bodice with embroidered rosebuds. As if she knew it was her special day, Netta took her first steps, tottering over to her father, holding up her arms to him, and he had a rare moment of pure joy. January was dominated by preparations for Up Helly Aa, which was being revived after the war. Osie and Henry took part. At the meeting of all the guizers (which was held a day or two before the event in order to finalise arrangements), Henry was elected Jarl for the following year – a matter of great pride for him, and for the family. Meanwhile everyone did their best to make the 1920 event "the best ever" except for Isaac - who was unable to get home - and Sam, who did not feel up to "jollifications", as he put it.

The next meeting was due in March, so Sam spent the first part of the year preparing for it. He threw himself into his assigned task as if it were purely an intellectual exercise, and had no further implications for him. That was the only way he could handle the situation. Letting the family think that he was preparing for his pharmaceutical exams, he sat every evening at the kitchen table beside Grace and Joe and drew neat columns with neat headings, and painstakingly filled them in.

He classified the first group of poisons as "substances used in the home or garden". He included cleaning and laundry products as well as pesticides and garden products such as fumigants, insecticides and weed killers. Next he listed "poisons used in medical treatments", for many lethal substances were beneficial in small doses. Finally, he listed poisonous plants. Beside each item he noted its level of toxicity; the length of time it took to work; its reliability, on a scale of one to five; how it should be administered and in what quantity; what symptoms it produced and, finally, what clues it might leave – such as the almond smell of cyanide, or the dreadful rictus of strychnine or bulging eyes, skin discolouration, blistering of the mouth and other noticeable effects that many poisons produced.

It was a comprehensive piece of work, and the brothers were impressed – and not a little daunted by the sheer number of poisons available.

'Dis is a stalwart piece o work, Sam,' said Isaac, after a brief glance through the neatly written pages. 'I had nae idea dey wir sae mony dangerous substances aboot.'

'It's da section on Poisonous Plants at amazes me,' commented Osie, who enjoyed helping his father in their front garden whenever he could. 'Ta think at aa yon boannie flooers can kill a body – an lots o dem growin right here in Lerwick. It doesna seen right.' He began to read the list aloud. 'Rhododendron, Privet, Foxgloves, Monkshood, Aconite, Autumn Crocus – even Lily o da Valley an da spring bulbs at lightens wir herts. No, it doesna seem right.'

'So,' said Isaac, cutting Osie's comments short, 'what will we rule oot first, boys?'

'Everything at's no a hunder percent reliable,' said Henry, practical as ever.

They went through Sam's list, and soon it was considerably reduced.

'What next?' asked Isaac.

They considered a moment, then Henry suggested that they ought to decide how quickly they needed the poison to "do the necessary".

'I reckon we need somethin at'll tak nae langer as fower ooers, five at da most.'

Isaac agreed. 'We really want him ta be 'awa' while aabody is still sleepin. Say we get hame round six in da moarnin, we'll sleep till aboot dinner-time.'

'Five hours is cuttin it fine, is it no?' asked Henry. 'We hae ta get him ta bed, an gie him da poison. It might be seevin, or even eight o'clock afore da job is done.'

'Right,' said Isaac. 'We'll rule oot onything at taks mair as fower ooers – just ta be on da safe side.'

So they went through the list again, eliminating a great many more.

'What noo?' asked Isaac. 'Ony suggestions, Sam?'

Sam said they should also reject anything that had a strong smell or taste that Jamie might detect, and anything that might be difficult to administer.

'What does du mean?' asked Isaac.

'Weel, onything at has ta be gien in large doses, or haes ta be injected. It's no dat easy ta do, an it might laeve puncture marks or bruises.'

'Dat maks good sense,' was Henry's verdict. 'So we'll geng trow da list again an rule dem oot – an while wir at it, I think we should cut oot onything at's hard ta get. We dunna want ta mak problems for wirsels.'

After several hours of intense concentration they had

reduced Sam's list to two poisonous liquids – chloral hydrate and nicotine, and a number of common plants. Sam told them that the chloral hydrate was a common sleeping draught, easily mixed with whisky. The alcohol would increase its effect. Nicotine could be ingested or absorbed through the skin, and could lead to respiratory failure in anything between five minutes and four hours. Several plants could do the job in twenty to forty minutes, but they were seasonal and only effective at certain times of the year. The brothers decided they would leave their final decision till their next meeting.

At the end of March there was an unexpected turn of events. Peter became aware that he was having moments when he, as he put it, "went away". Anxious that he might be putting his ship and its passengers at risk, he consulted Doctor Robertson who diagnosed his absences as tiny strokes. He advised Peter to retire at once, for the strain of such a responsible job might bring on more serious attacks with more lasting effects – apart from the danger to others, which Peter had already identified. Isaac came home and was interviewed for the position, and Captain Jacobson, junior, replaced his father one month later.

It was then much easier for them to confer. Henry arranged a get-together in the first week of May. He had, he said, something exciting to tell them. He had had a brainwave, and just couldn't understand how they hadn't thought of it before. The others were impatient to hear what the brainwave was, and urged him to 'get on wi it'.

'You aa ken at A'm Guizer Jarl next year…'

'Yea, an du's no likely ta let wiz forget it…but what does dat hae ta dae wi wir plans?'

'Do you no see. Dis is da perfect carrot.'

'Come on, man,' Isaac prompted. 'We didna come ta speak about vegetables.'

Still teasing them, he asked, 'What was Jamie mad aboot when he was a bairn? Cast your minds back. What was he aye speakin aboot – when he wasna busy getting inta fights, or in trouble wi da police?'

Sam answered in a single word, 'Vikings.'

'Dat's it! Do you no see?' Henry was getting quite worked up. 'If I invite him ta be in my squad next Up Helly Aa, an tell him at da whole squad will be dressed as Vikings – no just me - do you no think he'd come hame for dat? Hoo could he resist da chance ta parade round da streets o Lerwick in full Viking dress, complete wi axe an shield - or maybe even a spear?'

'It's da very thing,' said Isaac. 'A splendid idea. So will du write ta him da night?'

'Dat sall I,' replied Henry, pleased that he had found the solution to the problem that had been with them since their very first meeting.

'Why do we no settle on da poison noo, while wir at it?' suggested Osie. 'Dan we'll be clear o decision-makkin for a while, an can concentrate on makkin wir suits.'

They quickly rejected poisonous plants, because most were dormant in January – no seeds, berries, or flowers, and they had no rhododendron in their garden.

'What aboot da chloral hydrate, dan? What does du think, Sam?' asked Isaac.

'We'd need a reason ta buy it, I suppose. We'd hae ta mak up a story aboot some-ean in da faimily at couldna sleep, an da purchase could aye be traced back, if ony ean wis suspicious.

But it wid be easy ta administer, an wid be highly likely ta do da job…'

'Highly Likely, du says. No certain?'

'Weel, it wid be hard ta ken hoo muckle ta gie him…'

'Dat's no good enough,' said Henry. 'We need somethin at's a hunder percent reliable.'

'In my opinion – if we hae ta do it…an I suppose we must – nicotine is da best choice, for we can distil it wirsels fae fag ends…'

'Fae fag ends?!' exclaimed Osie.

'Yea, it's dangerous stuff dis bacca.' Sam laughed, for Osie's face was a study. 'A'll hae ta work oot hoo mony we need ta get da liquid da right strength, but it can be done. It's easy ta administer – if he's dead drunk. We just hae ta pent it onta his skin, an he'll be awa afore very lang – maybe minutes, certainly under fower ooers. Da only sign will be a slight stainin' on his skin – but tink how sunbrunt he'll be, comin' fae Australia.'

'Nicotine it is, dan,' said Isaac. No incriminating purchases to be made, and no evidence left behind. The meeting was closed.

As the year drew to an end their gatherings were legitimate and sociable. Their number was increased by the people Henry invited as guest members of his squad. None of them knew about the "hidden agenda". Everyone was busy helping to make helmets, spears, shields and other accoutrements, and the evenings passed in a glorious mix of working together, laughing together, telling anecdotes and listening to fiddle music.

Looking back, Kirsty reflected that relationships within

the household had evolved and changed, not least her own relationship with "Daddie Peter" – which was now warm and close. She now called him Daddie, without the added Peter, for Geordie had never come back, and Peter was the only father she had. She sensed his love and support, and confided in him. She knew that he, more than anyone else, understood what Sam was going through. He said little, other than to assure her that Sam would find his way back from his "dark place". His conviction was a comfort to her. He'd been there, so he knew. She was particularly pleased that Sam had agreed to take part in next year's Up Helly Aa. She thought this was a good sign. He seemed very involved in the preparation for it, and she reckoned the company of other young fellows would help to "bring him out of himself".

How would he cope with seeing Jamie again? She worried about that, and prayed it wouldn't be a set-back to his recovery. She wasn't very sure how she would cope with it either…or Joe. But they'd have to play the part. After all they'd given Mammie Jean their solemn word, and a promise like that could not be broken. For Daddie's sake they would pretend to make Jamie welcome.

Chapter Twenty-Four

The Hero Returns

January 1920

It was a beautiful still morning. The early frost had not yet melted. It lay white on leaves and grasses, and sparkled on rooftops and the ground beneath their feet. Peter, Isaac, Osie, Henry and Sam stood together on the pier, waiting to welcome the hero home. Their faces were white, their fingers and toes nipping with the cold.

The Aussie sunshine has done him good, thought Sam, as a confident and smiling Jamie strode down the gangway. He looked as if he were accustomed to being treated as somebody special – and expected them to treat him like that too. This was a different Jamie from the one he'd seen two and a half years ago.

He'd obviously risen early and taken time to present himself well. His hair was neatly cut, carefully combed and gleaming with macassar-oil, and he was newly shaved – his tanned skin smooth and shining. He smelt good too, expensively good, and he was immaculately dressed. His thick wool travelling coat was open, revealing a smartly cut suit in a very loud check – in marked contrast to the conservative taste of Shetland men, who favoured sober grey and black, or practical homespun working clothes. He wore a wrist-watch – a sure sign of affluence, and when he took off his soft kid gloves to shake them by the hand, they all noticed the ostentatious gold ring he wore, and its large black opal that seemed to spit out fiery glints. He oozed money, and wanted everyone to know it.

Peter hugged him, and said rather huskily, 'Welcome hom, Jamie boy. Welcome hom.' His pride was obvious. 'I only wish at dee midder was here ta see dee.'

As they walked up the hill, Sam noted that Jamie coughed now and then as the cold air caught in his throat and, by the time they reached the house, he was wheezing noisily.

'Is du aa right, boy?' his father asked anxiously.

'I'm fine,' he said. 'Dinkum. It'll pass when I've had a little sit-down, and maybe a drop of this.' He produced a silver hip-flask engraved with his name, and some sort of inscription Sam couldn't make out. 'Medicinal purposes, Daddie.' He took a generous swallow. 'That'll do the trick.'

The brother's exchanged glances. Drinking in their father's house – that was a taboo none of them would break. Jamie was showing no regard for their father's principles.

He made straight for his father's chair by the fire and sat down in it, as if it were his right. *Nothin but da best for him*, Sam thought, as their father took the smaller chair at the other side.

When his wheezing attack had passed he told them it was the result of having been gassed. 'Damaged the lungs and the tubes. The old ticker's a bit iffy too. It's no great problem though. It's not as if I need to work, my money'll work for me.' He laughed heartily and ended up coughing again. Another slug from his hip-flask and he was ready to continue. 'I just take it easy for a while, and hire a pretty little nurse to look after me.' He winked suggestively. 'Know what I mean?'

Dat soonds mair like da Jamie we ken, Sam thought. *Fancy spaekin like yon in front o Daddie! He has nae respect.* He looked at his father to see how he was taking it, but Peter's face was inscrutable.

Jamie was obviously used to holding court, so they sat round him, and listened while he told them about the "stunt" that had earned him his medal.

It's excitin stuff aa right, but – God forgie me – I wonder if it really happened da wye at he says? Sam knew his brother well.

'A'm prood o dee, Jamie,' said Peter. 'Fair prood.'

'So what's it been like for dee since du geed back ta Australia,' asked Henry, and Jamie was only too pleased to tell them about his changed circumstances.

'A'll hae ta hear dee news eftir A'm done my rounds,' said Peter. 'Da fock'll be expectin me, an I canna let dem doon.' He shrugged on his coat and picked up his bag. 'A'll see you aa at dinner-time.' His eyes rested on Jamie for a moment. 'A'm blyde at du's come hame.'

When he'd gone, Jamie asked what he meant by his "rounds". He seemed irritated that his father had found them more important than listening to him. They reminded him of his father's interest in nature's medicines.

'He used ta geng oot when he was hame on Saturdays, but noo at he's retired he gengs oot nearly every day,' Sam explained, and waited while Jamie lit a cigarette. 'Since da war it seems at der mair fock at need somethin ta help dem ta sleep, an der aye plenty wi aches an pains. He's ower blyde ta try an help dem.'

'Oh,' said Jamie, blowing out a cloud of smoke. Then he got back to talking about himself. 'You wouldn't believe it, mate, but they welcomed me back with bunting, and bands, and speeches, and lunches, and showered me with gifts like this.' He got out the hip-flask again and had another drink. 'I'm living the life of Riley, boys. Couldn't be better.'

He went on to explain that he spent much of his time on a round of house parties. 'They want to treat me, and why not? I'm a celebrity, and it does them no harm to let people know I'm their friend. I live well – fine food and fine wines - and I don't have to pay for it, so that can't be bad, eh boys?' He laughed heartily. 'And there are other benefits too.' He tapped the side of his nose. 'The "sheilas" will do anything for a hero.' Another quick slurp from the flask. 'And I've made a pile of money – a couple of big wins on the horses, and some lucky investments. Got myself a fine big fruit farm, and a stake in an opal mine. Labour is cheap – Abos don't need much, and they're good workers if you keep them at it. Small outlay and quick returns.'

'Just listen ta him!' said Kirsty to Beckie – the pair of them eaves-dropping through the open scullery door. 'Brag! Brag! Brag!' And, trembling, she braced herself for meeting him face to face.

'Hello, Jamie,' she said, as she came through to put the soup on the stove. 'Did du hae a fine journey? It's a lang wye ta come.'

'Yes, it was pleasant enough. If you grease a few palms, you get the extra little comforts.' He smiled at her as if there was no ugly history between them.

When she left the room he asked, 'Was that the little servant-maid who did the washing for Mammie? Impertinent little madam, if I remember right.'

Fighting hard for composure, Sam replied, 'Her name is Kirsty. She is my wife, Jamie, an I couldna hae a better ean.'

He doesna seem ta mind me, Kirsty thought, utterly amazed. Maybe he had blocked it out. Grace said that people could do that - pretend things had never happened – things they were ashamed of, or things they couldn't bear to remember. In her studies she'd come across several cases like that among ex-soldiers. She said it was the psychiatrist's job to bring these memories to the surface and help the patient to deal with them. If they kept them locked up inside it caused all sorts of problems – mental problems like depression or violent behaviour.

Whenever she was home at Christmas she'd talked endlessly to Kirsty about her studies. She was completely absorbed in them – the only woman in a class of men – but she could hold her own. So much was being discovered about the human mind through the close examination of war victims, she said. It was exciting to be part of such a new branch of medical science...and she had Jamie to thank for it, for it was his shell-shock that had prompted her to make this her career. She intended to write up his case for her research paper when that time came, if her tutors gave their approval. She was convinced that his taste for violence, even in childhood, indicated a latent psychosis. Perhaps it was a genetic thing, or perhaps it was as a result of emotional insecurity and his inability to recognise or respond to love. Whatever the cause, it only needed the right trigger to release the psychosis. For Jamie the trigger was the war. His experiences in France had led not only to his neurasthenia, but also to his psychotic behaviour. Until then, it had lain within him like an unexploded bomb. That was her theory, and she wanted to prove it. Grace's biggest worry was that the money would run out before she had finished her degree. Her scholarship money would soon run out. What then? Kirsty hoped fervently that a solution would be found, for it would be a tragedy if all that enthusiasm and hard work were to go to waste.

'Come on, boys. Show me my Viking suit,' Jamie demanded, once he'd temporarily exhausted his supply of "me" stories.

They climbed the stairs to the attic room with its row of six beds, and Henry brought the suit from the boxroom across the landing.

'What does du think o dis, dan?' he asked with pride in his voice, as he laid the various conponents on the bed for inspection. 'Try it on. I hoop du's no pitten on ony weight since du sent wiz dee measurements!'

Jamie put on the kirtle, and the breastplate, then sat down and criss-crossed the thongs over his leggings. Sealskin shoes, a feathered helmet and a warm wool cloak completed the outfit. He picked up the shield with its raven motif, and the spear with its highly polished, sharp-pointed blade.

'How do I look?' he asked, as he struck a pose. It felt good. He was a warrior...but he no longer felt the need to seek a hero's death. A hero's life was proving to be equal to his idea of Valhalla.

After the mid-day meal, he set off – to stretch his legs, he said. Gentle exercise and fresh air were good for his chest and heart – or so his doctor had told him. *Maybe not in these temperatures*, he thought, *but I'll wrap up warmly*. He couldn't wait to go out among people, and see the respect in the eyes of those who'd barely acknowledged him before. He was happy. He was accepted. He wasn't an outsider any more. He considered for a minute. Perhaps he was still an outsider, but of a different kind. He still wasn't one of them. He was above them - and the best thing of all was that they knew it. He had a medal to prove it.

While he was out, Henry took Isaac aside. 'I was thinkin it might be a good idea if we got da doctor ta come an see Jamie – ta soond his chest an tak his pulse an da like. We could say at wir worried aboot his wheezing.' He looked meaningly at Isaac.

'I see what du's getting at,' Isaac said. 'If da doctor kens hoo bad his chest is, an maybe his hert, he'll no be overly surprised… It's an excellent idea, boy. A'll go an see da doctor right away.'

Dr Robertson came later that afternoon, and Jamie needed little encouragement to tell him about his medal, and all about being gassed. The doctor examined him, and nodded his head. 'Take care, lad,' he said, 'and don't overdo it.'

That night, when everybody was asleep. Sam rose and took the full ash-tray from the side of Jamie's chair through to the scullery, and added the butts to those he had already collected in a small jar with a screw-top lid. He'd calculated that he'd need a minimum of twenty, so he'd gathered thirty to be safe. It was ridiculously easy. All he had to do was soak them in a small quantity of water. The resulting liquid would be highly toxic. He added the water. It was ironic that Jamie had provided the means to his own end, Sam thought wryly. Next he tied a small sponge firmly to the end of a stick. This would serve as an applicator. It wouldn't do if the person who applied the poison should get it on his own skin. All that remained to do now was to strain off the liquid when it was needed. He crept out to the wash-house and hid the jar on the shelf behind the other jars.

The festival was just as Jamie remembered it – but better. The Viking element had grown. The galley had become the centre-piece, with its imposing dragon's head and tail, its striped sail, its raven banner, and its mast with the blood-stained hand. Henry, as the Viking Chief, or Jarl, rode in the vessel, which was pulled through the town - and he invited Jamie to join him. Whether this was showing respect for him, or saving him a long walk carrying heavy equipment, Jamie wasn't sure. Either way he loved every minute of it. He was a Viking, and at the centre of a cheering crowd.

The marching was better too, not just a straggling band of disorganised followers, but men who had been well-drilled in the forces or in the reserves. They knew about straight backs, straight lines and keeping in step. The music too was rousing. Instead of the thin sound of a few scattered fiddles, the procession was led by a well-rehearsed Brass Band. The guizers sang Haldane Burgess' stirring words – which Jamie had loved as a boy – to a new and spirited tune. He tried to sing as lustily as the others.

Roll their glory down the ages,
Sons of warriors and sages,
Where the fight for freedom rages,
Be bold and strong as they.

However, he was short of breath and ended up coughing.

After the burning of the galley, the night was spent in revelry, visiting the halls and open houses, enjoying the music, the dancing and the generous hospitality. But in every brother's mind, excepting Jamie's, was the hidden agenda.

As the first streaks of light spread across the sky, they made their way back to the house. It was a clumsy home-coming as Jamie was drunk and obstreporous, lurching unsteadily into the flower beds, and shrugging off their offers of support. Now and again he burst into snatches of "Grand old Vikings ruled upon the ocean vast", while the others tried to hush him in stage whispers. At last they got him into the kitchen, where he dropped his spear with a clatter, and slumped into their father's chair in a stupor – his helmet at a rakish angle. Isaac and Osie helped him to his feet, and virtually carried him upstairs while Henry followed with shield, helmet and the spear, which he propped against the wall.

While they undressed him, Sam went to the wash-house and brought in the jar and the applicator. He strained the liquid into a clean jar, and put the discarded sludge into the fire. He put the used jar back into the wash-house. He's wash it out later. All the murderer had to do was to apply the brownish liquid to Jamie's face, neck and hands - any skin that was exposed.

Back in the kitchen all four brothers were restless and troubled.

'I hoop you didna waken Joe,' Sam said.

'Naa, naa. He was soond sleepin. He's at wan side o da room an Jamie at da idder. Der plenty o empty beds atween dem,' Henry assured him.

They were reluctant to take that final step, now the moment had come.

'You ken wir right, boys,' said Isaac. 'He has ta pay da price for what he's done, an der nae point in pittin it aff. Just mind at wha-ever does da deed is nae mair guilty as da rest o wiz. Wir in it tagidder, for better or worse. Agreed?' He looked at them each in turn.

'Osie?'

'Yea'

'Henry?'

'Yea.'

'Sam?'

'Yea.' His voice was no more than a whisper. An iron band was crushing his chest and he could hardly breathe. How had he allowed himself to be trapped like this?

'Right,' said Isaac. 'Dis is what we'll do.'

He strode over to the dresser, and took a pack of cards from the top drawer. He riffled through them and took out the four knaves, which he laid face down on the table.

'Sh,' said Henry, suddenly alert.

'What is it?' asked Isaac.

'I thought I heard fitsteps on da stair.'

They held their breath and listened intently.

'Der naebody dere. It's dee nerves playin tricks on dee,' said Isaac. 'Come on noo, let wiz get dis job done. I want every wan o you ta move da cairds around, so der nae chance at ony o wiz 'll ken what ean is what.'

Slowly, hesitantly, they each took their turn.

'Noo we'll each tak a caird, but we'll no look at him yet.'

Osie was first to take his card, then Henry, then Sam.

'Da last ean is for me,' said Isaac. 'Wha-ever has da Jack o Spades will do da deed. Agreed?'

They all nodded.

'We'll turn dem ower on da coont o three.' He counted slowly, 'Wan, two, three...'

With trembling hands they turned their cards over. Sam. It was Sam.

'Here,' said Isaac, handing him the bottle and the applicator. 'Du kens what ta do - an God be wi dee.'

Blinded by tears and praying for mercy, Sam took the poison from him and made his way to the stairs.

Chapter Twenty-Five

An End, and New Beginnings

As Sam reached the foot of the stairs he thought he saw a shadowy movement ahead of him. *Imagination,* he told himself, and crept up – stopping every time one of the treads creaked, till he was sure no-one had heard him. The bedroom door was ajar. He pushed it open, and stopped in his tracks. Two figures were silhouetted in the lamplight. Frozen to the spot, he tried to make sense of the eerie tableau.

Joe was standing beside Jamie's bed, spear in hand – and Daddie was there too. What was going on? The light was glinting off the polished blade. Joe raised the spear, ready to plunge it into Jamie's chest.

'Bad, bad man,' he said in his strange expressionless voice.

'No, Joe. Der nae need for yon,' said Peter calmly. 'Gie me da spear.'

'Bad, bad man,' Joe repeated dully, and tightened his grip.

'Der nae need for dee ta dae dis,' Peter said. 'Jamie's dead.'

'Dead?' whispered Sam from the doorway.

'Dead?' echoed Joe, uncomprehending.

'Gie me da spear,' Peter repeated gently. 'Jamie's dead.'

The tension went out of Joe's body, and he let his father take the weapon from him.

'I wanted ta kill him. What'll dey do ta me?' He slumped into his father's arms. 'I wakened up, an I saa da spear, an I minded…' He lifted his head. 'Dan da spear was in my hand. I wanted ta kill him.' He started to cry.

Sam watched and listened. He'd never heard Joe string so many words together before, and he'd never seen him allow anyone to hold him. He must be desperate. What was going on?

'Du's done nothin wrang, Joe. Naebody's goin ta dae onything ta dee. Naebody will ever ken.' He looked over the boy's head and caught Sam's eye. 'Right, Sam?'

Sam nodded. He took a step into the room – still trying to make sense of it.

'Is Jamie really dead, Daddie? Are you sure?'

'Yiss, he's gone, poor fellow. Aa da excitement an da dancin an da drink is surely been mair as his hert could cope wi.' He tried to free himself from Joe's grasp. 'Come, Joe. Come doon da stair. Da boys'll get dee a hot drink, dan du can sleep in my room wi me.' He led the boy toward the door where Sam still stood, staring in disbelief at Jamie. He'd been reprieved. His prayers had been answered.

'We'll hae ta tell da boys,' he mumbled and, turning, led the way downstairs.

The news was greeted with stunned silence. The brothers exchanged shocked glances, as they tried to take in what they had been told. Divine intervention – and just in the nick of time. Their relief was overwhelming. They'd come within a hair's breadth of committing the most heinous of crimes. All that righteous determination, all that inner torment, all that planning and preparation – all for nothing. It was as though they'd been forcing themselves to steel their resolve for so long that they were unable to let go.

They sat at the fire, minds reeling, still in their Viking dress – quite unable to get to grips with what had happened. *Thank God,* thought Sam. *Thank God that Daddie was dere ta stop peerie Joe.*

Peter was the strong one. He took charge and told them what to do.

'We should try ta get some rest,' he began.

'Should we no get da doctor?' asked Sam.

'What for?' countered his father. 'Der nothin at he can do for da poor boy noo. Let da doctor get his night's sleep. We'll send for him when we get up.'

'What aboot da lasses?' asked Henry. 'Should dey no be telt?'

'Surely dat can wait an aa. What good wid it dae ta waken dem?' He glanced at the clock. 'We'll go an get a couple o hours sleep, dan we'll be better able ta think aboot what has ta be done.'

There was an air of authority about him that inspired confidence and obedience.

Of coorse, thought Sam, as he lay beside Kirsty, wide awake. *He's used ta bein in command.* This was a side of his father that Sam had rarely seen, for when he was at home he'd always been content to leave the running of the house – and the upbringing of the children - in their mother's capable hands. The only time he'd intervened was when he'd tried to correct Jamie's wayward behaviour. His attitude to Jamie had changed when he was awarded his medal. *Daddie sees him as a shinin example noo. If he only kent da truth…*

He pictured his brothers lying upstairs in the room with Jamie's body. What must they be thinking? Had it sunk in yet that the nightmare was over? The Lord had surely been watching over them, and had intervened to stop them from carrying out their plan. What a glorious relief. His last thought before he dozed off was about his father. It struck him as odd that he had shown no grief. In fact he'd shown no feeling at all, other than sympathy and understanding for peerie Joe. Strange…and how lucky it was that he'd gone upstairs to prevent Joe from…it didn't bear thinking about.

When they had rested, they had their dinner with the rest of the family, and waited for Peter to give them their lead. The girls were totally unaware of the body lying upstairs, and simply assumed that Jamie was sleeping late – exhausted by the night's festivities. They bombarded their brothers with questions. Who had danced with whom? What did the other squads wear? What acts had the squads done to entertain the hosts and hostesses – musical turns or topical skits? The boys' lack-lustre replies were put down to tiredness, and the girls looked forward to more animated accounts later in the day.

When the meal was over, Peter folded his napkin, rolled it neatly and put it in his napkin ring. He turned to Isaac and nodded. Isaac excused himself from the table and went to fetch Dr Robertson. Then Peter cleared his throat, and the girls looked at him expectantly, sensing that he had something important to say.

'I hae some sad news, lasses. Jamie passed away in da night.'

The girls gasped, horrified that they had sat there enjoying their food and making frivolous conversation, when Jamie lay dead upstairs. Their questions came thick and fast. What had happened? Had there been an accident? Why hadn't they been told sooner? Had the doctor been to see him?

'Stop!' he said. 'Gie me a chance.'

He told them that Jamie had died in his sleep. His heart hadn't been strong enough for all the excitement and merry-making, and had simply given out. As to why he'd left it till now to tell them, he said he had wanted them to have rest and sustenance to help them through the difficult days ahead. 'Wid you a taen up your gruel if you kent aboot him lyin up da stair?'

They all looked sheepish and shook their heads

'Noo, maybe you could clear awa da breakfast afore da doctor comes. Isaac's geen ta fetch him. I saa nae point in getting da poor man oot o his bed when dey wir nothin he could do for Jamie. We should be thankful at Jamie died here among his faimily, an dat he had da chance ta geng oot wi da boys at Up Helly Aa. We aa ken hoo he felt aboot da Vikings, an it must a been ean o da highlights o his life – so he wid a died a happy man. It was good at Henry thought ta invite him.'

When Dr Robertson arrived, Peter took him upstairs. He checked his pulse as a matter of routine, took the body temperature to estimate the time of death. Then he bent over the body and sniffed – no odour other than alcohol. No signs of trauma – not that he expected to find anything untoward in this decent Christian home - besides he'd examined the poor boy only a couple of days ago. The gas had certainly left its legacy. *Still*, he thought, *you have to go through the motions*.

'I just have one question, Peter. Why did you not send for me as soon as you found him?'

'Weel Doctor, it was obvious what was happened – an dey wir nothin at could bring him back. So I thought I wid leave you ta get a good night's sleep. Eftir aa, wir no getting ony younger, are we?'

The doctor laughed, and thanked him for being so considerate. Then he wrote out the death certificate indicating that Jamie had died of cardial infarction, a contributory cause being gas poisoning.

'You won't get away with a quiet funeral, Captain Jacobson,' said the undertaker gently 'A lot of people will want to pay their respects - him being a war hero. No doubt the council will want to be represented, and the armed services. People need to celebrate their heroes.'

The minister endorsed this view. So the Jacobsons were carried along on the wave of public opinion, and the funeral was conducted with due pomp and ceremony. Hiding their true feelings behind expressionless faces, the brothers listened to the eulogy, where local dignitaries contributed to the praise. They paid tribute to his courage and the "exemplary selflessness of one of Shetland's worthy sons", and Jamie was laid to rest beside his mother, who had tried so hard to love and understand him.

In early April Peter received an important-looking legal document.

'Read dis ta me, Sam. Du kens I was never ony good wi lang words,' he said.

Sam read it carefully several times. He wanted to be sure that he understood it properly – that he wasn't making a mistake. It seemed that, as Jamie left no wife or family, everything he owned would come to his father. Peter was now an extremely wealthy man. Sam thought that it was probably dirty money, obtained through dishonest – maybe even violent means. But his father would not suspect that from a decorated soldier.

'What does it say? Du looks as if du's been struck by lightnin. Come on, boy. Tell me what it says.'

'It's Jamie's will, Daddie. Everything he possessed is yours noo. Do you ken what dis means?'

Peter was speechless. He shook his head.

'You're a very rich man, Daddie. Very rich.'

Peter was dazed. 'What am I wantin wi a lot o money? I hae everything I need.' He set little store by material things.

'You'll think o somethin ta dae wi it wance you're had time ta think it ower,' said Sam.

And think about it he did. He thought long and hard. Eventually he called them all together, and said he'd decided what to do with his fortune. Every one of them would get something that would help them to achieve their dreams.

To Isaac he gave the fruit farm, for he'd often said he wanted to leave the sea and settle in Australia after the war. To Osie and Henry he gave money to buy shares in a brand new fishing boat. To Beckie he gave money to set up her dress-making business – complete with the latest in modern sewing machines. To Joe he gave money for art lessons, and for a studio to be built in the garden. To Grace he gave enough money to cover all her educational expenses, so she could complete her degree and even go on to further study. To Sam he gave a sum of money to spend as he pleased on education – either for himself, or Kirsty or Netta. There was a moment's silence while they all digested what their father had said, then he went on.

'I want Robert's share to go to Catherine – half o it ta help wi her travellin back and fore ta France, for I dunna think she'll ever gie up looking for him'. He gave a heavy sigh, then went on, 'Da idder half is to be spent on peerie Berta in whatever wye Catherine thinks best'

The family began to murmur their thanks, but Peter wasn't finished yet.

'I coodna think what to do wi Henry's share, dan I heard your midder's voice telling me. She minded me hoo he loved ta play his fiddle an hoo it lichtened wir herts to hear it. *Du cood help young eens at canna afford ta buy a fiddle – eans at hae da music in dem sammas Henry did. Dat wye du'll keep his speerit alive. Gie dem fiddles an fin someen ta learn dem.* As usual your midder wis right. So A'm goin to get someen ta help me set up da "Henry Jacobson Fiddle Fund". I ken dare'll be a lock ta do afore it's up an runnen, but it'll be worth it. Robert'll live on in peerie Berta, an Henry'll live on in da music. You understand at I coodna leave dem oot for aa at dir no wi wiz ony mair?'

There was a murmur of agreement, and a confusion of thanks and admiration for all the careful thought that their father had put into the sharing out of his wealth.

'What aboot yoursel, Daddie. Was der nothin at you wanted?' asked Sam, eager to lift the mood a little.

'Yea,' answered Peter with a broad smile. 'A'm goin ta get a bathroom wi hot watter, an an inside W.C. An A'm ordered...' he paused dramatically, while they waited, intrigued, 'a motor car. A Model T, dey caa it. Alex Carter is seein ta it.'

They all burst into gales of laughter. This was the last thing they had expected.

'But you canna drive,' said Sam, when things quietened down.

'No, but du can. Du can tak me oot on Sundays. I want ta go ower every rodd in Shetland – and Kirsty an Netta will come wi wiz, an Joe if he wants an peerie Berta. I want you aa ta see every corner o dis lovely place at God made for wiz ta live in – every burn an every beach, every loch an every hill, every stack an every voe.' He turned to Kirsty. 'Du'll be able ta fill in yon map at du was workin on wi Grace.' He turned to Joe, 'An du'll paint picters o da boanniest places in da world.'

The old man was happy.

Epilogue
Poetic Justice

As the year wore on, the healing process was at work in Sam's heart. Eventually, as the distance between them closed, he felt able to tell Kirsty everything. He wanted her to understand why he, who loved her more than life itself, had allowed the rift to come between them. She listened, appalled – and wept for his suffering, and for the fact he'd endured it alone.

'I nearly committed murder, Kirsty. Hoo am I goin ta live wi dat? If da Good Lord hadna stepped in an taen Jamie when he did…'

'So, so love,' she said holding him in her arms. 'Dunna distress deesel. Du didna do it, an dat's aa dat maitters. An ta my mind a sin is no sae black if it's done in da name o love. It was dy love for me, an Joe, an dee midder, an dee faither at drave dee inta da trap. Du has a hert at's foo o love.' She held up her face for his kiss. In her heart she whispered, *Welcome back, hjarta. Welcome back.*

After a lot of deliberation and discussion with Kirsty, Sam told her he had decided what they'd do with his share of Jamie's money. They'd set up an education fund for Netta.

'An ean for her peerie bridder or sister,' added Kirsty.

'Does du mean…?'

'Yiss,' she replied, smiling, 'An dis time du'll enjoy every minute o it – wi nae haddin back.'

He held her in his arms. 'You ken, Kirsty, der a kind o poetic justice in dis. Jamie did his best ta destroy wiz aa, but noo every ean o wiz is gotten somethin we only dreamed aboot… somethin ta improve wir lives. His end is led ta a lot o new beginnins.'

'Getting dee back was da only improvement at I could ever wish for,' said Kirsty happily, snuggling up to him, 'but I ken what du means.'

After the distribution of his life-changing gifts, Peter seemed to age rapidly. He spent most of his days sitting by the fire. Often he would sleep, and sometimes he was confused, but there were days when he was clearer in his mind. It was on one of his better days – when he was watching Joe and Netta play with his dominoes on the hearth rug – that he suddenly said, 'Dat's what we wir like.'

'What do you mean, Daddie?' Kirsty glanced up from her book.

'We wir like Joe's dominoes.'

Kirsty looked puzzled. He tried to explain.

'Du kens hoo he likes ta set dem up in a row, dan push da first ean…an watch while dey aa faa?'

Kirsty nodded and Peter continued.

'An he's never pleased till every wan is doon?'

'Yea,' said Kirsty. 'Dat's right.'

'Weel, I was thinkin at we wir like da dominoes, an Jamie was da finger at pushed wiz. Du was da first ean ta faa, an I was da last.'

Later as they lay in bed, Kirsty recounted this strange little conversation to Sam.

'What does du mak o it?' she asked,

He thought about it for a long while, so long that she had fallen asleep.

'Kirsty,' he said, shaking her gently. 'I think I ken what Daddie was speakin aboot.' He sounded a bit shaken, agitated even.

She sat up, rubbing the sleep from her eyes.

'Did'n he say at we wir like da dominoes?' he asked.

'Yea.'

'An did'n he say at every wan fell doon?'

'Yea.'

'An did'n he say at it was Jamie at caased wiz ta faa?'

'Yea.'

'Does du no see?' he said excitedly. 'He must a kent, Kirsty. Daddie kent what Jamie was done ta wiz aa.'

Kirsty looked at him in astonishment. 'Ken dis?' she said. 'I believe du's right.'

They discussed the matter long into the night, and came to the conclusion that Peter must have overheard when Sam had his first meeting with his brothers, on the night of Jean's funeral.

'I telt dem da whole story dan, every last detail - an he must a heard it.'

They thought about the implications of this. He knew what they'd been through - and how they'd been forced to deal with it, in order to protect him.

'Da bit at I dunna understand is what he meant by "Du was da first an I was da last" ' said Kirsty, as she settled back to sleep.

Sam turned it over in his mind. It was clear enough that

Daddie knew Kirsty was Jamie's first victim – the first to fall from grace. "I was da last" implied that he had sinned too – after all the rest of them had fallen. What was his sin? Sam wondered. It couldn't have been anything serious. Daddie was such an intrinsically good man.

Sam yawned and snuggled down, moulding himself to his sleeping wife's back. *Da clues are dere,* he thought. *A'll just hae ta fin dem.*

In the middle of the night he woke, his mind sharp and clear. He was back at the door of the attic room, on the night Jamie died. Something was not right. What was it? It was a miracle that Daddie was there to stop Joe, he thought… then it came to him. *Dat's it. Dat's what's wrang. Why was Daddie dere?* He was a heavy sleeper, and wouldn't have heard them come in. Why was he awake at that hour, and why was he upstairs? He never went up there. He must have had a reason. Sam had no answer to his own questions, and other things were beginning to bother him. Why had Daddie delayed fetching the doctor? It was a strange thing to do, even if his explanation was plausible. Letting the doctor get a "good night's rest" - what if there had been some other reason? He argued with himself, unwilling to go in the direction his reasoning was leading him.

He got up and went through to the kitchen to have a smoke. That would help him to think more clearly. At last he forced himself to ask the question – had Daddie ushered them quickly down the stairs because there was something to hide? Something to do with the body? Some evidence of… some evidence that would disappear in a few hours? Had he been playing for time? Sam went to the back door and looked up at the stars. Could his father have killed Jamie? The answer, of course was "Yes, he could." He had the knowledge, and probably the means, in that "Saturday bag" of his. But why would he do it?

The answer, when it came, was blindingly clear. He'd done it to pre-empt them. So they wouldn't have to live with the guilt. He'd done it in order to carry their burden for them. Tears dripped down his cheeks – not exactly tears of sadness, but of relief, gratitude and overwhelming love for his father, and for the enormous sacrifice he'd made for them. What it must have taken for this devout and committed Christian to break the most important commandment, "Thou shalt not kill". If indeed he did.

Sam crept back to bed. He would keep his suspicions locked in his heart. After all it was pure speculation. All he knew for certain was that his burden had been lifted, and that Jamie's end had given each one of them chance of a new beginning.

The End

Author's Note

Here is some of the factual background against which I have set my work of fiction.

Captain H. G. Alston was appointed Senior Naval Officer at Lerwick in March 1915. His remit was to establish a shore base to support the work of the Tenth Cruiser Squadron, in enforcing the naval blockade which deprived Germany of supplies. Their job was to intercept and board any enemy or neutral ships which they thought were attempting to run the blockade. They conducted a preliminary examination and if they were still suspicious, would escort the ship to Lerwick or Kirkwall for more rigorous investigation.

This meant that Lerwick Harbour was a very busy place. One day there were seven full-rigged ships anchored there, and on their busiest day 139 vessels were waiting inspection.

Captain Alston also organised the work of the Auxiliary Patrol whose main job was to seek out and deter enemy submarines. In January 1917 the approaches to the harbour were mined by a U Boat which was known to lurk at the back of Bressay. Captain Alston instigated a mine patrol which swept the harbour twice daily, but no sooner had they cleared it than UC40 crept in and laid more mines. Thus the harbour was always dangerous to shipping.

Here is a list of some of the ships known to have been victims of UC40 between September and December 1917, when Part One of this novel takes place.

September 10th	Parkmill torpedoed and sunk off Bressay.
September 12th	Another ship (nameless) torpedoed and sunk off Bressay.
September 24th	Trawler, Asia, struck a mine and sank off Bressay Lighthouse.
October 19th	Russian steamer, Slavonic, struck a mine off the Bard. It was taken in tow, but sank 30 minutes later.
October 20th	Anglo-Dane (Copenhagen) struck a mine and sank close to Kirkabister.
October 21st	Flyndenborg (Denmark) torpedoed and sunk SE of Kirkabister.
October 21st	Novington (UK cargo ship) torpedoed off the Bard. Beached, then refloated.
October 24th	Woron (Russia) torpedoed and sunk at south entrance to the harbour.
December 12th	Trawler, Anadavat, mined and sunk off Bressay.
December 12th	SS Leonatus torpedoed 2 miles off Kirkabister.

I was quite shocked when I realised that the noise of these explosions would have been heard by the people of Lerwick, including my grandparents and my mother who was a little girl at the time. Many people would have been aware of the activity involved in bringing survivors to the hut which had been built at Captain Alston's request by the Church Army. It was run by the women of Lerwick, who provided food and clothing.

Despite trawling through the local papers I found no

reference to these events, and when I started writing the book my mental image did not include these explosions or the volume of shipping. I discovered later that the papers had issued a statement earlier saying they would not report the movement of shipping for security reasons.

My list of ships sunk was provided initially by the late Captain Robert Manson. It was verified by studying *Shipwrecks 1917* on Wikipedia and *Shipwrecks of the North of Scotland* by R M Baird (published by Birlinn).

My view of Lerwick 1917 was based on my grandfather's early photos and the discussions we had when I was a teenager, also:

Lerwick's Waterfront History by Douglas Sinclair
Old Lerwick People and Places by Douglas Sinclair
A Lerwick Miscellany by E S Reid Tait
Lerwick During the Last Half Century 1867 – 1917 by Thomas Manson

More general information came from Captain H G Alston's lecture on his time in Lerwick, given in 1920, and published in the *Shetland News* on 21 and 28 December 1939. I was directed to this by staff at Shetland Museum and Archives. Thank you.

Finally, *Deadly Doses: a writer's guide to poisons* by Serita Deborah Stevens with Anne Klarner informed the brothers' discussions on how to get rid of Jamie!

Acknowledgments

Firstly, I must thank Karen Fraser, manager of the Shetland Library for her advice, enthusiasm, belief and hard work and her decision to publish. Without her this book would never have seen the light of day. I'd also like to thank Library staff members Pat Leask (for her patience) and Michaela Goodlad (for her enthusiasm).

Tracey Hawkins gave invaluable help with all IT issues, which are a mystery to me. Jacqui King did a most detailed and diligent job of proof reading.

A number of writing friends have given stalwart support. Firstly, Laureen Johnson and Mary Blance read, commented, advised, made suggestions and nagged me to 'get on with it' for years, and Laureen did the first edit. Love and thanks to you both.

The late, and much missed, Alex Cluness gave lots of encouragement at the start. Kevin MacNeil, friend and tutor, taught me much about structure and pace and a great deal more besides. His interest and enthusiasm did much to boost my confidence. My formidable friend, the late Molly Hunter, drove me on relentlessly and gave lots of advice, particularly on the use of dialect.

My dear friend, the late Captain Robert Manson, took a lively interest and provided information on maritime affairs.

Members of the Lerwick Writers' Group have listened, discussed and spurred me on, as did the Westside Writers' Group. I appreciate all their comments.

I also want to thank my late husband Harry, who urged me

on, even in his darkest days; and Robert Alan Jamieson who said I must finish the book for his sake.

Lastly, thanks to my family – Denise, Rhona and Robbie; Mairi and Mark; James and Jennifer; Liam and Sandra; and Scott – for believing that some day I'd finish it. Here it is. Lang lippened come at last.

Christian S. Tait